Routledge Revivals

Waltharius and Ruodlieb

Waltharius and Ruodlieb

edited and translated by
DENNIS M. KRATZ

Volume 13

First published in 1984 by Garland Publishing, Inc.

This edition first published in 2018 by Routledge
2 Park Square, Milton Park, Abingdon, Oxon, OX14 4RN
and by Routledge
52 Vanderbilt Avenue, New York, NY 10017, USA

Routledge is an imprint of the Taylor & Francis Group, an informa business

© 1984 by Dennis M. Kratz

All rights reserved. No part of this book may be reprinted or reproduced or utilised in any form or by any electronic, mechanical, or other means, now known or hereafter invented, including photocopying and recording, or in any information storage or retrieval system, without permission in writing from the publishers.

Publisher's Note
The publisher has gone to great lengths to ensure the quality of this reprint but points out that some imperfections in the original copies may be apparent.

Disclaimer
The publisher has made every effort to trace copyright holders and welcomes correspondence from those they have been unable to contact.
A Library of Congress record exists under ISBN:

ISBN 13: 978-0-367-18185-7 (hbk)
ISBN 13: 978-0-367-18188-8 (pbk)
ISBN 13: 978-0-429-05997-1 (ebk)

The Garland Library of Medieval Literature

General Editors
James J. Wilhelm, Rutgers Univesity
Lowry Nelson, Jr., Yale University

Literary Advisors
Ingeborg Glier, Yale University
Guy Mermier, University of Michigan
Fred C. Robinson, Yale University
Aldo Scaglione, University of North Carolina

Art Advisor
Elizabeth Parker McLachlan, Rutgers University

Music Advisor
Hendrik van der Werf, Eastman School of Music

Two scenes from Prudentius' *Psychomachia*: Faith with Martyrs (top) and Modesty battling Lust (bottom). Page 70 from Codex 264 of the Burgerbibliothek Bern. (Courtesy of the Burgerbibliothek Bern)

Waltharius and *Ruodlieb*

edited and translated by
DENNIS M. KRATZ

Volume 13
Series A
GARLAND LIBRARY OF MEDIEVAL LITERATURE

Garland Publishing, Inc.
New York and London
1984

Copyright © 1984 by Dennis M. Kratz
All rights reserved

Library of Congress Cataloging in Publication Data
Main entry under title:
        Waltharius and Ruodlieb.

        (The Garland library of medieval literature ; v. 13.
        Series A)
        Bibliography: p.
        1. Latin poetry, Medieval and modern—Translations into
        English. 2. English poetry—Translations from Latin.
        3. Latin poetry, Medieval and modern. 4. Epic poetry,
        Latin—Translations into English. 5. Epic poetry, Latin.
        6. Christian poetry, Latin—Translations into English.
        7. Christian poetry, Latin. I. Kratz, Dennis M.,
        1941–   . II. Ekkehard I, Dean of St. Gall, d. 973.
        Waltharius manu fortis. 1984. III. Ruodlieb. 1984.
        IV. Series: Garland library of medieval literature ;
                        v. 13.
        PA8164.W34   1984   873'.03'08   80-8958
                ISBN 0-8240-9444-1 (alk. paper)

Printed on acid-free, 250-year-life paper
Manufactured in the United States of America

The Garland Library of Medieval Literature

Series A (Texts and Translations); Series B (Translations Only)
1. Chrétien de Troyes: *Lancelot, or The Knight of the Cart.* Edited and translated by William W. Kibler. Series A.
2. Brunetto Latini: *Il Tesoretto.* Edited and translated by Julia Bolton Holloway. Series A.
3. *The Poetry of Arnaut Daniel.* Edited and translated by James J. Wilhelm. Series A.
4. *The Poetry of William VII, Count of Poitiers, IX Duke of Aquitaine.* Edited and translated by Gerald A. Bond; music edited by Hendrik van der Werf. Series A.
5. *The Poetry of Cercamon and Jaufre Rudel.* Edited and translated by George Wolf and Roy Rosenstein; music edited by Hendrik van der Werf. Series A.
6. *The Vidas of the Troubadours.* Translated by Margarita Egan. Series B.
7. *Medieval Latin Poems of Male Love and Friendship.* Translated by Thomas Stehling. Series A.
8. *Barthar Saga.* Edited and translated by Jon Skaptason and Phillip Pulsiano. Series A.
9. Guillaume de Machaut: *Judgment of the King of Bohemia.* Edited and translated by R. Barton Palmer. Series A.
10. *Three Lives of the Last Englishmen.* Translated by Michael Swanton. Series B.
11. Giovanni Boccaccio: *The Elegy of Lady Fiammetta.* Translated by Mariangela Causa-Steindler. Series B.
12. Walter Burley: *On the Lives and Characters of the Philosophers.* Edited and translated by Paul Theiner. Series A.
13. *Waltharius* and *Ruodlieb.* Edited and translated by Dennis Kratz. Series A.
14. *The Writings of Medieval Women.* Translated by Marcelle Thiébaux. Series B.
15. *The Rise of Gawain (De Ortu Waluuani).* Edited and translated by Mildred Day. Series A.
16, 17. *The French Fabliau*: B.N. 837. Edited and translated by Raymond Eichmann and John DuVal. Series A.
18. *The Poetry of Guido Cavalcanti.* Edited and translated by Lowry Nelson, Jr. Series A.

19. Hartmann von Aue: *Iwein*. Edited and translated by Patrick M. McConeghy. Series A.
20. *Seven Medieval Latin Comedies*. Translated by Alison Goddard Elliott. Series B.
21. Christine de Pizan: *The Epistle of the Prison of Human Life*. Edited and translated by Josette Wisman. Series A.
22. Marie de France: *Fables*. Edited and translated by Harriet Spiegel. Series A.
23. *The Poetry of Cino da Pistoia*. Edited and translated by Christopher Kleinhenz. Series A.
24. *The Lyrics and Melodies of Adam de la Halle*. Edited and translated by Deborah Nelson; music edited by Hendrik van der Werf. Series A.
25. Chrétien de Troyes. *Erec and Énide*. Edited and translated by Carleton Carroll. Series A.
26. *Three Ovidian Tales*. Edited and translated by Raymond J. Cormier. Series A.
27. *The Poetry of Guido Guinizelli*. Edited and translated by Robert Edwards. Series A.
28. *Meier Helmbrecht*. Edited by Ulrich Seelbach; introduced and translated by Linda B. Parshall. Series A.
29. *Pathelin and Other Farces*. Edited and translated by Richard Switzer and Mireille Guillet-Rydell. Series A.
30. Christine de Pizan: *Lyric Poetry*. Edited and translated by Nadia Margolis. Series A.
31. Gerald of Wales (Giraldus Cambrensis): *The Life of St. Hugh of Avalon*. Edited and translated by Richard M. Loomis. Series A.
32. *L'Art d'Amours*. Translated by Lawrence Blomquist. Series B.
33. Boccaccio: *Ameto*. Translated by Judith Serafini-Sauli. Series B.
34, 35. *The Medieval Pastourelle*. Selected and edited by William D. Paden, Jr. Series A.
36. Thomas of Britain: *Tristan*. Edited and translated by Valerie Roberts. Series A.
37. *Graelent* and *Guingamor*: Two Breton Lays. Edited and translated by Russell Weingartner. Series A.

Preface of the General Editors

The Garland Library of Medieval Literature was established to make available to the general reader modern translations of texts in editions that conform to the highest academic standards. All of the translations are original, and were created especially for this series. The translations attempt to render the foreign works in a natural idiom that remains faithful to the originals.

The Library is divided into two sections: Series A, texts and translations; and Series B, translations alone. Those volumes containing texts have been prepared after consultation of the major previous editions and manuscripts. The aim in the editing has been to offer a reliable text with a minimum of editorial intervention. Significant variants accompany the original, and important problems are discussed in the textual notes. Volumes without texts contain translations based on the most scholarly texts available, which have been updated in terms of recent scholarship.

Most volumes contain Introductions with the following features: (1) a biography of the author or a discussion of the problem of authorship, with any pertinent historical or legendary information; (2) an objective discussion of the literary style of the original, emphasizing any individual features; (3) a consideration of sources for the work and its influence; and (4) a statement of the editorial policy for each edition and translation. There is also a Select Bibliography, which emphasizes recent criticism on the works. Critical citations are often accompanied by brief descriptions of their importance. Selective glossaries, indices, and footnotes are included where appropriate.

The Library covers a broad range of linguistic areas, including all of the major European languages. All of the important literary forms and genres are considered, sometimes in anthologies or selections.

The General Editors hope that these volumes will bring the general reader a closer awareness of a richly diversified area that has for too long been closed to everyone except those with precise academic training, an area that is well worth study and reflection.

James J. Wilhelm
Rutgers University

Lowry Nelson, Jr.
Yale University

For
ABBY
and
MATTHEW

Contents

Introduction	xiii
Select Bibliography	xxxix
Waltharius	1
Ruodlieb	73
Textual Notes	201

Introduction

The *Waltharius* and *Ruodlieb* are considered by many scholars to be among the finest works of medieval Latin literature. Both the *Waltharius*, composed probably in the ninth century by a German monk, and the *Ruodlieb*, composed by an anonymous eleventh-century poet from southern Germany, are heroic narratives that provide examples of the creative transformation of the Latin epic tradition into a vehicle for the expression of Christian values. The *Ruodlieb*, in addition, is widely regarded as a bridge between the epic and the emerging genre of romance.

Although they have long been of particular interest to students of medieval Latin and German literature, unfortunately neither poem is well known outside those areas of specialization. In part, this neglect can be attributed to the lack of available translations. Neither work has ever been translated into English poetry. The only complete translation into English of the entire *Waltharius* is a prose version published in 1950 and out of print for many years. The *Ruodlieb* has been translated twice into English prose, the more recent version having appeared in 1965.

WALTHARIUS

Authorship

Both the date and the authorship of the *Waltharius* have been the subject of much debate. We can say with assurance only that the poet was a monk, since he addresses the poem to his "brothers" (line 1: tertia pars orbis, fratres, Europa vocatur). Scholars have placed the writing of the *Waltharius* at various points in the ninth and tenth centuries. Several authors have been suggested, most often Ekkehard

I of St. Gall and a certain Gerald, who composed a 22-verse preface to the epic which appears in several manuscripts.

The identification of Ekkehard I as the poet was first proposed by Jacob Grimm (1838, pp. 57–64), who based his argument on a statement by Ekkehard IV of St. Gall, in the eleventh-century chronicle *Casus Sancti Galli*, that he had reshaped and polished a work about "Waltharius manu fortis" (strong in hand) which the earlier Ekkehard had composed as a school exercise. Is the work to which he refers the epic poem *Waltharius*? Although numerous scholars have challenged that assumption, Ekkehard IV's statement remains the most positive piece of evidence about the composition of the poem; and many scholars contend that the *Waltharius* was in fact composed by Ekkehard in the tenth century.

Other scholars have argued that the *Waltharius* was composed in the ninth century. For example, although the poet makes reference to numerous classical and medieval authors, no work later than 900 is cited (Schumann). References to the Carolingian writers Theodulf of Orléans and Rabanus Maurus establish 820 as the earliest date of the poem. Historical evidence, such as the poet's description of Châlon as the capital of Burgundy and of Metz as a *metropolis*, suggest that the *Waltharius* was composed before 890 (Von den Steinen). The identification of Gerald as the author has been both affirmed (Von den Steinen, Schumann, Reeh) and denied (Schaller 1965, Krammer) on the basis of a comparative analysis of the style of the *Waltharius* and his prefatory verses. Recently it was even suggested that the poem was composed in the ninth century by Grimald, teacher of the famous Carolingian poet Walafrid Strabo (Önnerfors). Even if one maintains that Gerald is the author, the problem of identifying Erkambald has not been solved. We do know of an Erkambald who was Bishop of Eichstätt in Bavaria from 880 to 912. However, there are strong arguments against accepting him as the recipient of Gerald's dedication, one of which is the fact that the main textual tradition of the *Waltharius* has little to do with Bavaria.

The controversy continues; and until further evidence emerges, we must be content with conjecture. On the basis of the available evidence, I favor a ninth-century date and lean toward accepting Gerald as the author. The poet's knowledge of classical literature, his attempt to recreate the epic, and his resolution of the problem of transforming the classicizing epic into a vehicle for the presentation of a Christian theme strike me as basically Carolingian in spirit. On

Introduction

the other hand, it is quite possible that the poem was composed in the tenth century. Whatever the truth may be, it is important that the issue of date and authorship not overshadow the artistic excellence of this remarkable narrative.

Artistic Achievement

The *Waltharius* combines Germanic, classical, and Christian elements. The story and its characters are drawn from the same body of legends that produced the *Nibelungenlied*. Composed in Latin hexameters, the *Waltharius* is told in the form of a classical epic. Its style and language reflect the poet's desire to place the *Waltharius* in the Latin epic tradition. The nature of the poem's Christian content, as we will see, lies in the poet's criticism of the values traditionally associated with the heroism of epic literature.

The narrative has three parts, approximately equal in length. In the first section (1-418), the army of Attila the Hun sweeps through western Europe. Three kings ransom their kingdoms with tribute and hostages. These hostages are Walter of Aquitaine, his betrothed Hildegund of Burgundy, and the Frankish warrior Hagen, who is sent in place of the infant prince Gunther. In time, all three hostages rise to positions of prominence in Attila's court, especially Walter, the greatest of Attila's warriors and now the commander of his army. Hagen, however, flees the land of the Huns after learning that Gunther has become king of the Franks and abrogated his treaty with Attila. Shortly thereafter, Walter also flees, taking with him Hildegund and two coffers crammed with treasure taken from the Huns. His successful plan of escape has involved inviting the Huns to a banquet and running off during the night while they are sunk in drunken slumber.

In the second section (419-1061), Walter and Hildegund pass through the land of the Franks. While Hagen is delighted to learn that his friend has escaped, the greedy Gunther thinks only of wresting away the treasure that the fugitives are transporting. Despite Hagen's objections and warnings, Gunther gathers eleven warriors and sets out. Though named one of this band, Hagen refuses to participate. Walter and Hildegund, meanwhile, have taken refuge in a narrow mountain pass. Gunther orders his men to attack Walter; but, ensconced in his stronghold, he can be approached by only one warrior at a time. In a series of individual combats, he kills each of the men sent against him, until only Gunther and Hagen remain.

In the final third of the narrative (1062–1456), Gunther convinces Hagen to join with him against Walter. Hagen agrees to fight to avenge the death of his nephew, one of the warriors who had been sent against Walter. He and Gunther lure Walter onto open ground, then charge him. In the ensuing fight, each man is grievously wounded. Walter hacks off Gunther's right leg. Hagen, however, intercepts the next blow, and Walter's sword shatters against his helmet. When Walter angrily throws away the hilt of his shattered weapon, Hagen cuts off his outstretched right hand. With his left hand, Walter grasps a short sword and puts out Hagen's right eye as well as six of his teeth. At this point the men abruptly lay down their weapons. Walter orders Hildegund to serve them wine, and the men make jokes about each other's wounds before they depart for their respective homes. The poet mentions that Walter will reach home, marry Hildegund and rule happily in Aquitaine.

The structural design of the *Waltharius* is based on a successive narrowing of focus and on the number three. The epic falls naturally into its three parts. The first section begins with all of Europe, indeed a statement that Europe is one of three parts of the world. Then the narrative turns to the three kingdoms that send hostages to Attila. The core of the second section is Walter's fight against Gunther's men. In the final third, three warriors—Gunther, Hagen, and Walter—fight among themselves. Perhaps this recurrence of the number three is intended as a hint that the poet is exploiting his Germanic subject matter for a Christian purpose. Within this basic scheme, the poet is careful not to betray any trace of sloppy craftsmanship (Brinkmann). He even interrupts the narrative to remind the reader of his artistic control. Early in the tale he promises that Gunther will figure in the later action (15). Later, when he introduces the use of a seemingly anachronistic weapon, he hastens to say that the Franks had weapons of that type at the time of the story (910). When Walter flees Pannonia, he girds a one-edged sword on his right thigh (336–338). When he grabs this sword at a critical moment in his battle against Hagen and Gunther, the poet reminds the reader that he had already mentioned the weapon (1389–1392).

That the *Waltharius* should be seen as part of the continuum of the Latin epic tradition is undeniable. It is written in Latin dactylic hexameter, the meter of the epic genre. In language, form, and content it reflects the poet's imitation of two classical epics, Vergil's *Aeneid* and the *Thebaid* of Statius, and of a fourth-century allegorical epic, Prudentius' *Psychomachia*, which recounts a series of individual combats in which personified Virtues defeat corresponding Sins. No small part of the poet's art lay in his knowledge of and ability to imitate classical literature (Stackmann).

The *Waltharius* includes imitations of both general epic conventions and specific scenes from earlier works. The description of warfare, both massed battles and individual combats, is an expected element in any epic poem. The battle scenes in the *Waltharius* reflect with particular clarity the poet's knowledge of his classical models (Andersson, pp. 133–144). The poet also includes the simile, an obligatory feature of the epic style. Eight similes occur in the *Waltharius*. The longest (1337–1343) provides a good example of the poet's relationship to his literary models. The apparent source for this simile, which compares Walter under attack to a Numidian bear surrounded by hunting dogs, is Vergil's comparison of the warrior Mezentius to a boar that has been attacked by dogs (*Aeneid* 10.707–715); but the poet seems also to have had in mind a simile from the *Thebaid* (4.396–400). Statius uses the image of two bulls fighting as a fulfillment of an earlier vision which was interpreted as foretelling the final confrontation of Polynices and Eteocles. The same pattern is repeated in the *Waltharius*; for the comparison of Walter to a bear serves to fulfill the truth of a dream in which Hagen sees a bear tear off Gunther's leg. Finally, the simile in the *Waltharius* depicts the hero as surrounded by dogs, an alteration of the Vergilian model; and this change introduces a Christian element, since it calls to mind the image of Christ surrounded by his tormentors (see Marrow).

In addition to his more general imitations of epic themes and style, the poet models some episodes on specific scenes from earlier epics. The banquet at which Walter induces such drunkenness among the Huns that they fail to notice his escape is based on the banquet given by Dido in honor of Aeneas (*Aeneid* 1.637–756). Attila's complaint upon his discovery of Walter's departure (380–401) is based largely on Vergil's description of the lovesick

Dido (*Aeneid* 4.1–89). The concluding episode of the *Waltharius*, in which the warriors put down their weapons and drink, is based on a scene in the *Psychomachia* in which the victorious Virtues rest and refresh themselves (606–663).

The *Waltharius* represents a skillful re-creation of the classical epic genre. On this issue there is little serious disagreement. There remains an important question, however, concerning which less agreement is to be found. How and to what extent, if at all, was the poet able to fashion his material into a work that presents a Christian theme? Answers to this question have varied. A few scholars have labeled the Christian elements of the *Waltharius* as inconsequential or defined the ethos of the work as hardly Christian at all (Grimm, Jones 1959). Most, however, find the poem to be essentially, even totally, Christian in spirit (Brinkmann, Von den Steinen, Schumann, Katscher).

Most judgments about the underlying ethos of the *Waltharius* have been based on an assessment of Walter's behavior and values. Those who have seen the poem as a reconstruction of Germanic legend without significant Christian coloring have emphasized Walter's concern for vengeance, reputation, and worldly goods. A hero who kills eleven men, four of whom he decapitates, to protect a treasure is hardly a positive model of moral excellence, especially in a work intended for monks. Others have argued that in the poet's portrait of Walter can be seen a new type of heroism that reflects Christian values. They point specifically to his various expressions of contrition and especially to the scene in which Walter, during a respite from the attacks against him, fits the heads of his decapitated foes to their appropriate trunks and prays for his victims.

An alternative reading would accept a portion from both the other approaches (see Kratz 1980, pp. 15–60). It sees the *Waltharius* as an essentially Christian work but agrees that Walter himself is not a Christian hero. It is possible to read the *Waltharius* as an epic that offers a different solution to the problem of filling the old bottle of epic with a new wine of Christian values. This reading suggests that the poet has inverted the traditional function of epic by attacking rather than celebrating the actions of his apparently heroic characters, and that the Christian theme of the poem is to be found in its criticism of the values traditionally associated with the Germanic and classical epic traditions. In this interpretation, the *Waltharius* is

Introduction

perhaps best described as a mocking epic, for it mocks the values of epic and the characters who hold those values. Instead of offering a positive exemplar of heroic behavior, it emphasizes the flaws that prevent its characters from serving as models for its original readership of monks.

The poet's ironically critical attitude toward heroism is evident not only in his treatment of the main characters—Hagen, Gunther, and Walter—but also in his treatment of a lesser character, Attila. When Attila discovers that Walter and Hildegund have fled, he is deeply distressed; but the description of his anger is filled with mocking humor. His anger, for example, is compared to storm-whipped Aeolic winds; but the passage has been shown to contain a reference to a mocking description by Venantius Fortunatus of the digestive woes of a gluttonous abbot (Dronke 1971, p. 161). Moreover, a series of allusions to the *Aeneid* connects Attila's rage not with a heroic act but with the meanderings and distresses of the lovesick Dido.

In like manner, the poet undermines the apparent excellence of the three main characters. His disdain for Gunther is the most obvious; for he is depicted as cowardly, stupid, and greedy. His greed is central to the story that unfolds (Wehrli 1965). When Gunther learns of Walter's presence in the territory of the Franks, he thinks not of friendship or hospitality but only of the opportunity to deprive the traveler of the treasure he is transporting. Connected with Gunther's greed is his pride. The epithet "haughty" is regularly applied to him (for example, see 468, 720). On two occasions (513–515, 530) he is even described in language that echoes the personification of Pride in the *Psychomachia*.

The criticism of Hagen is more subtle. Praised by the poet for his intelligence as well as his prowess as a warrior, he refuses at first to join in the ill-fated venture against Walter. When his nephew Batavrid attacks Walter, Hagen delivers an impassioned condemnation of the greed for wealth and fame that leads so many warriors to their death (857–877). However, when Hagen is drawn into the battle, he expresses his own desire for glory (1275–1279). He tells Walter, moreover, that he is fighting specifically to avenge his nephew; and this motive has significance for the wounds Hagen suffers at the end of the tale.

Walter, the central figure in the epic, has, as I mentioned, often been seen as an exemplary character. He is a brave, even awesome, fighter. He is described, along with Hagen, as surpassing all the Huns in intelligence. He seems in other respects to be a good man by Christian standards. During the many days and nights of the flight from Pannonia, Walter refrains from sexual contact with the beautiful Hildegund, earning the poet's praise for his continence (426–427). Unlike Gunther, he controls his pride. After uttering an arrogant boast just prior to the first attack by one of Gunther's men, he immediately begs God's forgiveness for his words (559–565).

Avarice, the concern for worldly goods and glory, prevents both Hagen and Walter from being models of Christian virtue. Walter kills Gunther's eleven men, in his own words, to avoid dishonor and to keep his possessions (1214–1218). When he explains his plan of escape to Hildegund, he instructs her first to procure armor, then to fill two coffers with treasure. During the central section of the narrative, this treasure is Walter's primary concern. When Hildegund first sees the approaching Franks, she mistakes them for Huns and asks Walter to kill her before they rape her. After consoling her, Walter recognizes the insignia of the Franks but thinks immediately about protecting his gold so that no Frank can "boast to his wife" about taking it (561–563). Walter's motives involve keeping his wealth and avoiding the shame of losing it.

Concern for reputation is a recurring theme of the sequence of attacks against Walter by Gunther's men. For example, when one of his foes manages to shave off a lock of Walter's hair, the hero decapitates him even as the wounded man begs for mercy, to prevent him from boasting that he gave Walter a bald spot (979–981). He tells another warrior, as he kills him, to report to his friends in the Underworld his failure to avenge Walter's murder of them (1056–1058). The desire for fame through vengeance spurs on several of the attackers as well. The second warrior, for example, fights to avenge the first (691); and the death of Hagen's nephew Batavrid prompts both an immediate act of vengeance by Gerwit (914) and the later attempt by Hagen.

Even the scene in which a remorseful Walter prays for the salvation of his enemies demonstrates his failure to act according to Christian ideals of compassion and forgiveness; for the next morning Walter carefully despoils those same victims (1191–1197). He immediately re-enters the fray in order that, in his own words, his

Introduction xxi

right hand may not have slain many enemies in vain, that he may avoid dishonor, and that he may hold on to his possessions (1214–1218).

Although none of its characters is an exemplar of Christian heroism, the *Waltharius* is a Christian epic. The basic theme of the poem lies in its criticism of the values associated with the epic tradition. The poet portrays glory and wealth as the twin motives of the warriors in the heroic society described in the *Waltharius*. The goal of the heroic individual is to gain glory—that is, a reputation for excellence, through the performance of brave acts. Material wealth is a tangible symbol of the esteem that he has earned. The importance of these two factors can be seen in the poet's comment that none of Attila's warriors dared to pursue the fleeing Walter despite the desire to win long-lasting fame (411: virtute sua laudem captare perennem) and money-bags filled with treasure (412: gazam infarcire cruminis). The innovation of the *Waltharius* is to subject that ethos to criticism by connecting the desire for both wealth and glory with avarice. Presumably the Germanic legend had emphasized the theme of Hagen's conflicting loyalties. The *Waltharius* suppresses this theme, emphasizing the greed of Walter and Gunther and accusing Hagen of greed through the equation of avarice with the quest for glory. The whole poem, then, undercuts the apparently heroic stature and pronouncements of its characters by exposing their actions as misguided because they are prompted by values that are merely a manifestation of sinfulness.

The key to this criticism of epic heroism is to be found in the poem's brilliantly conceived final scene in which the three remaining warriors are injured. This scene has long perplexed readers of the *Waltharius*, both those who see it as a Christian work and those who believe its Christian elements to be superficial. The conclusion has been dismissed as a "trick ending" (Jones 1959, p. 18); and it has been suggested that the poet, forced to include the episode because it was part of the Walter legend, used it in spite of its implausibility (Von den Steinen, p. 19). In fact, as I mentioned earlier, there is no evidence that the mutilation of the warriors was part of the Walter legend. Our poet seems to have invented it.

The climactic scene employs direct moralizing combined with purposeful allusions to the Bible and the *Psychomachia* to draw together the disparate threads of the preceding narrative and make clear the basic moral point of the whole epic. The Christian references are used specifically to cast a mocking light on the poem's heroic motifs. The scene includes two main episodes. In the first occurs the disfiguring of the warriors; in the second, they desist from the feud and refresh themselves. The scene seems based on a scene from the *Psychomachia* (606–663); for after Greed has been killed, victorious Good Works announces that a time for celebration has arrived. She tells the Virtues to put down their weapons and rest, now that the lust for wealth has been defeated.

In the *Waltharius*, the wounds received by the three warriors have symbolic meaning. Hagen, we recall, entered the fight against Walter to avenge the death of his nephew. His wounds, the loss of an eye and several teeth, are ironically appropriate; for what monk could fail to be reminded of the Biblical injunction regarding "an eye for an eye, a tooth for a tooth" (Exodus 21: 22-25)? The poet himself intrudes into the narrative to make his own position clear when he lists the wounds suffered by the men (1401–1404):

> The fight is ended; marks of honor branded each.
> King Gunther's foot was lying there, and Walter's hand
> Was lying there, and also Hagen's twitching eye.
> Thus, thus the men have shared the treasure of the Avars!

The vividness of this gruesome list and the poet's exclamation call attention to its importance; and yet the list is inaccurate, an odd lapse for a poet who seems to pride himself on his artistic control. It fails to mention Hagen's teeth; moreover, although Walter had sliced off Gunther's entire leg, the catalogue makes note only of his foot. The omission and change, however, direct the reader to another scriptural reference (Mark 9: 42-48):

> And if your hand causes you to sin, cut it off; it is better for you to enter life maimed than with two hands to go to Hell, to the unquenchable fire. And if your foot causes you to sin, cut it off; it is better for you to enter life lame than with two feet to be thrown into Hell. And if your eye causes you to sin, pluck it out; it is better for you to enter the kingdom of God with one eye than with two eyes to be thrown into Hell, where the worm does not die, and the fire is not quenched.

This allusion allows us to regard the wounds suffered by the men as symbolic punishments for yielding to temptation, while the allusion to the *Psychomachia* suggests greed as the specific sin. In a sense, the punishment was inevitable. The men were acting on the motivation inherent in the heroic code, a code that the poet has characterized as being based on greed for worldly goods and fame.

The scene in the *Psychomachia* contains another element that has significance for both our reading of the *Waltharius* and our response to Walter. After inviting the Virtues to rest, Good Works describes the true rest that is possible only to those without greed. She exhorts her fellows to moderation and in this speech advises her colleagues when setting out on a journey not even to carry a wallet but to trust in God to provide for their needs. How different was Walter's attitude in taking so much treasure when he fled Attila!

The conclusion of the narrative is consistent with the overall design and ironic tone of the *Waltharius*. The poet, utilizing the language and trappings of epic poetry, has turned the genre to a new use. He has resolved the problem of welding Christian content to classical form by attacking the values of apparently heroic figures and rendering them, in essence, ridiculous. The poem is rich in humor. The characters themselves are fond of jokes and puns (see Morgan). In the heat of battle, one of Gunther's men puns on Walter's name to call him Walt-herr, that is, a wood-sprite (756–778). On two occasions Walter himself makes puns on Hagen's name. In German, *Hagedorn* means hawthorn. Walter, therefore, refers to Hagen as both thorny (1421: spinosus) and a hawthorn (1351: O paliure). In the poem's final scene, of course, Walter and Hagen make cruel jests at each other's expense. I have mentioned, moreover, the poet's humorous undercutting of Attila's anger and despair at Walter's escape. In a sense, the entire work is an extended joke on the characters and their misguided values. But we as modern readers should not forget that the butt of the poet's humor is sin, and in the ridicule of sin lies the poem's serious Christian spirit.

Sources and Influences

Various hypotheses for the source of the story recounted in the *Waltharius* have been proposed. Grimm (1838) suggested that the Latin poem was merely a translation of a specific Old High German

"Waltharilied." Panzer (1948), on the other hand, argued that the Latin poet invented the entire story, and that the *Waltharius* is the first work of literature to include Walter of Aquitaine. Both of these hypotheses have long since been discarded in favor of the view that the Latin poet was familiar with pre-existing Germanic sagas about Walter and Attila and refashioned the tale to his own purposes. Hauck (1954, pp. 23–26) has shown that it was not unusual for a monk in the ninth century to be familiar with stories from Germanic sagas. Indeed, the famous complaint "Quid Hinieldus cum Christo?" (What has Ingeld to do with Christ?) uttered by Charlemagne's adviser Alcuin refers specifically to the popularity in monasteries of tales about German heroes.

The *Waltharius* is in fact but one of numerous appearances of the same basic story about Walter of Aquitaine in medieval literature (see Learned, Smyser and Magoun, Carroll 1952). Earlier than the *Waltharius* are two fragments of the Old English poem *Waldere*. Composed probably in the eighth century, the *Waldere* recounts two scenes which seem to belong to the moments immediately preceding Walter's battles with Gunther's men.

Walter is mentioned three times in the *Nibelungenlied*. In the first passage Etzel, that is, Attila, recalls the time when Walter, Hagen, and Hildegund were his hostages (1756, Canto 28). In this passage, however, Etzel says that he sent Hagen home, whereas in the *Waltharius* Hagen escapes. Elsewhere in the *Nibleungenlied* a warrior makes note of the triumphs won by Hagen and Walter fighting together in Etzel's service (1797, Canto 29); and finally another warrior reproaches Hagen for "sitting on his shield" while Walter slew so many of his friends (2344, Canto 39).

It is unlikely that the author of the *Nibelungenlied* knew the Latin *Waltharius*. The evidence suggests rather that both poets drew on the same widely known body of legendary material. Indeed, the *Waltharius* cannot be said to have had a major influence on later literature. The poem, as its manuscript tradition attests, was known but far from famous during the eleventh and twelfth centuries. Most significant is the fact that no other work of medieval literature mentions the disfigurement of the three warriors which plays so prominent a role in the *Waltharius*. The most reasonable assumption would seem to be that the author of the *Waltharius* did invent this portion of the story.

RUODLIEB

Authorship

The *Ruodlieb* is a Latin narrative poem composed in southern Germany, probably between the years 1050 and 1075. It is of extraordinary value both as a work of art and as a "unique and precious testimony for important aspects of medieval life in Germany during the eleventh century" (Gamer 1955, p. 65); however, we know nothing certain about its author.

Our statements about the author must be limited to conjectures based on his poem; for he neither finished nor made public the *Ruodlieb*. Its very survival for the modern reader, as we will see, was a happy accident. The poet seems to have been a monk at Tegernsee, where the fragmentary manuscript of the narrative was discovered and in all probability where it was composed. Monks are treated very favorably in the work; and Braun (pp. 18–44) has argued convincingly that it reflects the ideals of Cluniac monasticism. The poem reflects also the poet's familiarity with the imperial court. It is possible, therefore, that he spent time in the court of Henry II, who became emperor in 1046 and died in 1056. Indeed, Henry has been proposed as the poet's model for the idealized Greater King into whose court Ruodlieb is welcomed (Hauck).

Beyond these comments, we can say only that the author was a keen observer of the world, able to depict the behavior of both nobles and rustics. We are not sure even how widely read he was. The evidence of the poem has generated radically different hypotheses. Brunhölzl (1965) found him ignorant of all literature other than the *Aeneid*. Braun (1962), on the other hand, saw in the *Ruodlieb* allusions to a wide range of literature that included Terence, Ovid, Petronius, Venantius Fortunatus, and even the *Waltharius*. The truth lies between these extreme views. I would agree with Brunhölzl that allusions only to the *Aeneid* can be verified. However, it is foolish to assume on that account that the author's reading was limited to Vergil. He does, after all, cite Pliny by name (II. 27), even though the passage involved attributes statements to Pliny not found among his extant works. Certain themes in the *Ruodlieb*, like the complaints about old age in Fragment XV and the formulaic "as many/so many" passage about love that appears in Fragment XVII (11–14) have a long history in literature (Walther). The education at Tegernsee is known to have included such rhetorical themes based on Christian Latin writers (Gamer 1955, pp. 96–97). This fact helps explain their presence in the *Ruodlieb* and suggests that the poet was acquainted with a fairly wide range of classical and Christian literature.

Artistic Achievement

The *Ruodlieb* is a unique and captivating work of art which has resisted all attempts to categorize it. Perhaps the best measure of the poem's originality exists in the diversity of critical responses to it. The *Ruodlieb* has been variously called the first courtly romance (Wilmotte), the earliest courtly novel (Zeydel), the first realistic novel (Gamer 1955), a classicizing epic (Brunhölzl), and a Christian epic (Kratz 1973). It has even been called a totally individualistic work divorced from any literary tradition (Manitius, p. 533). Given the enormous narrative diversity of the poem, from realistic depictions of everyday life to fairy-tale encounters with dwarves, we are perhaps best advised to approach the *Ruodlieb* as a "poetic experiment" that illustrates a movement away from the values of epic toward those to be associated with romance (Dronke 1970).

The narrative, of which approximately 2500 verses survive in fifteen fragments of various lengths, recounts the adventures of a young man who, inadequately rewarded by his lords, leaves home to avoid feuds and better his fortunes. He leaves behind his widowed mother. Upon reaching the court of a foreign king, the man (who is not identified by name until later in the tale) distinguishes himself as a hunter, warrior, and diplomat. This foreign monarch is identified only as the Greater King. The hero first ingratiates himself by demonstrating his skill as a fisherman and a hunter with the herb called *bugloss*. Later, a war breaks out between the people of the Greater King and a neighboring country ruled by a Lesser King. After leading the army of the Greater King to victory, Ruodlieb later acts as his ruler's emissary in the ensuing peace negotiations.

Shortly thereafter, a letter from his mother, who reports that all his enemies have been eliminated, prompts Ruodlieb to seek the

Introduction

king's permission to leave the court and return home. The king's rewards to Ruodlieb for his service include both gnomic counsels and a generous supply of treasure. Ruodlieb's journey home includes several episodes that demonstrate the correctness of the king's advice, particularly his warning against redheaded men. Later, Ruodlieb stops at the castle of a widow, who turns out to be his mother's godchild and arranges the marriage of her daughter with his nephew. At home, Ruodlieb gains great honors. He follows his mother's advice and seeks to marry, but the woman suggested to him as a suitable wife is found to be dissolute and unworthy. At this point Ruodlieb's mother has a dream that prophesies even greater successes for her son. The scene changes radically now. Ruodlieb has just captured a dwarf who promises to reveal the location of a substantial treasure and a beautiful princess (whom the hero presumably will marry). Here the manuscript breaks off.

The *Ruodlieb* is written in Latin leonine hexameters, that is, hexameters in which there occurs an internal rhyme between the last syllable of the line and the last syllable of a word near the middle of the line, usually in the third foot. The poet had, at best, a tenuous mastery of Latin prosody; for the poem abounds in such errors as long syllables made short (e.g., XII.39: matre) and short syllables made long (e.g., V.198: bōna). The poet constantly changes the tenses of verbs within a sentence, usually for metrical reasons. The Latin of the *Ruodlieb*, that of an eleventh-century German, presents enormous difficulties to a reader familiar only with classical Latin. A few German, Romance, and even Greek words occur. In four instances, Latin words are given German glosses. Unusual forms of Latin words appear; gerunds and gerundives are used in ways unknown to classical authors; the subjunctive and indicative forms of verbs are often used without apparent distinction. The Latin, in summation, is decidedly odd. In part, this oddness can be attributed to the natural evolution of Latin; in part, to misunderstandings and errors by the poet; in part, to the demands of writing in Latin hexameter. Fortunately, an excellent critical discussion of the poet's Latin, including a comprehensive glossary of unusual words in the narrative, is available (Ford 1966).

Although the Latin of the *Ruodlieb* is difficult and occasionally even ungrammatical, it possesses an exceptional vitality and attractiveness. The author is particularly adept at characterization through dialogue. The interrogation of the exile by the huntsman of the king in the first fragment (73–117), for example, is a model of tact. On the other hand, the episode in which the redhead (VII. 33–129) bullies his old host and crudely propositions the man's young wife is filled with dramatic tension and coarse humor. The language of the poem has been attacked as an unsuccessful attempt to recreate Vergilian style (Brunhölzl); however, I believe that it is a more accurate and fairer assessment to praise the author for creating a language suited to the unique nature of his subject matter and his apparent attempt to forge a new literary genre (Dronke 1970). A comparison of the Latin of the *Ruodlieb* with that of the *Waltharius* is instructive. The latter work, which recreates a classical genre, aims at a Latin close to the classical norms. The former work, which makes allusions to but rejects the classical epic tradition, is written in a new Latin that is enriched by words and constructions taken from other languages.

Because the *Ruodlieb* has survived only in a fragmentary and incomplete form, no conclusive statement can be made concerning its overall design. We do not know whether the poet completed the work. It is more likely, since the narrative breaks off abruptly in the middle of an episode, that he did not. Two assumptions about the lost, or, more likely, unwritten conclusion of the work seem most plausible. One assumption is that the series of maxims that the Greater King gives Ruodlieb on the eve of his departure was intended as a frame for the remainder of the tale. Certainly the episode following the giving of the maxims provides a convincing example of the wisdom of the king's warning against redheaded men. The other assumption is that the poet had abandoned this design. The applicability of the other maxims to the rest of the narrative is less obvious. The sudden change of the story in the final fragments may indicate that the poet had decided to alter radically the nature of his narrative, and he may have meant it to conclude with Ruodlieb's acquisition of the treasure and a bride.

Another apparent inconsistency in the narrative is the poet's use of personal names. For most of the tale, the characters seem intended as types rather than individuals. The central character is called at different times the man, soldier, exile, and envoy. Neither the Greater King nor the Lesser King is given a name. In XII, however, the hero is called Ruodlieb, a name drawn from Germanic legend. This name also is written over·an erasure in V, perhaps added by the author after he decided to name his hero. In XIII, the Greater King's realm is described as African, although with this term the author probably is referring to southern Italy. The final fragment gives names to the princess and to the two kings about whose treasure Ruodlieb is told. It has been suggested that the poet changed his mind about using names as he composed the narrative (Langosch); but his delayed identification of his hero may have been part of his original design, for the practice has parallels in later romance narratives.

As a narrative poem, the *Ruodlieb* invites immediate comparison with the *Aeneid*, the only classical work to which the poet makes an unmistakable allusion. The poet's choice of Latin hexameters to recount the adventures of a central heroic figure is the first indication of his epic intent. Moreover, the first strokes of his portrait of Ruodlieb bear significant resemblances to Vergil's Aeneas. The opening line of each poem identifies its hero simply as "a man." Both men are exiles from their native lands who, suffering numerous hardships, travel through foreign realms. Each man is a mighty warrior who eventually triumphs. As Aeneas will marry Lavinia, we have little doubt that Ruodlieb will wed the fair princess about whom he is told in the final fragment of the narrative.

The *Ruodlieb*, however, differs drastically from the *Aeneid* in its content and language. It stands apart from the *Waltharius* and other classicizing epics particularly in the wealth of material from folklore and contemporary life with which the poet has enriched his tale. Moreover, the poet eschews the scenes of warfare that figure so prominently in the Latin epic tradition. The battle between the forces of the Greater King and the Lesser King is not described. Instead, the poet focuses attention on the lengthy peace negotiations that follow the victory of the forces led by Ruodlieb. The poet's interest seems to lie far more in scenes of everyday life that demonstrate proper human relations.

Despite the fragmentary state of the *Ruodlieb*, a tentative conclusion about its intent can be drawn. I agree with Vollmann (1981) that it is a didactic work, a mirror of knighthood. The focus of the narrative is upon Ruodlieb's growth toward a new kind of heroism based upon Christian principles and courtly behavior. His primary model for this new heroism is the Greater King, whose court serves as an example of the proper relationship between a ruler and his subjects. The various episodes of the story provide either positive or cautionary examples for proper behavior. Therefore, in its basic theme the *Ruodlieb* has less in common with the epic tradition than with the genre of romance which would emerge in the next century. The poet reveals a knowledge of and intense interest in proper courtly behavior. Ruodlieb, like Tristan, is not only an accomplished hunter and fighter but also a skillful musician. Amusements of court life, from chess to trained birds, are described in detail; and depictions of jewelry and elegant clothing abound. At the heart of the narrative is the poet's attempt to fashion a new vision of heroism appropriate for the new circumstances of his time.

At the beginning of the narrative, Ruodlieb is pictured as already proficient as a hunter and a warrior but unfortunate in that he has served unworthy lords who have cheated him of his rightful rewards. Nonetheless, he cannot be described as a truly Christian hero, since he has been willing to serve his lords as an avenger, in contrast to Christ's teaching concerning vengeance (Matthew 5:38–42).

Ruodlieb's sojourn at the court of the Greater King serves to teach him a new, better model of values and behavior. The life at the court of this king is marked by gaiety, congeniality, and generosity. The Greater King's treatment of his men is presented as a contrast to the ignoble behavior of the lords in Ruodlieb's homeland. The effect of the Greater King on Ruodlieb's values is evident almost immediately; for after the war with the soldiers of the Lesser King, he refuses to punish them because the Greater King has specifically forbidden vengeance. The Greater King's treatment of his vanquished enemies reflects his *virtus*, *sophia*, *pietas*, and *clementia* (Gamer 1957–58). These concepts of "virtue, wisdom, piety, and forgiveness" figure prominently throughout the narrative. They clearly are the foundation of a new Christian definition of heroism; for the Greater King, who embodies these qualities most obviously, is himself described by the defeated Lesser King as the earthly representative of Christ (IV.154: tu solus es in vice Christi). Ruodlieb, when he is about to leave the king's court, even states that every day there has been Easter to him (V.303–307).

The Greater King emphasizes that excellence involves both inward values and outward behavior. He chides Ruodlieb for gaining wealth by defeating the Lesser King and his nobles at chess during the peace negotiations. When the Lesser King offers an extraordi-

Introduction

nary array of presents to the victors, the Greater King declines. He accepts only the symbolically rich gift of a pair of dancing bears that seem to signify harmony and the control of base desires (Dronke 1970, pp. 44–46).

Ruodlieb learns not only forgiveness but also wisdom from the Greater King. When he announces his desire to return home, he is given a choice of wisdom or wealth as his departing gift. Ruodlieb chooses wisdom; and this choice leads to his receiving both wisdom and treasures. The treasure is in the form of a generous supply of gold and jewels hidden in what seem merely loaves of bread which the king instructs Ruodlieb not to break open until he reaches home. The wisdom takes the form of twelve maxims.

That portion of the narrative depicting Ruodlieb's journey home contains several exemplary episodes. The Greater King, for example, specifically warns against redheaded men; and on the journey a redhead joins Ruodlieb. Although Ruodlieb refuses to become the redhead's friend, he allows the man to travel with him; and soon the redhead manages to steal Ruodlieb's cloak. Later, the two men reach a village. Following another of the king's maxims, Ruodlieb seeks lodging at the home of a young man with an old wife. The redhead, however, seeks out an old man with a young wife.

The adventures of Ruodlieb and the redhead are parallel. The redhead seems in part to represent pride, for he is described as vain and excessively haughty (VI.177: vanus nimiumque superbus). The redhead engages in sexual intercourse with his host's wife, and the lovers murder the old man. At the ensuing trial, the wife repents and is pardoned; but the redhead presumably will be executed for his crime. Ruodlieb, meanwhile, discovers at his place of lodging still another example of correct social behavior. The same ideal of generosity and festivity that prevailed at the court of the Greater King exists in the lowlier house of this young man and his wife. As Ruodlieb called his time with the Greater King "Easter," so too the young man says that he regards any day that Christ sends him a guest as Easter (VII.1–15).

In the final part of his journey home, Ruodlieb meets and befriends a young nephew of his. When the two of them stop at a castle, the youth falls in love with the daughter of the châtelain. The sojourn at the castle has two interrelated episodes. The youth and the maiden fall in love; and Ruodlieb, who helps arrange the match, demonstrates his mastery of proper courtly behavior. He demonstrates his skill as hunter and musician. Taking up a harp, he provides the music as the young man and girl dance. As he is compared to a falcon, she is likened to a swallow. The image not only symbolizes his strength and her graceful beauty but also foreshadows the nature of his attempts to snare her in wedlock. Indeed, he does not win but is won by her. The two play at dice. First she wins. When she loses a game, she takes a ring from her finger and tosses it to him. This ring does not fit him, but he can wear it if he is willing to adjust it. This little scene, especially with its emphasis on the girl's lack of submissiveness, prefigures the wedding of the two that occurs later in the narrative.

At home, Ruodlieb arranges the wedding of his nephew, an episode that is linked thematically with the hero's own search for a wife. The wedding of the youth and maiden includes a remarkable interchange in which she demands that he swear fidelity to her and that their marriage be based on mutual trust without deceit rather than on her subjugation to him. The maiden is aware that the young man had been shamefully involved with a courtesan; and, as earlier she defeated him with dice, in this scene she conquers him with arguments, among them the fact that God fashioned only one woman for Adam out of his rib. The poet comments with approval on the couple's future, saying that he has little cause for anxiety about their future harmony.

Ruodlieb's attempt to find a suitable wife, on the other hand, proves unsuccessful, perhaps because he depends upon the advice of his relatives. And yet Ruodlieb's willingness to seek a wife at the prompting of his mother is related to the apparent main theme of the narrative at this point; for when he reaches home, Ruodlieb is able to reflect in his behavior the lessons he has learned at the court of the Greater King. When he and his mother break open the loaves and discover the treasure within, Ruodlieb realizes that he has been richly honored. This episode recalls the fact that Ruodlieb had left his homeland originally because his lords had withheld from him those honors that he deserved. He responds with humility and a prayer that God grant him the wisdom to make the best use of his new wealth. Hirsh (1973) has suggested that the existence of the Greater King suggests the role of the Greatest King, that is, God; and that the final section of the narrative is meant to show the rewards of

God to Ruodlieb for putting into practice the values taught him by the Greater King.

In the last major surviving section of the work, Ruodlieb's mother has a dream that prophesies that God will further honor Ruodlieb, although his mother will die before the events take place. We are told that her good deeds have helped win these honors for Ruodlieb; and in this way the poet's control over his narrative becomes even clearer. Her intense grief at her son's departure is now replaced by her joy at the knowledge of his future greatness. The episode with the dwarf, during which the poem ends abruptly, was intended, I believe, to demonstrate the correctness of the mother's dream.

The skill with which the poet has fashioned his portrait of Ruodlieb and his depiction of Ruodlieb's education refutes once and for all any notion that the poet was incapable of organizing his diverse material into a coherent meaningful whole (Brunhölzl; see replies by Dronke 1970 and Langosch 1972). Ruodlieb is a new hero, whose qualities reflect a step away from epic heroism toward the heroism of the romance genre. He learns to act in accordance with the four qualities of *virtus, pietas, clementia*, and *sophia*. These qualities he encounters in the person of the Greater King, whose court is a model of the ideal society. From the Greater King he also receives for the first time the honors of which he previously had been unjustly deprived in his homeland. Upon his return home from the king's court, he gains, through his own noble actions and those of his mother, even greater honors from God.

Despite the differences in their tone and their use of classical models, the *Ruodlieb* has much in common with the *Waltharius*. Both works extend the capabilities of Latin epic by making it a suitable vehicle for the expression of Christian values. The *Waltharius* is an ironic epic, whose basic Christian theme, the condemnation of greed, is inextricably bound up with a denial of classical standards of heroic action. The *Ruodlieb*, on the other hand, attempts to provide a new model of heroism in the person of Ruodlieb. Both works specifically condemn the destructive power of avarice, the desire for vengeance, and the concern with worldly fame. In Walter and Ruodlieb, they also have created two of the most striking characters in Latin literature.

Sources and Influence

The range of material included in the *Ruodlieb* is most impressive. Gamer (1955), in particular, has listed the possible sources for the various episodes and elements of the narrative. Perhaps the most important source for the poet was folklore. His narrative contains dwarves who know the whereabouts of treasures, prophetic dreams, folk maxims, an herb that can not only blind wolves but also prevent fish from swimming under water, and instructions for creating a precious gem from the urine of a caged lynx.

The name of the hero can be connected with other Germanic legends. One version of the *Eckeliet*, for example, mentions a king named Ruotliep, who is given a sword stolen from three dwarves. Similarly, one thread of the *Thidrekssaga* concerns a dwarf and a king named Rozeleif (Gamer 1955, pp. 83–84). Schneider, who believed the poem to be based on a pre-existing German "Ruodliebslied," has shown that the connection between a hero and a dwarf, such as occurs at the end of the *Ruodlieb*, is a common element of Germanic saga (1925, pp. 167, 263).

Among the many episodes that seem to reflect the poet's use of oral traditions, the dream of Ruodlieb's mother (XVII.89–101) is of particular interest. This dream, in which she sees her son first threatened by wild boars and then crowned by a dove as he sits in a linden tree, has much in common with other prophetic dreams in German sagas. Schach (1954) has pointed out parallels in works ranging from the *Nibelungenlied* to the Norse *Heimskringla*.

There are of course many folk tales about the adventures of a young man who goes abroad to seek his fortune. Seiler (1882) and Braun (1962) have investigated in detail examples of tales in which the adventurer is offered wisdom in the form of maxims and in which these maxims form the framework, so to speak, for further adventures. Sources for specific maxims and episodes in the *Ruodlieb* have been found in literature ranging from Greek romances (Burdach) to Arabic tales (Löwenthal), from Irish-Cornish tales (Seiler, p. 52) to Christian hagiographic legends (Gamer 1955, pp. 99–101).

Folk traditions were but one of the sources from which the author drew his material. The *Ruodlieb* is also a rich source of information about everyday life in eleventh-century Germany. It

Introduction   xxxv

contains, for example, detailed and realistic descriptions of a judicial proceeding (Vollmann 1979), of a marriage ceremony (Gellinek), and of the proper greeting and treatment of guests. The episode at the court of the Lesser King includes one of the earliest descriptions of chess to be found in Western literature (Gamer 1954); and the poet offers detailed pictures of his characters' clothing and jewels, as well as their entertainments and style of dancing.

The *Ruodlieb* had no influence, of course, on later literature. The author did not complete it, and no other writer either borrows from or makes reference to it. Our knowledge of it, as the discussion in the following section will show, is the result of a fortuitous set of circumstances.

Editorial Policy for This Text and Translation

The textual and editorial histories of both the *Waltharius* and *Ruodlieb* have led me to adopt a conservative policy with regard to proposing new readings. Every modern reader of the *Waltharius* owes an inestimable debt of gratitude to the labors of Karl Strecker, whose magisterial edition of the poem has provided the basis for my edition. The *Ruodlieb* has also been edited by, among others, Friedrich Seiler, Edwin Zeydel, and Gordon B. Ford, Jr. I consulted Ford's excellent edition, in particular, while preparing my own.

The *Waltharius* survives wholly in four and partially in another eight manuscripts described by Strecker (1951, pp. 3–16). The four manuscripts containing the entire *Waltharius* are:

B—Brussels, Bibl. Royale, 5380-84, late 11th or early 12th century.

P—Paris, Bibl. Nationale, Latin 8488A, late 11th century.

K—Karlsruhe, Landesbibl. Rastatt 24, 12th century.

T—Trier, Stadtbibl. 2002, fifteenth century.

Three of the complete manuscripts (BPT) are descended from a common archetype. All three include the 22-line dedicatory poem by the monk Gerald. The fourth of the complete manuscripts (K) is from another, less reliable archetype.

In preparing this edition, I have relied heavily on the two oldest complete manuscripts (B and P). The latter was copied, perhaps at

Fleury, in the last quarter of the eleventh century. The former was copied, probably at Gembloux, in the late eleventh or early twelfth century. As Strecker showed, these manuscripts represent the most reliable textual tradition of the poem. I have also made constant reference to Strecker's edition of the *Waltharius*. I have adopted his numbering of the lines, and I have indicated in the Textual Notes all those instances in which I have offered a reading that differs from Strecker's suggestion. The recent edition of the *Waltharius* prepared by A. K. Bate is seriously flawed and of little use.

The *Ruodlieb*, as I mentioned earlier, survives only in a fragmentary form. While we may regret that the poet, for whatever reason, did not complete the *Ruodlieb*, we must be grateful that the work survived at all. The text was first discovered in 1803 by B. J. Docen of the Royal Bavarian Library in Munich. It was written on irregularly cut parchment strips in the bindings of manuscripts from Tegernsee. Docen began the work of copying these fragments. Andreas Schmeller, Docen's successor as librarian, continued this copying and also discovered more fragments. The fragments that were collected now constitute the "Munich" manuscript (Clm 19486 in the Bayerische Staatsbibliothek). In 1840, a fragment of another manuscript, evidently copied from the Munich manuscript, was also discovered in St. Florian, near Linz. This fragmentary manuscript is now housed in the St. Florian Chorherrenstift. It was first published in Moriz Haupt's *Exempla Poesis Medii Aevi* in 1834. Schmeller and Jacob Grimm published the Munich manuscript and the St. Florian fragment in their *Lateinische Gedichte des X. und XI. Jahrhunderts* (1838).

The first critical edition of the poem was published by Seiler in 1882. His edition took into account both the Munich and St. Florian fragments and included a discussion on the nature of the narrative and its language. A major issue in editing the *Ruodlieb* involves the necessity to offer conjectured completions of the poem's numerous mutilated lines. Seiler's conjectures were generally plausible. The following year Ludwig Laistner (1883) published a long review of Seiler's edition in which he suggested numerous corrections and a different arrangement of the fragments.

Three editions of the *Ruodlieb* have appeared in the twentieth century. Karl Langosch's edition, published in 1956, was basically a reprinting of Seiler's version but with the ordering of the fragments

Introduction   xxxvii

suggested by Laistner. In 1959, Edwin Zeydel published an edition. The most recent edition was prepared by Gordon B. Ford, Jr. Ford's edition, which also includes a linguistic introduction and a comprehensive glossary, offers many new conjectures about unfinished lines and is far superior to those of Seiler and Zeydel. A facsimile of both manuscripts of the poem has also been published. The edition presented here is based on my own transcription of the Munich manuscript. I have also worked from the facsimile edition. In preparing my edition of the *Ruodlieb*, I have adopted most of the conjectures found in Ford's critical edition. Since the *Ruodlieb* exists in one manuscript, and that in the author's own hand, the problem of deciding between alternate manuscript readings does not exist. The primary area of debate lies in the conjectured completions of lines. I have indicated in the Textual Notes section those places in which I differ from Ford. Generally, either reading is possible. In V.1, however, I believe that Ford's conjecture (*cancellis*) is impossible, because the letters "*eg*" are discernible in the lacuna. In XII.1 I have adopted a reading suggested by Benedikt Vollmann (1981). Following a long tradition among editors of the *Ruodlieb*, I have used brackets to set off the beginnings and endings of lines that are conjectures. I have also adopted the practice of all other editors of referring to the fragments by Roman numerals. To aid the reader, I have followed Ford's practice of giving the classicized spelling of the diphthongs *-ae* and *-oe*. For both poems I have distinguished *i* from *j* and *u* from *v*, and I have provided capitalization and punctuation where required. Discussion of issues concerning emendation, interpretation, and the translation of ambiguous or particularly vexing passages will be found in the Textual Notes. I have not identified the numerous references in the *Waltharius* to other works of literature. Strecker (1951) has compiled this information in his edition of the poem.

As a translator, I have endeavored to provide English versions of the *Waltharius* and *Ruodlieb* that are faithful not only to the literal meaning but also to the rich poetic texture of these two works. For that reason, I have attempted a verse translation. Neither the *Waltharius* nor *Ruodlieb* has previously been translated into English poetry; and the existing prose versions, though useful, fail to communicate the vitality of either poem. In order to give a line-by-line translation, I have adopted a basic twelve-syllable iambic line, with occasional feminine line endings. This longer line has permitted me to preserve the meaning of each line while attempting to capture, however imperfectly, the dramatic and poetic life of the original. On a few occasions it was necessary for me to use two lines of English to render one line of Latin.

I have tried to fashion translations that recreate both the virtues and the faults of the originals. Of the two works, the *Ruodlieb* presented the greater difficulties. The language is idiosyncratic, sometimes puzzling. The quality of the poetry ranges from the dynamic cleverness of its dialogue to extreme awkwardness in several narrative sections. I have tried to avoid the temptation of "improving" the less artful passages. I have not attempted to recreate the internal rhyme of the poet's leonine hexameters; nor have I followed the poet's practice of switching between the past and present tenses in the same sentence.

I am grateful to the Deutscher Akademischer Austauschdienst for a fellowship that enabled me to travel to Germany, where I examined major manuscripts and consulted with medieval Latinists about issues involved in editing and translating the *Waltharius* and *Ruodlieb*. My colleague and friend Rainer Schulte, Director of the Center for Translation Studies at The University of Texas at Dallas, provided invaluable advice and encouragement. Lowry Nelson, Jr., solved several problems for me and made numerous suggestions that have markedly improved the translation. Finally, I wish to express my thanks to Eleanor Oberwetter and Sheryl St. Germain for their careful and efficient typing, and to Sandra Schulte for proofreading the entire manuscript.

Richardson, Texas   D.M.K.

Select Bibliography

WALTHARIUS

I. Major Editions

Lateinische Gedichte des X. und XI. Jahrhunderts. Ed. Jacob Grimm and Andreas Schmeller, 1838; rpt. Amsterdam, Rodopi, 1967. Contains both *Waltharius* and *Ruodlieb*.

Waltharii Poesis. Das Waltharilied Ekkehards I. von St. Gallen nach den Geraldushss. Ed. Hermann Althof. Leipzig: Dietrich, 1905.

Waltharius. Ed. Karl Strecker. Berlin: Weidmann, 1947. Includes preface by Gerald.

Waltharius. Ed. Karl Strecker. Monumenta Germaniae Historica, Poetae Latini Aevi Carolini. Vol. 6, Pt. 1. Weimar: Böhlau, 1951. An authoritative critical edition based on all known manuscripts. Supersedes all earlier editions. Does not include Gerald's preface.

Waltharius, Ruodlieb, Märchenepen. Lateinische Epik des Mittelalters mit deutschen Versen. Ed. Karl Langosch. A reprint of Strecker's 1951 edition. Includes a facing German verse translation.

II. English Translations

Jones, Charles W. *Medieval Literature in Translation.* New York: McKay, 1950, pp. 192–208. Includes lines 1–571 and 1332–1455 translated into verse by Jones. The translation is free and often inaccurate.

Smyser, H. M., and F. P. Magoun, Jr. *Walter of Aquitaine: Materials for the Study of His Legend.* New London: Connecticut College Monographs

III. Critical Writings

Andersson, Theodore. *Early Epic Scenery*. Ithaca: Cornell, 1976. A study of the epic tradition through the depiction of scenic backgrounds. "Spatial Design in the Carolingian Epic," pp. 104–144, includes an analysis of the major mass battle scene in the *Waltharius*.

Brinkmann, Hennig. "Ekkehards Waltharius als Kunstwerk." *Zeitschrift für deutsche Bildung*, 43 (1928), 625–636. The poem is not a school exercise but a carefully designed work of art in which the poet calls attention to his control.

Carroll, Benjamin H. "An Essay on the Walther Legend." *Florida State University Studies*, 5 (1952), 123–179.

———. "On the Lineage of the Walther Legend." *Germanic Review*, 28 (1953), 34–41.

Dronke, Peter. "Functions of Classical Borrowing in Medieval Latin." *Classical Influences on European Culture: A.D. 500–900*, Ed. R. R. Bolgar. Cambridge: Cambridge University, 1971, pp. 159–164. The depiction of Attila's hangover undercuts his anger by making him seem ridiculous.

Elliott, Alison Goddard. Review of *Mocking Epic*, by Dennis M. Kratz. *Speculum*, 57 (1982), 387–389.

Hauck, Karl. "Das Walthariusepos des Bruders Gerald von Eichstätt." *Germanisch-Romanische Monatsschrift*, 4 (1954), 1–27.

Jones, George Fenwick. "The Ethos of the *Waltharius*." *Middle Ages–Reformation, Volkskunde: Festschrift for John G. Kunstmann*. Chapel Hill: North Carolina Studies in the Germanic Languages and Literatures, 1959, pp. 1–20. Walter is a pagan hero, the *Waltharius* a pagan poem.

Katscher, Rosemarie. "Waltharius—Dichtung und Dichter." *Mittellateinisches Jahrbuch*, 9 (1976), 48–120. The Christianity of the poem lies in the new values exemplified by Walter. A detailed, thoughtful essay.

Krammer, Hedwig. *Die Verfasserfrage des Waltharius*. Vienna: Wissenschaftliche Gesellschaft, 1973. Dates the poem in the tenth century.

Select Bibliography

Contains a thorough review of literature concerning date and authorship.

Kratz, Dennis M. *Mocking Epic: Waltharius, Alexandreis and the Problem of Christian Heroism.* Studia Humanitatis. Madrid: Porrúa, 1980. The narrative attacks the values associated with epic heroism.

Learned, Marion Dexter. *The Saga of Walther of Aquitaine.* 1892; rpt. Westport, Conn.: Greenwood, 1970. A survey of all known references in literature to the Walter legend. Generally outdated by subsequent scholarship.

Morgan, Gareth. "Walther the Wood-Sprite." *Medium Aevum*, 41 (1972), 16–19. In 756–778 Ekivrid is punning on Walter's name in German. "Trans-language" word play is a mark of the poet's style.

Önnerfors, Alf. *Die Verfasserschaft des Walthariusepos aus sprachlicher Sicht.* Opladen: Westdeutscher, 1979. In addition to proposing Grimald as the author, offers guidelines for determining the poet's borrowings from other works.

Panzer, Friedrich. *Der Kampf am Wasichenstein.* Speyer am Rhein: Verlag Historisches Museum der Pfalz, 1948. The story is the poet's invention, and is based on the ambush of Theseus in Statius' *Thebaid*; this thesis is now discredited.

Pickering, F. P. *Augustinus oder Boethius?* 2 vols. Philologische Studien und Quellen, 39, 80. Berlin: De Gruyter, 1967–76.

Ploss, Emil Ernst, ed. *Waltharius und Walthersage: Eine Dokumentation der Forschung.* Hildesheim: Olms Studien 10, 1969. A broad anthology of the major works of German scholarship concerning the *Waltharius*.

Reeh, Rudolf. "Zur Frage nach dem Verfasser des Walthariliedes." *Zeitschrift für deutsche Philologie*, 51 (1926), 413–431.

Schaller, Dieter. "Geraldus und St. Gallen. Zum Widmungsgedicht des 'Waltharius.'" *Mittellateinisches Jahrbuch*, 2 (1965), 74–84. The prefatory poem does not establish Gerald as the author of the *Waltharius* but offers to Erkambald the work of another poet.

———. "Fröhliche Wissenschaft vom 'Waltharius.'" *Mittellateinisches Jahrbuch*, 16 (1981), 54–57. A review that dismisses Bate's edition, especially the introduction, as frivolous.

Schieffer, R. "Silius Italicus in St. Gallen—ein Hinweis zur Lokalisierung des 'Waltharius.'" *Mittellateinisches Jahrbuch*, 10 (1974), 7–19.

Schumann, Otto. "Zum *Waltharius*." *Zeitschrift für deutsches Altertum*, 83

(1951), 12–40. The Waltharius, composed in the ninth century, presents a Christian hero.

Stackmann, Karl. "Antike Elemente im *Waltharius*." *Euphorion*, 45 (1950), 231–248. An important study of the ways in which the poet not only imitates but also transforms his classical models.

Steinen, Wolfram von den. "Der *Waltharius* und sein Dichter." *Zeitschrift für deutsches Altertum*, 84 (1952), 1–47. The poem reflects, in its depiction of Walter, the values of the Carolingian Renaissance.

Wagner, Hans. *Ekkehard und Vergil*. Heidelberg: Quellen und Studien zur Geschichte und Kultur des Altertums und des Mittelalters. Reihe D.9, 1939. Documents specific lines from the *Aeneid* that are imitated or alluded to in the *Waltharius*.

Wehrli, Max. "*Waltharius*: Gattungsgeschichtliche Betrachtungen." *Mittellateinisches Jahrbuch*, 2 (1965), 63–73. Discusses the theme of greed.

RUODLIEB

I. Major Editions

Lateinische Gedichte des X. und XI. Jahrhunderts. See listing under *Waltharius*.

Ruodlieb: Der älteste Roman des Mittelalters. Ed. Friedrich Seiler. Halle: Weisenhaus, 1882. The first critical edition, with extensive introduction and a glossary of unusual words.

Waltharius, Ruodlieb, Märchenepen. Lateinische Epik des Mittelalters mit deutschen Versen. See listing under *Waltharius*. Basically reprints, with a differing order of the fragments, Seiler's edition.

Ruodlieb: The Earliest Courtly Novel (after 1050). Introduction, Text, Translation, Commentary and Textual Notes. Ed. Edwin H. Zeydel. Chapel Hill: North Carolina Studies in the Germanic Languages and Literatures 23, 1959. A critical edition based on a re-examination of the Munich and St. Florian manuscripts.

The Ruodlieb: Linguistic Introduction, Latin Text, and Glossary. Ed. Gordon B. Ford, Jr. Leiden: Brill, 1966. A carefully prepared critical edition offering many new conjectures.

Ruodlieb: Faksimile-Ausgabe des Codex latinus Monacensis 19486 der Bayerischen Staatsbibliothek München und der Fragmente von St. Florian. Ed. Walter Haug. Vol. 1, Pt. 2. Wiesbaden: Reichert, 1974.

Ruodlieb: Mittellateinisch/Deutsch. Ed. Fritz Peter Knapp. Stuttgart: Reclam, 1977. Reprints Ford's edition, but with extensive critical notes and a full bibliography. Contains a facing German translation.

II. English Translations

Ford, Gordon B., Jr. *The Ruodlieb: The First Medieval Epic of Chivalry From Eleventh Century Germany.* Leiden: Brill, 1965. A prose translation, more readable and reliable than Zeydel's version.

Zeydel, Edwin H. *Ruodlieb: The Earliest Courtly Novel (after 1050).* See listing above. An awkward, overly literal translation.

III. Critical Writings

Braun, Werner. *Studien zum Ruodlieb.* Quellen und Forschungen zur Sprach- und Kulturgeschichte der Germanischen Völker. Neue Folge 7 (131). Berlin: de Gruyter 1962. *Ruodlieb* expresses an ideal of knighthood influenced by Cluniac monasticism.

Brunhölzl, Franz. "Zum *Ruodlieb.*" *Deutsche Vierteljahrsschrift für Literaturwissenschaft und Geistesgeschichte,* 39 (1965), 506–552. Poet attempted but failed to fashion a Vergilian epic. An unsympathetic essay that has prompted numerous critical responses.

Burdach, Konrad. *Vorspiel: Gesammelte Schriften zur Geschichte des deutschen Geistes.* Halle: Waisenhaus, 1925. Greek romances influence the style and content of the narrative.

Dahinten, Kurt. "Zum Problem der literaturhistorischen Stellung des *Ruodlieb,*" *Historische Vierteljahrsschrift,* 28 (1934), 503–512. The *Ruodlieb* as a work of German rather than Latin literature.

Dronke, Peter. *Poetic Individuality in the Middle Ages.* Oxford: Clarendon, 1970. See *"Ruodlieb:* The Emergence of Romance," pp. 33–65.

Gamer, Helena M. "The Earliest Evidence of Chess in Western Literature: The Einsiedeln Verses." *Speculum,* 29 (1954), 734–750.

---. "The *Ruodlieb* and Tradition." *ARV: Journal of Scandinavian Folklore*, 11 (1955), 65–103. Studies the poet's use of matter drawn from literature, everyday life, and folklore.

---. "Studien zum *Ruodlieb*." *Zeitschrift für deutsches Altertum*, 88 (1957–58), 249–266. The Greater King is the model for the four virtues on which the poet's new vision of heroism is based.

Gellinek, Christian. "Marriage by Consent in Literary Sources of Medieval Germany." *Studia Gratiana*, 12 (1967), 554–579.

Giesebrecht, Wilhelm von. *Geschichte der deutschen Kaiserzeit*. Volume 1. Leipzig: Duncker und Humblot, 1889. Work reflects conditions in the court of Henry II.

Hauck, Karl. "Heinrich III. und der *Ruodlieb*." *Beiträge zur Geschichte der deutschen Sprache und Literatur*, [PBB] 70 (1948), 372–419.

Hirsh, John. "The Argument of *Ruodlieb*." *Classical Folia*, 27 (1973), 74–83. The poem is meant to be read symbolically, with the Greater King's court a reflection of divine harmony.

Knapp, Fritz Peter. "Bemerkungen zum *Ruodlieb*." *Zeitschrift für deutsches Altertum*, 104 (1975), 189–204. Discusses issues of genre and the didactic nature of the poem.

---. *Similitudo: Stil- und Erzählfunktion von Vergleich und Exempel in der lateinischen, französischen und deutschen Grossepik des Hochmittelalters*. Volume 1. Philologica Germanica 2. Vienna: Braumüller 1975. Studies the use of similes and exempla in selected medieval Latin epics. The chapter on *Ruodlieb*, pp. 191–221, emphasizes the work's tenuous relation to the epic tradition.

Kratz, Dennis M. "Ruodlieb: Christian Epic Hero." *Classical Folia*, 27 (1973), 252–266. The *Ruodlieb* is an epic poem offering a Christian redefinition of heroism.

Laistner, Ludwig. Review of Seiler's edition of *Ruodlieb*. *Anzeiger für deutsches Altertum*, 9 (1883), 70–106.

Langosch, Karl. "Zum Stil des *Ruodlieb*," *Zeiten und Formen in Sprache und Dichtung: Festschrift für Fritz Tschirch*. Ed. K. H. Schirmer and B. Sowinski. Cologne: Böhlau, 1972, pp. 17–41. Attacks Brunhölzl's interpretation.

Löwenthal, Fritz. "Bemerkungen zum *Ruodlieb*." *Zeitschrift für deutsches Altertum und deutsche Literatur*, 64 (1927), 128–134.

Manitius, Max. *Geschichte der lateinischen Literatur des Mittelalters.* Volume III. Munich: Beck, 1923, pp. 552–554. *Ruodlieb* as a unique work that belongs in no existing genre.

Ottinger, Hans, "Zum Latein des *Ruodlieb*." *Historische Vierteljahrsschrift*, 26 (1931), 449–535.

Schach, Paul. "Some Parallels to the Tree-Dream in *Ruodlieb*." *Monatshefte für deutschen Unterricht*, 46 (1954), 353–364.

Schneider, Hermann. *Heldendichtung, Geistlichendichtung, Ritterdichtung.* Heidelberg: Winter, 1925.

Vollmann, Benedikt K. "Der Strafprozess im VIII. Fragment des *Ruodlieb*." *Befund und Deutung. Zum Verhältnis von Empirie und Interpretation in Sprach- und Literaturwissenschaft: Festschrift für Hans Fromm.* Ed. Klaus Grubmüller and others. Tübingen: Niemeyer, 1979, pp. 193–227.

———. "'Ruodlieb' Fragment XII," *Lateinische Dichtungen des X. und XI. Jahrhunderts. Festgabe für Walther Bulst.* Ed. Walter Berschin and Reinhard Düchting. Heidelberg: Lambert Schneider, 1981, pp. 227–248. Reinterprets XII in light of his view of the poem as a reworking of saga into a didactic description of knighthood. An important essay.

Walther, Hans. "Quot-tot. Mittelalterliche Liebesgrusse und Verwandtes." *Zeitschrift für deutsches Altertum*, 65 (1928), 257–289.

Wehrli, Max. *Formen mittelalterlicher Erzählung.* Zurich/Freiburg i. Br.: Atlantis, 1969. Examines the role of animals in the *Ruodlieb* (pp. 127–139).

Wilmotte, Maurice. "'Le *Ruodlieb*,' Notre Premier Roman Courtois." *Romania*, 44 (1915–17), 373–406. The poet was French; the work is the first courtly romance. A long-discredited theory.

Winterfeld, Paul von. "Der Mimus im *Ruodlieb*." *Deutsche Dichter des lateinischen Mittelalters.* Ed. Winterfeld and Hermann Reich. Munich: Beck, 1922, pp. 491–502.

IV. Lexicons

Du Fresne, Charles, Sieur du Cange. *Glossarium mediae et infimae latinitatis.* 10 vols. Paris: Niort, 1883–87. [Du Cange]

Mittellateinisches Wörterbuch bis zum ausgehenden 13. Jahrhundert. Bayerische Akademie der Wissenschaften und Deutsche Akademie der Wissenschaften zu Berlin. Munich: Beck, 1967.

Niermeyer, J. F. *Mediae Latinitatis lexicon minus.* Leiden: Brill, 1954–1976.

Waltharius

DEDICATORY PREFACE

Omnipotens genitor, summae virtutis amator,
iure pari natusque amborum spiritus almus,
personis trinus, vera deitate sed unus,
qui vita vivens cuncta et sine fine tenebis,
pontificem summum tu salva nunc et in aevum   5
claro Erchamboldum fulgentem nomine dignum,
crescat ut interius sancto spiramine plenus,
multis infictum quo sit medicamen in aevum.
Praesul sancte dei, nunc accipe munera servi,
quae tibi decrevit de larga promere cura   10
peccator fragilis Geraldus nomine vilis,
qui tibi nam certus corde estque fidelis alumnus;
quod precibus dominum iugiter precor omnitonantem,
ut nanciscaris factis, quae promo loquelis,
det pater ex summis caelum terramque gubernans.   15
Serve dei summi, ne despice verba libelli,
non canit alma dei, resonat sed mira tyronis,
nomine Waltharii, per proelia multa resecti.
Ludendum magis est dominum quam si rogitandum,
perlectus longaevi stringit inampla diei.   20

Sis felix sanctus per tempora plura sacerdos,
sit tibi mente tua Geraldus carus adelphus.

DEDICATORY PREFACE

Almighty Father, Lover of the highest virtue,
And Kindly Spirit, born of both, with equal rule,
Threefold in persons, one in true divinity,
Alive in life, You will hold all things without end.
May You protect the exalted Bishop now and always,   5
Resplendent, worthy of his bright name, Erkambald,
That he may grow within, filled with the Holy Spirit,
To be a useful remedy for many, always.
God's holy Bishop, now accept your servant's gifts,
Which from long effort he resolved to offer you—   10
A sinner, weak, unworthy, known by name of Gerald;
For he is your true-hearted and your faithful pupil.
What I with prayers continually ask the all-thundering Lord,
That you perform in deeds what I express in words,
May God who from on high rules earth and heaven, grant.   15
God's servant, do not scorn the words of my slight book.
It sings, not of God's grace, but of a young man's exploits.
His name is Walter; he was slashed in many battles.
It is for playing more than praying to the Lord.
Read through, it makes the lengthy day a little
    shorter.   20
Be happy, reverend priest, for many days to come;
And may you think of brother Gerald with affection.

Tertia pars orbis, fratres, Europa vocatur,
moribus ac linguis varias et nomine gentes
distinguens, cultu tum relligione sequestrans.
Inter quas gens Pannoniae residere probatur,
quam tamen et Hunos plerumque vocare solemus. 5
Hic populus fortis virtute vigebat et armis,
non circumpositas solum domitans regiones,
litoris oceani sed pertransiverat oras,
foedera supplicibus donans sternensque rebelles.
Ultra millenos fertur dominarier annos. 10
Attila rex quodam tulit illud tempore regnum,
impiger antiquos sibimet renovare triumphos.
Qui sua castra movens mandavit visere Francos,
quorum rex Gibicho solio pollebat in alto,
prole recens orta gaudens, quam postea narro: 15
namque marem genuit, quem Guntharium vocitavit.
Fama volans pavidi regis transverberat aures,
dicens hostilem cuneum transire per Hystrum,
vincentem numero stellas atque amnis arenas.
Qui non confidens armis vel robore plebis 20
concilium cogit, quae sint facienda requirit.
Consensere omnes foedus debere precari
et dextras, si forte darent, coniungere dextris

obsidibusque datis censum persolvere iussum;
hoc melius fore quam vitam simul ac regionem 25
perdiderint natosque suos pariterque maritas.
Nobilis hoc Hagano fuerat sub tempore tiro
indolis egregiae, veniens de germine Troiae.
Hunc, quia Guntharius nondum pervenit ad aevum,
ut sine matre queat vitam retinere tenellam, 30
cum gaza ingenti decernunt mittere regi.
Nec mora, legati censum iuvenemque ferentes
deveniunt pacemque rogant ac foedera firmant.
Tempore quo validis steterat Burgundia sceptris,
cuius primatum Heriricus forte gerebat. 35
Filia huic tantum fuit unica nomine Hiltgunt,
nobilitate quidem pollens ac stemmate formae.
Debuit haec heres aula residere paterna
atque diu congesta frui, si forte liceret.
Namque Avares firma cum Francis pace peracta 40
suspendunt a fine quidem regionis eorum.
Attila sed celeres mox huc deflectit habenas,
nec tardant reliqui satrapae vestigia adire.
Ibant aequati numero, sed et agmine longo,
quadrupedum cursu tellus concussa gemebat. 45

A third part of the world is called Europe, brothers:
By customs, tongues and name dividing various peoples,
Then separating them by their religious practice.
Among them lived the people of Pannonia,
Whom we are generally accustomed to call Huns.   5
This brave folk flourished both by courage and by arms;
Subduing not just those lands which surrounded theirs,
They had extended even to the seashore's limits;
They granted pacts to suppliants, but crushed resisters.
They held sway, it is said, more than a thousand years.   10
At one time King Attila ruled that realm, intent
Upon renewing for himself their ancient triumphs.
He broke camp, ordered them to move against the Franks,
Whose king, Gibicho, governed from his lofty throne,
Rejoicing in his newborn heir (of whom more later);   15
For he had fathered a male child, whom he called Gunther.
A rumor, flying, reached the frightened monarch's ears,
Announcing that a hostile force had crossed the Danube,
In number greater than the stars or river's sands.
The king, not trusting in his people's arms or strength,   20
Then calls a council and asks what ought to be done.
They all agreed a treaty should be asked for, and,
If they would grant it, that right hands be clasped in
    right,
That hostages be given, a stated tribute paid:
For better that than lose not just their lives and lands   25
But also lose their children and their wives as well.
At that time noble Hagen was a youthful soldier;
Of excellent character, he came from Trojan stock.
And him (since Gunther had not reached the age when he,
Without his mother, could sustain his tender life)   30
They chose to send with a huge treasure to the king.
Without delay the envoys, bearing tribute and
The youth, arrive; they sue for peace and sign the treaty.
At that time Burgundy was under a strong monarch;
By chance King Hereric was wielding power there.   35
He had an only daughter, Hildegund her name,
Distinguished by nobility and crowning beauty.
His heir, she was to live within her father's hall
And long enjoy, if chance permitted, the riches there.
The Huns, a firm pact now concluded with the Franks,   40
Stand ready at the very border of their land.
At once Attila turned swift reins in that direction,
Nor were his satraps slow to follow in his tracks.
They went deployed in companies, in a long column.
The earth was groaning, shaken by the tramp of horses.   45

Scutorum sonitu pavidus superintonat aether.
Ferrea silva micat totos rutilando per agros.
Haud aliter primo quam pulsans aequora mane
pulcher in extremis renitet sol partibus orbis.
Iamque Ararim Rodanumque amnes transiverat altos   50
atque ad praedandum cuneus dispergitur omnis.
Forte Cabillonis sedit Heriricus, et ecce
attollens oculos speculator vociferatur
"Quaenam condenso consurgit pulvere nubes?
Vis inimica venit, portas iam claudite cunctas!"   55
Iam tum quid Franci fecissent, ipse sciebat
princeps et cunctos compellat sic seniores
"Si gens tam fortis, cui nos similare nequimus,
cessit Pannoniae, qua nos virtute putatis
huic conferre manum et patriam defendere dulcem?   60
Est satius pactum faciant censumque capessant.
Unica nata mihi, quam tradere pro regione
non dubito. Tantum pergant, qui foedera firment."
Ibant legati totis gladiis spoliati,
hostibus insinuant, quod regis iussio mandat: 65
ut cessent vastare rogant. Quos Attila ductor,
ut solitus fuerat, blande suscepit et inquit
"Foedera plus cupio quam proelia mittere vulgo.
Pace quidem Huni malunt regnare, sed armis
inviti feriunt, quos cernunt esse rebelles.   70
Rex ad nos veniens dextram det atque resumat."
Exivit princeps asportans innumeratos
thesauros pactumque ferit natamque reliquit.
Pergit in exilium pulcherrima gemma parentum.
Postquam complevit pactum statuitque tributum,   75
Attila in occiduas promoverat agmina partes.
Namque Aquitanorum tunc Alphere regna tenebat,
quem sobolem sexus narrant habuisse virilis,
nomine Waltharium, primaevo flore nitentem.
Nam iusiurandum Heriricus et Alphere reges   80
inter se dederant, pueros quod consociarent,
cum primum tempus nubendi venerit illis.
Hic ubi cognovit gentes has esse domatas
coeperat ingenti cordis trepidare pavore,
nec iam spes fuerat saevis defendier armis.   85
"Quid cessemus" ait "si bella movere nequimus?
Exemplum nobis Burgundia, Francia donant.
Non incusamur, si talibus aequiperamur.
Legatos mitto foedusque ferire iubebo
obsidis inque vicem dilectum porrigo natum   90
et iam nunc Hunis censum persolvo futurum."

The frightened air resounded with the crash of shields.
An iron forest flashes, lighting all the fields,
Just as the lovely sun that strikes the waves at dawn
Reflects its light into the farthest lands of earth.
And now they had crossed the deep rivers Rhone and Saone;   50
The whole force is deployed for plundering the land.
King Hereric then happened to be at Chalon.
Behold, the watchman, lifting up his eyes, cries out
"What is this thick-packed cloud of dust that rises up?
A hostile force is coming; now close all the gates!"   55
Because he knew already what the Franks had done,
The king made this address to all his counsellors:
"If that bold tribe, to whom we cannot be compared,
Has yielded to the Huns, with what strength do you think
That we will battle them, defending our sweet land?   60
No, better that they make a pact, exacting tribute.
I have one daughter, whom I am not slow to give
To save our land. Now let them speed to strike a pact!"
The envoys, who were stripped of all their swords, set out.
They tell the enemy what their king's order bids: 65
They ask them to cease ravaging; the chief, Attila,
Received them courteously, as he was wont, and said,
"I wish for treaties more than bringing wars to people.
The Huns prefer to reign in peace, but strike with arms
Reluctantly those whom they see to be rebellious.   70
Your king may come to us, give and receive a hand."
King Hereric set out, transporting countless treasures;
He struck a treaty; and he left behind his daughter.
Then into exile went her parents' loveliest jewel.
Once he had made the treaty and had set the tribute,   75
Attila marched his army into western parts.
In those days Alphere ruled the Aquitanians' realms.
They say he had one child, whose sex was masculine;
Resplendent in the flower of youth, his name was Walter.
The kings, Alphere and Hereric, had sworn an oath   80
Between themselves that they would then unite their children
As soon as they had reached the age of marrying.
When he learned that these peoples had been overcome,
The king began to tremble with great fear of heart;
There was no hope now in defense by savage weapons.   85
"Why should we wait," he says, "if we cannot wage war?
For France and Burgundy provide us an example.
To be compared to them brings no rebuke to us.
I will send envoys with commands to strike a pact
And offer my beloved son to be a hostage,   90
And pay the Huns immediately their future tribute."

Sed quid plus remorer? Dictum compleverat actis.
Tunc Avares gazis onerati denique multis
obsidibus sumptis Hagenone, Hiltgunde puella
nec non Walthario redierunt pectore laeto. 95
Attila Pannonias ingressus et urbe receptus
exulibus pueris magnam exhibuit pietatem
ac veluti proprios nutrire iubebat alumnos.
Virginis et curam reginam mandat habere,
ast adolescentes propriis conspectibus ambos 100
semper adesse iubet, sed et artibus imbuit illos
praesertimque iocis belli sub tempore habendis.
Qui simul ingenio crescentes mentis et aevo
robore vincebant fortes animoque sophistas,
donec iam cunctos superarent fortiter Hunos. 105
Militiae primos tunc Attila fecerat illos,
sed haud immerito, quoniam, si quando moveret
bella, per insignes isti micuere triumphos;
idcircoque nimis princeps dilexerat ambos.
Virgo etiam captiva deo praestante supremo 110
reginae vultum placavit et auxit amorem,
moribus eximiis operumque industria habundans.
Postremum custos thesauri provida cunctis
efficitur, modicumque deest, quin regnet et ipsa;
nam quicquid voluit de rebus, fecit et actis. 115
Interea Gibicho defungitur, ipseque regno
Guntharius successit et ilico Pannoniarum
foedera dissolvit censumque subire negavit.
Hoc ubi iam primum Hagano cognoverat exul,
nocte fugam molitur et ad dominum properavit. 120
Waltharius tamen ad pugnas praecesserat Hunos,
et quocumque iret, mox prospera sunt comitata.
Ospirin elapsum Haganonem regia coniunx
attendens domino suggessit talia dicta
"Provideat caveatque, precor, sollertia regis, 125
ne vestri imperii labatur forte columna,
hoc est, Waltharius vester discedat amicus,
in quo magna potestatis vis extitit huius;
nam vereor, ne fors fugiens Haganonem imitetur,
idcircoque meam perpendite nunc rationem: 130
cum primum veniat, haec illi dicite verba:
'servitio in nostro magnos plerumque labores
passus eras ideoque scias, quod gratia nostra
prae cunctis temet nimium dilexit amicis.
Quod volo plus factis te quam cognoscere dictis. 135
Elige de satrapis nuptam tibi Pannoniarum
et non pauperiem propriam perpendere cures.

But why stretch out my tale? He did just as he said.
The Avars, loaded down at last with many treasures—
Their hostages received, the maiden Hildegund
And Hagen, also Walter—returned with happy hearts.   95
Once in Pannonia and greeted by his city,
Attila showed great kindness to the exiled children,
And ordered them brought up as if they were his own;
And he commanded the queen to take care of the girl,
But ordered both the young boys to be in his presence   100
At all times, and he also taught them many skills,
Especially the games one plays in time of war.
The boys, who grew in both age and intelligence,
Surpassed the strong in strength, the wise in intellect,
Until they were by far the best of all the Huns.   105
Attila made them captains of his army then—
And with good reason, since whenever wars arose,
They were conspicuous with their outstanding triumphs.
And so the prince had grown extremely fond of both.
And with the help of God, the captive maiden too—   110
Abounding in good character and diligence—
Was pleasing in the queen's sight and increased her love.
At last the prudent girl was placed in charge of all
Supplies, and she was little short of being queen
Herself; for she did what she wished concerning things.   115
Gibicho, meanwhile, passed away, and that same Gunther
Succeeded to the throne. At once he broke the treaty
Made with the Huns, refusing to pay further tribute.
When the exile Hagen learned that he had done this, he
Made his escape by night and hurried to his lord.   120
However, Walter stayed to lead the Huns in battle;
Wherever he would go success was quick to follow.
The king's wife, Ospirin, while pondering the flight
Of Hagen, offered her lord these words of advice:
"The shrewdness of the king, I pray, should be alert   125
And keep the pillar of your empire from collapsing;
That is, it should keep your friend Walter from departing,
The man in whom the great strength of our kingdom rests.
I am afraid he may by fleeing copy Hagen.
And for that reason now consider well my plan.   130
As soon as he returns, you say these words to him:
'In serving us you often have endured great hardships,
And therefore you should know that we, in our esteem,
Have loved you far above all of our other friends.
I want you to know this in deeds more than in words.   135
Choose from the Avars' noble families a bride,
And do not be concerned about your poverty.

Amplificabo quidem valde te rure domique,
nec quisquam, qui dat sponsam, post facta pudebit,
Quod si completis, illum stabilire potestis." 140
Complacuit sermo regi coepitque parari.
Waltharius venit, cui princeps talia pandit,
uxorem suadens sibi ducere; sed tamen ipse
iam tum praemeditans quod post compleverat actis,
his instiganti suggestibus obvius infit 145
"Vestra quidem pietas est, quod modici famulatus
causam conspicitis. Sed quod mea segnia mentis
intuitu fertis, numquam meruisse valerem.

Sed precor ut servi capiatis verba fidelis:
si nuptam accipiam domini praecepta secundum, 150
vinciar in primis curis et amore puellae
atque a servitio regis plerumque retardor;
aedificare domos cultumque intendere ruris
cogor, et hoc oculis senioris adesse moratur
et solitam regno Hunorum impendere curam. 155
Namque voluptatem quisquis gustaverit, exin
intolerabilius consuevit ferre labores.
Nil tam dulce mihi quam semper inesse fideli
obsequio domini; quare precor absque iugali
me vinclo permitte meam iam ducere vitam. 160
Si sero aut medio noctis mihi tempore mandas,
ad quaecumque iubes, securus et ibo paratus.
In bellis nullae persuadent cedere curae
nec nati aut coniunx retrahentque fugamque movebunt.
Testor per propriam temet, pater optime, vitam 165
atque per invictam nunc gentem Pannoniarum
ut non ulterius me cogas sumere taedas."
His precibus victus, suasus rex deserit omnes,
sperans Waltharium fugiendo recedere numquam.
Venerat interea satrapae certissima fama 170
quandam, quae nuper superata, resistere gentem
ac bellum Hunis confestim inferre paratam.
Tunc ad Waltharium convertitur actio rerum.
Qui mox militiam percensuit ordine totam
et bellatorum confortat corda suorum, 175
hortans praeteritos semper memorare triumphos
promittensque istos solita virtute tyrannos
sternere et externis terrorem imponere terris.
Nec mora, consurgit sequiturque exercitus omnis.
Ecce locum pugnae conspexerat et numeratam 180
per latos aciem campos digessit et agros.

I will reward you amply with a home and lands.
Who gives a bride to you will later feel no shame.'
If you fulfill your part, then you can keep him here."   140
The king, pleased by her words, began the preparations.
When Walter came, the king unveiled these thoughts to him,
Encouraging his marriage; he, however, was
Already making plans he later would accomplish.
With these words he responded to Attila's urging: 145
"It is indeed a mark of your own goodness that
You should perceive the motive for my modest service;
However, never could I have deserved that you
Take notice of the sluggish efforts of my mind.
I pray that you accept your faithful servant's words.
If, following my lord's command, I take a wife,   150
I will be bound first by my love and care for the girl
And often kept away from service to the king.
The need to build a house and supervise my farmland
Will hinder me from being present in your sight
And giving to the Huns' realm my accustomed care.   155
Whoever once has tasted pleasure then becomes
Accustomed to find hardships unendurable.
For nothing is so sweet to me as always being
In faithful obedience to my lord. I ask you, therefore,
To let me lead my life free of the yoke of marriage.   160
If late or in the dead of night you summon me,
I'll go wherever you command, prepared, unhindered.
In battle, no anxieties will urge retreat—
Not wife nor children will restrain or make me flee.
I beg you, best of fathers, by your very life   165
And still unconquered tribe of the Pannonians,
Do not continue to force me to take a wife."
Defeated by these prayers, the king abandoned all
His urging, hoping Walter never would take flight.
Meanwhile, a definite report came from a satrap: 170
That tribe which recently was conquered was rebelling,
Prepared to wage immediate war against the Huns.
The conduct of affairs is placed in Walter's hands.
He quickly mustered all the troops in battle ranks
And fortified the hearts within his warriors,   175
Exhorting them to think always of former triumphs,
And vowing he, with his accustomed bravery,
Would slay those tyrants, terrorize the foreign lands.
Without delay, he sets out; all the army follows.
Now he surveyed the battle site and then deployed   180
His battle-line, arrayed to fight, through fields and
    plains.

Iamque infra iactum teli congressus uterque
constiterat cuneus; tunc undique clamor ad auras
tollitur, horrendam confundunt classica vocem,
continuoque hastae volitant hinc indeque densae. 185
Fraxinus et cornus ludum miscebat in unum,
fulminis inque modum cuspis vibrata micabat.

Ac veluti boreae sub tempore nix glomerata
spargitur, haud aliter saevas iecere sagittas.
Postremum cunctis utroque ex agmine pilis 190
absumptis manus ad mucronem vertitur omnis;
fulmineos promunt enses clipeosque revolvunt,

concurrunt acies demum pugnamque restaurant.
Pectoribus partim rumpuntur pectora equorum,
sternitur et quaedam pars duro umbone virorum. 195
Waltharius tamen in medio furit agmine bello,
obvia quaeque metens armis ac limite pergens.
Hunc ubi conspiciunt hostes tantas dare strages,
ac si praesentem metuebant cernere mortem,
et quemcumque locum, seu dextram sive sinistram, 200
Waltharius peteret, cuncti mox terga dederunt
et versis scutis laxisque feruntur habenis.
Tunc imitata ducem gens maxima Pannoniarum
saevior insurgit caedemque audacior auget,
deicit obstantes, fugientes proterit usque, 205
dum caperet plenum belli sub sorte triumphum.
Tum super occisos ruit et spoliaverat omnes.
Et tandem ductor recavo vocat agmina cornu
ac primus frontem festa cum fronde revinxit,
victrici lauro cingens sua tempora vulgo, 210
post hunc signiferi, sequitur quos cetera pubes.
Iamque triumphali redierunt stemmata compti
et patriam ingressi propria se quisque locavit
sede, sed ad solium mox Waltharius properavit.
Ecce palatini decurrunt arce ministri 215
illius aspectu hilares equitemque tenebant,
donec vir sella descenderet inclitus alta.
Si bene res vergant, tum demum forte requirunt.
Ille aliquid modicum narrans intraverat aulam,
(lassus enim fuerat) regisque cubile petebat. 220
Illic Hiltgundem solam offendit residentem.
Cui post amplexus atque oscula dulcia dixit
"Ocius huc potum ferto, quia fessus anhelo."
Illa mero tallum complevit mox pretiosum
porrexitque viro, qui signans accipiebat 225

Within a spear's throw of each other stand the two
Assembled armies; from both sides a noise arises
Into the air: the trumpets blare their awful sound;
At once from everywhere dense clouds of weapons fly.   185
Now ash and cornel-wood joined in a single game.
The lance, once hurled, would flash just like a lightning
   bolt.
Just as the snow swirls thickly in the winter time,
Not otherwise the warriors cast their savage weapons.
At last, when every javelin from both the lines   190
Was thrown, then every hand is reaching for a sword.
They draw their flashing blades and swing their shields
   around;
At length, the battle lines converge, renew the fray.
Some of the horses charge and shatter breast to breast;
Some of the riders are unhorsed by a hard shield.   195
Among the warring host, however, Walter rages;
He surges forward, hacking down all in his path.
His foes, when they observe what slaughter he deals out,
As if afraid to see their death so close at hand,
Whatever place that Walter sought, to right or left,   200
Immediately all fling their shields across their backs,
Let loose their horses' reins, turn tail and flee away.
Then copying their chief, the mighty tribe of Huns,
More fierce, advances and, more bold, extends the carnage;
It cuts down those resisting, slaughters those who run   205
Until it gains full victory in the lot of war.
Then rushing to the corpses it despoils them all.
At last the leader calls the troops with his curved horn;
And he was first to bind his brows with festive leaves,
In public wreathe his temples with triumphant laurel;   210
The standard-bearers after him, and then the others.
And now, bound with triumphal garlands, they returned.
Once in the homeland, each went to his dwelling place,
But Walter hastened to the royal throne at once.
The king's attendants rushed down from the citadel,   215
Delighted at the sight of him, and held his horse,
Until the famous man dismounted from his saddle;
And only then they asked if things have turned out well.
Recounting but a little, he entered the hall,
For he was weary, and sought out the royal chamber.   220
And he found Hildegund there sitting by herself.
He first embraced and kissed her sweetly, then he said,
"Bring drink here quickly; I am gasping with exhaustion."
At once she filled a precious beaker with strong wine
And gave it to the man, who, as he took it, crossed   225

virgineamque manum propria constrinxit; at illa
astitit et vultum reticens intendit herilem,
Walthariusque bibens vacuum vas porrigit olli
— Ambo etenim norant de se sponsalia facta—
provocat et tali caram sermone puellam 230
"Exilium pariter patimur iam tempore tanto,
non ignorantes quid nostri forte parentes
inter se nostra de re fecere futura.
Quamne diu tacito premimus haec ipsa palato?"
Virgo per hyroniam meditans hoc dicere sponsum 235
paulum conticuit, sed postea talia reddit
"Quid lingua simulas quod ab imo pectore damnas,
oreque persuades, toto quod corde refutas,
sit veluti talem pudor ingens ducere nuptam?"
Vir sapiens contra respondit et intulit ista 240
"Absit quod memoras! Dextrorsum porrige sensum!
Noris me nihilum simulata mente locutum
nec quicquam nebulae vel falsi interfore crede.
Nullus adest nobis exceptis namque duobus.
Si nossem temet mihi promptam impendere mentem 245
atque fidem votis servare per omnia cautis,
pandere cuncta tibi cordis mysteria vellem."
Tandem virgo viri genibus curvata profatur
"Ad quaecumque vocas, mi domne, sequar studiose
nec quicquam placitis malim praeponere iussis." 250
Ille dehinc "Piget exilii me denique nostri
et patriae fines reminiscor saepe relictos
idcircoque fugam cupio celerare latentem.
Quod iam praemultis potuissem forte diebus,
Si non Hiltgundem solam remanere dolerem." 255
Addidit has imo virguncula corde loquelas
"Vestrum velle meum, solis his aestuo rebus.
Praecipiat dominus, seu prospera sive sinistra
eius amore pati toto sum pectore praesto."
Waltharius tandem sic virginis inquit in aurem 260
"Publica custodem rebus te nempe potestas
fecerat, idcirco memor haec mea verba notato.
Inprimis galeam regis tunicamque, trilicem
assero loricam fabrorum insigne ferentem,
diripe, bina dehinc mediocria scrinia tolle. 265
His armillarum tantum da Pannoniarum,
donec vix unum releves ad pectoris imum.
Inde quater binum mihi fac de more coturnum,
tantundemque tibi patrans imponito vasis.
Sic fors ad summum complentur scrinia labrum. 270
Insuper a fabris hamos clam posce retortos.

Himself, and pressed the maiden's hand with his; but she
Just stood there, silent, staring at her master's face.
Then Walter drained the cup and gave it back to her
(Both knew of the betrothal set concerning them)
And with these words he spoke to his beloved girl: 230
"Together we have suffered exile for so long,
Although we are not ignorant of what our parents
Arranged among themselves about our future state.
How long shall we suppress these thoughts in silent mouths?"
Believing her betrothed said this ironically,   235
The maiden paused a moment, then made this reply:
"Why feign in speech what you condemn deep in your breast,
And with your mouth urge what you spurn with all your heart,
As if it were a great shame to wed such a bride?"
The clever man replied in turn and spoke these words: 240
"May what you say be wrong! Now hear the proper meaning.
Know that I did not speak with a deceitful mind.
Believe that nothing vague or false was intermixed;
For there is no one present but the two of us.
If I knew you would show a sympathetic spirit   245
And in all ways be faithful to my clever plans,
Then I would show you all the secrets of my heart."
At this the maiden, stooping to his knees, then spoke:
"Where you direct, my lord, I'll follow eagerly.
For I would not place anything above your orders."   250
Then he: "I have at last grown tired of our long exile,
Remembering often my homeland's forsaken borders.
And therefore I desire to speed my stealthy escape.
I could perhaps have done this many days ago,
Were I not grieved that Hildegund be left alone."   255
The maiden spoke these words from deep within her heart:
"Your wish is mine; for these things only I am burning.
My lord commands, and I stand ready to endure,
For love of him, with my whole heart, success or failure."
Then Walter whispered this into the maiden's ear;   260
"Her majesty has made you guardian of goods;
So therefore hear attentively these words of mine:
First steal the helmet and three-layered byrnie of
The king, I mean the corselet which bears the mark
Of smiths; and then obtain two coffers—fairly large,   265
And fill these with so many arm-rings of the Huns
That you can scarcely lift one just up to your breast.
Then make me, in the usual way, four pairs of shoes—
Preparing four for you—and place them in the boxes.
And so the coffers may be filled up to the top.   270
Moreover, secretly ask fish-hooks from the smiths;

15

Nostra viatica sint pisces simul atque volucres,
ipse ego piscator, sed et auceps esse coartor.
Haec intra ebdomadam caute per singula comple.
Audisti, quid habere vianti forte necesse est. 275
Nunc quo more fugam valeamus inire, recludo.
Postquam septenos Phoebus remeaverit orbes,
regi ac reginae satrapis ducibus famulisque

sumptu permagno convivia laeta parabo
atque omni ingenio potu sepelire studebo, 280
donec nullus erit, qui sentiat hoc, quod agendum est.
Tu tamen interea mediocriter utere vino
atque sitim vix ad mensam restinguere cura.
Cum reliqui surgant, ad opuscula nota recurre.
Ast ubi iam cunctos superat violentia potus, 285
tum simul occiduas properemus quaerere partes."
Virgo memor praecepta viri complevit et ecce
praefinita dies epularum venit, et ipse
Waltharius magnis instruxit sumptibus escas.
Luxuria in media residebat denique mensa, 290
ingrediturque aulam velis rex undique saeptam.
Heros magnanimus solito quem more salutans
duxerat ad solium, quod bissus compsit et ostrum.
Consedit laterique duces hinc indeque binos
assedisse iubet; reliquos locat ipse minister. 295
Centenos simul accubitus iniere sodales,
diversasque dapes libans conviva resudat.

His et sublatis aliae referuntur edendae,
atque exquisitum fervebat migma per aurum.
Aurea bissina tantum stant gausape vasa 300
et pigmentatus crateres Bachus adornat.
Illicit ad haustum species dulcedoque potus.
Waltharius cunctos ad vinum hortatur et escam.
Postquam epulis depulsa fames sublataque mensa,
heros iam dictus dominum laetanter adorsus 305
inquit "In hoc, rogito, clarescat gratia vestra,
ut vos inprimis, reliquos tunc laetificetis."
Et simul in verbo nappam dedit arte peractam
ordine sculpturae referentem gesta priorum,
quam rex accipiens haustu vacuaverat uno, 310

confestimque iubet reliquos imitarier omnes.
Ocius accurrunt pincernae moxque recurrunt,
pocula plena dabant et inania suscipiebant.
Hospitis ac regis certant hortatibus omnes.

For as we travel let our food be fish and fowl;
And I am forced to be both fisherman and fowler.
Do these things one by one—with caution—in a week.
You have heard what is necessary for our journey.   275
And now I will reveal how we can start our flight.
As soon as Phoebus has completed seven circuits,
For both the king and queen (and satraps, captains,
    servants)
I will prepare at great expense a festive banquet
And try with all my guile to bury them in drink   280
Until there is none who knows what is going on.
But meanwhile you partake of wine in moderation,
And at the table take care just to quench your thirst.
Then, when the rest arise, resume your usual tasks;
But when the power of the drink undoes them all,   285
Let us at once make haste to seek the western parts."
The maiden, mindful, carried out the man's instructions.
And so the day appointed for the feast arrived,
And he himself, at great expense, arranged the dishes.
At length extravagance reigned among the tables.   290
The king steps in the hall adorned with tapestries;
With customary greeting the great-hearted hero
Led him up to the throne, which purple and fine cloth
Adorned. He sits and bids two lords to sit down there
On either side; the seneschal then seats the rest.   295
The guests together occupied a hundred seats.
Each guest, from eating different dishes, breaks out
    sweating.
When these were taken off, still other foods were brought,
And choicest wine was gleaming in a golden bowl;
For on the linen cloth stand only golden vessels,   300
And aromatic Bacchus decorates the bowls.
The kind and sweetness of the wine entice their drinking,
And Walter goads them all on to the wine and food.
With hunger banished by the feasting, tables cleared,
The aforesaid hero cheerfully addressed his lord   305
And said: "In this, I ask, may your grace be revealed,
That first you give cheer to yourself, then to the rest,"
And with this word gave him an artfully made goblet
Which on a row of chasings lists his forebears' deeds.
The king, accepting this, then drained it in one
    draught,   310
And ordered all the rest to follow suit at once.
The serving men run quickly and they soon return;
For they were bringing full cups, taking empty ones.
All vie, with exhortations from their host and king,

Ebrietas fervens tota dominatur in aula, 315
balbutit madido facundia fusa palato,
heroas validos plantis titubare videres.
Taliter in seram produxit bachica noctem
munera Waltharius retrahitque redire volentes,
donec vi potus pressi somnoque gravati 320
passim porticibus sternuntur humotenus omnes.
Et licet ignicremis vellet dare moenia flammis,
nullus, qui causam potuisset scire, remansit.
Tandem dilectam vocat ad semet mulierem,
praecipiens causas citius deferre paratas. 325
Ipseque de stabulis victorem duxit equorum,
ob virtutem quem vocitaverat ille Leonem.
Stat sonipes ac frena ferox spumantia mandit.
Hunc postquam faleris solito circumdedit, ecce
scrinia plena gazae lateri suspendit utrique 330

atque iteri longo modicella cibaria ponit
loraque virgineae mandat fluitantia dextrae.
Ipseque lorica vestitus more gigantis
imposuit capiti rubras cum casside cristas
ingentesque ocreis suras complectitur aureis 335

et laevum femur ancipiti praecinxerat ense
atque alio dextrum pro ritu Pannoniarum:
is tamen ex una tantum dat vulnera parte.
Tunc hastam dextra rapiens clipeumque sinistra
coeperat invisa trepidus decedere terra. 340
Femina duxit equum nonnulla talenta gerentem,
in manibusque simul virgam tenet ipsa colurnam,
in qua piscator hamum transponit in undam,
ut cupiens pastum piscis deglutiat hamum.
Namque gravatus erat vir maximus undique telis 345
suspectamque habuit cuncto sibi tempore pugnam.
Omni nocte quidem properabant currere, sed cum
prima rubens terris ostendit lumina Phoebus,
in silvis latitare student et opaca requirunt,
sollicitatque metus vel per loca tuta fatigans. 350
In tantumque timor muliebria pectora pulsat
horreat ut cunctos aurae ventique susurros,
formidans volucres collisos sive racemos.
Hinc odium exilii patriaeque amor incubat inde.
Vicis diffugiunt, speciosa novalia linquunt, 355
montibus intonsis cursus ambage recurvos

And glowing Drunkenness rules in the entire hall. 315
From drunken mouths there gushes sottish eloquence;
And you could see strong heroes stagger on their feet.
Thus Walter kept on serving late into the night
His Bacchic gifts and held back those who wished to leave,
Until, subdued by the strong drink, weighed down by
　　sleep, 320
They all were strewn upon the ground throughout the hall.
And if he wished to give the walls to hungry flames,
There was nobody left who could have known what happened.
And then at last he summoned his beloved woman,
Instructing her to bring down quickly their provisions. 325
And from the stables he led forth his champion stallion,
Which he, because of its great valor, had named Lion.
The steed stands fiercely, chomping at its foaming bit.
Once he has fixed its trappings in the usual way,
On either side he hangs the coffers filled with
　　treasure, 330
And for the long trip packs a small supply of food;
And to the girl's right hand entrusts the slackened reins.
The man himself, clad in a byrnie, like a giant,
Then places on his head a crimson-crested helmet
And wraps his massive calves in greaves of gold; he
　　girds 335
A two-edged sword on his left thigh; and following
The manner of the Huns, another on his right:
This one, however, will wound only from one edge.
His right hand grasps a spear; his left hand grasps a
　　shield;
He sets out to depart that hated land in haste. 340
The woman led the horse which bore no little treasure;
And meanwhile in her hands she held a hazel-rod
From which the fisherman will cast a hook in water
For fish, who want the food, to swallow down the hook.
That awesome man was burdened everywhere by weapons; 345
He was in constant expectation of attack.
All night indeed they hastened on their way; but when
The reddening Phoebus showed his first rays to the lands,
They tried to hide in forests and seek dark recesses.
But vexing fear disturbs them even in safe places. 350
Dread beats against the woman's breast so much that she
Would tremble at each murmur of the breeze or wind,
In fear of birds or branches that would strike each other.
The hate of exile, love of home—both weigh on them.
They shun the towns, avoid the fine fields newly tilled, 355
Pursuing routes that snake and curve through wooded

sectantes tremulos variant per devia gressus.
Ast urbis populus somno vinoque solutus
ad medium lucis siluit recubando sequentis.
Sed postquam surgunt, ductorem quique requirunt, 360
ut grates faciant ac festa laude salutent.
Attila nempe manu caput amplexatus utraque
egreditur thalamo rex Walthariumque dolendo
Advocat, ut proprium quereretur forte dolorem.
Respondent ipsi se non potuisse ministri 365
invenisse virum, sed princeps sperat eundem
hactenus in somno tentum recubare quietum
occultumque locum sibi delegisse sopori.
Ospirin Hiltgundem postquam cognovit abesse
nec iuxta morem vestes deferre suetum, 370
tristior immensis satrapae clamoribus inquit
"O destestandas, quas heri sumpsimus, escas!
O vinum, quod Pannonias destruxerat omnes!
Quod domino regi iam dudum praescia dixi,
approbat iste dies, quem nos superare nequimus. 375
En hodie imperii vestri cecidisse columna
noscitur, en robur procul ivit et inclita virtus:
Waltharius lux Pannoniae discesserat inde,
Hiltgundem quoque mi caram deduxit alumnam."
Iam princeps nimia succenditur efferus ira, 380
mutant laetitiam maerentia corda priorem.
Ex humeris trabeam discindit ad infima totam
et nunc huc animum tristem, nunc dividit illuc.
Ac velut Aeolicis turbatur arena procellis,
sic intestinis rex fluctuat undique curis, 385
et varium pectus vario simul ore imitatus
prodidit exterius, quicquid toleraverat intus,
iraque sermonem permisit promere nullum.
Ipso quippe die potum fastidit et escam,
nec placidam membris potuit dare cura quietem. 390
Namque ubi nox rebus iam dempserat atra colores,
decidit in lectum, verum nec lumina clausit,
nunc latus in dextrum fultus nunc inque sinistrum,
et veluti iaculo pectus transfixus acuto
palpitat atque caput huc et mox iactitat illuc, 395
et modo subrectus fulcro consederat amens.
Nec iuvat hoc, demum surgens discurrit in urbe,
atque thorum veniens simul attigit atque reliquit.
Taliter insomnem consumpserat Attila noctem.
At profugi comites per amica silentia euntes 400

mountains.
The two direct their trembling way through lonely parts.
The people of the city, slack with sleep and wine,
Lay sleeping to the middle of the following day.
But after they arise, they all seek out their leader   360
To offer thanks and greet him with their festive praise.
The king, Attila, while he grasps his head in both
His hands, departs his room in pain and summons Walter,
In order to complain about his misery.
The serving men reply that they have not been able   365
To find the man; the king, however, hopes that he,
Still held by sleep, is lying quietly and has
Selected for himself some hidden place for resting.
But after Ospirin learned that Hildegund was absent
And has not brought her clothes according to her custom,   370
She calls out sadly to her lord with mighty cries,
"Detestable that food which we ate yesterday!
O wine that has destroyed all the Pannonians!
What I, foreknowing, long since told my lord and king,
This day which we can not make good has brought to pass.   375
Oh yes, today we know the prop of your empire
Has fallen away, its strength and famous courage gone.
The beacon of Pannonia, Walter, has departed,
And taken too my precious daughter Hildegund!"
The crazed prince now is burning with excessive wrath;   380
A grieving heart replaces his former cheerfulness.
From shoulders to the hem he rips his royal robe,
And he directs his saddened mind now here, now there.
And as the sand is stirred up by Aeolus' winds,
The king is surging inwardly with warring cares.   385
The changes in his face reflect his changing feelings;
Outward, the man betrays his suffering within.
His wrath permitted him to speak no words at all.
That day, of course, the king rejected food and drink;
Anxiety stripped soothing quiet from his limbs.   390
For when the black night stole the color from all things,
He slumped into his bed but did not close his eyes,
Reclining now upon his right side, now his left.
As if his breast were pierced by a sharp-pointed spear,
He trembles and he shakes his head now here, now there,   395
And maddened now he sits bolt upright in his bed.
It does not help; he rises, wanders through the city.
Returning to his bed, he leaves as soon as he
Has reached it. Thus Attila spent a sleepless night.
But through the friendly silence went the fleeing
    comrades,   400

suspectam properant post terga relinquere terram.
Vix tamen erupit cras, rex patribusque vocatis
dixerat "O si quis mihi Waltharium fugientem
afferat evinctum ceu nequam forte liciscam,
hunc ego mox auro vestirem saepe recocto   405
et tellure quidem stantem hinc inde onerarem
atque viam penitus clausissem vivo talentis!"
Sed nullus fuit in tanta regione tyrannus
vel dux sive comes seu miles sive minister,
qui, quamvis cuperet proprias ostendere vires   410
ac virtute sua laudem captare perennem
ambiretque simul gazam infarcire cruminis,
Waltharium tamen iratum praesumpserat armis
insequier strictoque virum mucrone videre.
Nota equidem virtus, experti sunt quoque quantas   415

incolomis dederit strages sine vulnere victor.
Nec potis est ullum rex persuadere virorum,
qui promissa velit hac condicione talenta.
Waltharius fugiens, ut dixi, noctibus ivit,
atque die saltus arbustaque densa requirens   420
arte accersitas pariter capit arte volucres,
nunc fallens visco, nunc fisso denique ligno.
Ast ubi pervenit, qua flumina curva fluebant,
immittens hamum rapuit sub gurgite praedam,
atque famis pestem pepulit tolerando laborem.   425
Namque fugae toto se tempore virginis usu
continuit vir Waltharius laudabilis heros.
Ecce quater denos sol circumflexerat orbes,
ex quo Pannonica fuerat digressus ab urbe.
Ipso quippe die, numerum qui clauserat istum   430
venerat ad fluvium iam vespere tum mediante,
scilicet ad Rhenum, qua cursus tendit ad urbem

nomine Wormatiam regali sede nitentem.
Illic pro naulo pisces dedit antea captos
et mox transpositus graditur properanter anhelus.   435
Orta dies postquam tenebras discusserat atras,
portitor exurgens praefatam venit in urbem
regalique coco, reliquorum quippe magistro,
detulerat pisces, quos vir dedit ille viator.
Hos dum pigmentis condisset et apposuisset   440

regi Gunthario, miratus fatur ab alto
"Istius ergo modi pisces mihi Francia numquam
ostendit; reor externis a finibus illos.

In haste to leave behind them that distrusted land.
The day had scarcely broken when the king addressed
The gathered nobles, "If someone would bring to me
That fleeing Walter, tied up like a dog, soon I
Would clothe that man in many times resmelted gold,   405
On all sides weigh him down where he stands on the ground,
And block his path completely—as I live!—with wealth."
But there was not a noble in so great a land,
No, neither duke nor count nor knight nor serving man,
However much he wished to demonstrate his strength   410
And by his courage capture everlasting fame
And wish as well to stuff his money-bags with treasure,
Who would have dared pursue in arms an angry Walter,
Or dared to face that man when he had drawn his sword.
They knew his courage well, and knew what massive
 carnage   415
That he, unhurt, unwounded, had dealt out as victor.
The king could not persuade a single man of them
To wish for treasure offered under these conditions.
The fleeing Walter, as I said, moved on by night;
In daytime, seeking thickly wooded groves and gorges,   420
He used his skill to lure and then to capture birds,
Deceiving them at times with bird-lime or with snares.
But when their journey reached where winding rivers flowed,
He cast his hook and captured prey from that deep water;
And by enduring work dispelled the pang of hunger.   425
And that praiseworthy hero Walter, all the time
They fled, refrained from carnal use of Hildegund.
Behold, the sun had made its circuit forty times
Since they departed from the city of the Huns;
And on the very day that made the number forty,   430
As night was just approaching he came to a river,
The Rhine, that is, just where its course turns toward a
 town
Renowned because the king lived there—its name is Worms.
For passage, he paid fish that he had caught before,
And once across, then breathless hurried on his way.   435
As soon as dawn had driven back the shades of night,
The ferry-man arose, went to the forenamed city
And gave the royal cook, the master of all others
The fishes that the traveler had just given him.
The cook, when he had seasoned them with herbs, then
 served   440
Them to King Gunther who, amazed, said from his throne,
"Now fish of this sort France has never offered me!
I think that they have come from foreign parts. Tell me

Dic mihi quantocius: cuias homo detulit illos?"
Ipseque respondens narrat, quod nauta dedisset. 445
Accersire hominem princeps praecepit eundem;
et cum venisset de re quaesitus eadem
talia dicta dedit causamque ex ordine pandit
"Vespere praeterito residebam litore Rheni
conspexique viatorem propere venientem 450
et veluti pugnae certum per membra paratum.
Aere etenim penitus fuerat, rex inclite, cinctus
gesserat et scutum gradiens hastamque coruscam.
Namque viro forti similis fuit, et licet ingens
asportaret onus, gressum tamen extulit acrem. 455
Hunc incredibili formae decorata nitore
assequitur calcemque terit iam calce puella.
Ipsaque robustum rexit per lora caballum
scrinia bina quidem dorso non parva ferentem,
quae, dum cervicem sonipes discusserit altam 460
atque superba cupit glomerare volumina crurum,
dant sonitum, ceu quis gemmis illiserit aurum.
Hic mihi praesentes dederat pro munere pisces."
His Hagano auditis (ad mensam quippe resedit)
laetior in medium prompsit de pectore verbum 465
"Congaudete mihi quaeso, quia talia novi:
Waltharius collega meus remeavit ab Hunis."
Guntharius princeps ex hac ratione superbus
vociferatur, et omnis ei mox aula reclamat:
"Congaudete mihi iubeo, quia talia vixi! 470
Gazam, quam Gibicho regi transmisit eoo,
nunc mihi cunctipotens huc in mea regna remisit."
Haec ait et mensam pede perculit exiliensque
ducere equum iubet et sella componere sculpta
atque omni de plebe viros secum duodenos 475
viribus insignes, animis plerumque probatos

legerat, inter quos simul ire Haganona iubebat.
Qui memor antiquae fidei sociique prioris
nititur a coeptis dominum transvertere rebus.
Rex tamen econtra nihilominus instat et infit 480
"Ne tardate, viri, praecingite corpora ferro
fortia, squamosus thorax iam terga recondat.
Hic tantum gazae Francis deducat ab oris?"
Instructi telis, nam iussio regis adurget,
exibant portis, te Waltharium cupientes 485
cernere et imbellem lucris fraudare putantes.
Sed tamen omnimodis Hagano prohibere studebat,
at rex infelix coeptis resipiscere non vult.

At once: the man who brought them, where did he come from?"
The cook said that the ferry-man had given them. 445
The king commanded that the man be brought to him;
He, when he came and then was asked about the matter,
Gave this reply, and told the story all in sequence.
"Last evening, on the Rhine's bank, I was sitting down.
I saw a traveler approaching in great haste, 450
Equipped from head to foot as though expecting battle.
He was, distinguished king, completely clad in bronze
And as he walked he held a shield and gleaming spear.
He seemed a man of strength, for even though he bore
A heavy load, he still maintained a rapid pace. 455
A girl adorned with stunning radiance of beauty
Was following the man, and matched him stride for stride;
And by the reins the maiden led a mighty stallion
That bore indeed upon its back two quite large coffers
Which, when the stallion shook its lofty mane and wished 460
To rear up high and paw with haughty legs, gave forth
A sound as if someone were striking gold with gem-stones.
This was the man who gave to me those fish as payment."
When Hagen, who sat at the table, heard these words,
With joyful heart he broke into the conversation, 465
"Rejoice with me, I ask, that I have heard this news!
For my companion Walter is back from the Huns."
From this account Prince Gunther, in his haughtiness,
Exclaimed, and all the hall at once applauded him:
"That I lived to see this, rejoice with me, I ask! 470
The treasure which Gibicho sent the Eastern king
Now God Almighty has sent back into my realm!"
He spoke, kicked back the table, leaping up, and had
Them bring his horse and dress it with a carven saddle.
From all his troop he chose, including him, twelve men, 475
Distinguished for their strength, their courage often
    proved;
And he told Hagen he must go among these men.
He, mindful of his former pledge and his old friend,
Attempts to sway his lord from what he has begun.
The king, however, nonetheless stands firm and says 480
"Do not delay, my men! Gird your strong bodies with
A sword; now let a scaly corselet guard your backs!
Shall he remove from Frankish lands so great a treasure?"
Equipped with weapons (as the king's command required),
They left the gates in eagerness to see you, Walter, 485
And thinking they would cheat a weakling of his wealth.
Though Hagen strives in every way to hinder him,
The ill-starred king will not give up his undertaking.

Interea vir magnanimus de flumine pergens
venerat in saltum iam tum Vosagum vocitatum.   490
Nam nemus est ingens, spatiosum, lustra ferarum
plurima habens, suetum canibus resonare tubisque.
Sunt in secessu bini montesque propinqui,
inter quos licet angustum specus extat amoenum,
non tellure cava factum, sed vertice rupum,   495
apta quidem statio latronibus illa cruentis.
Angulus hic virides ac vescas gesserat herbas.
"Huc," mox ut vidit iuvenis, "huc" inquit "eamus,
his iuvat in castris fessum componere corpus."
Nam postquam fugiens Avarum discesserat oris,   500
non aliter somni requiem gustaverat idem
quam super innixus clipeo; vix clauserat orbes.
Bellica tum demum deponens pondera dixit
virginis in gremium fusus "Circumspice caute,
Hiltgunt, et nebulam si tolli videris atram,   505
attactu blando me surgere commonitato,
et licet ingentem conspexeris ire catervam,
ne excutias somno subito, mi cara, caveto,
nam procul hinc acies potis es transmittere puras.
Instanter cunctam circa explora regionem."   510
Haec ait atque oculos concluserat ipse nitentes
iamque diu satis optata fruitur requiete.
Ast ubi Guntharius vestigia pulvere vidit,
cornipedem rapidum saevis calcaribus urget,
exultansque animis frustra sic fatur ad auras   515
"Accelerate, viri, iam nunc capietis euntem,
numquam hodie effugiet, furata talenta relinquet."
Inclitus at Hagano contra mox reddidit ista
"Unum dico tibi, regum fortissime, tantum.
Si totiens tu Waltharium pugnasse videres   520
atque nova totiens, quotiens ego, caede furentem,
numquam tam facile spoliandum forte putares.
Vidi Pannonias acies, cum bella cierent
contra Aquilonares sive Australes regiones.
Illic Waltharius propria virtute coruscus   525
hostibus invisus, sociis mirandus obibat.
Quisquis ei congressus erat, mox Tartara vidit.
O rex et comites, experto credite, quantus
in clipeum surgat, quo turbine torqueat hastam."
Sed dum Guntharius male sana mente gravatus   530
nequaquam flecti posset, castris propiabant.
At procul aspiciens Hiltgunt de vertice montis

Meanwhile, the great-souled man, departing from the river,
Had reached a mountain woodland, then too called the
   Vosges: 490
A massive forest, spacious, having many lairs
Of beasts, accustomed to resound with dogs and horns.
Within a recess stand two mountains close together,
Between which lies a narrow, although pleasant, gorge:
Not hollowed from the earth, but formed by jutting
   cliffs.   495
Indeed that place is suited for bloodthirsty thieves.
This crevice had produced both green and tender grass.
"Let us head there," the youth said when he saw the place.
"I wish to rest my weary body in this stronghold."
For ever since he left the Avars' lands in flight,   500
He had not tasted of the rest of sleep unless
While leaning on his shield; he scarcely closed his eyes.
At last he put his heavy burdens down and said,
While resting on the maiden's lap, "Watch cautiously,
And, Hildegund, if you should see a dark cloud raised,   505
Then with a gentle touch warn me to rouse myself;
And even if you see a mighty troop approaching,
My dear, be careful not to wake me suddenly;
From here you can direct your sharp eyes quite a distance.
Scan this entire area attentively."   510
He spoke these words and then he closed his shining eyes
And now enjoyed the sleep he had so long desired.
But Gunther, when he saw their footprints in the dust,
Goads his swift-footed charger on with savage spurs;
Rejoicing vainly in his mind, he tells the winds: 515
"Hurry, men; soon now you will seize him on his way.
Today he'll not escape, but lose his stolen treasure."
But famous Hagen in reply said this at once:
"Just one thing will I say to you, most brave of kings;
If you had seen him fight and had seen Walter rage   520
With fresh-spilled blood as often as I have, perhaps
You would not think despoiling him so light a task.
I saw the forces of Pannonia, when they
Waged war against the northern or the southern regions.
And there, resplendent in his valor, Walter stalked,   525
A marvel to his friends, a terror to his foes.
Whoever faced that man soon saw the underworld.
O king and counts, trust one who knows how high he lifts
His shield, with what rapidity he hurls his spear."
While Gunther, burdened by an insane mind, could not   530
In any way be turned aside, they neared the stronghold.
But Hildegund, while watching from the mountain's crest,

pulvere sublato venientes sensit et ipsum
Waltharium placido tactu vigilare monebat.
Qui caput attollens scrutatur, si quis adiret. 535
Eminus illa refert quandam volitare phalangem.
Ipse oculos tersos somni glaucomate purgans
paulatim rigidos ferro vestiverat artus
atque gravem rursus parmam collegit et hastam
et saliens vacuas ferro transverberat auras 540
et celer ad pugnam telis prolusit amaram.
Comminus ecce coruscantes mulier videt hastas
ac stupefacta nimis "Hunos hic" inquit "habemus,"
in terramque cadens effatur talia tristis
"Obsecro, mi senior, gladio mea colla secentur, 545
ut, quae non merui pacto thalamo sociari,
nullius ulterius patiar consortia carnis."
Tum iuvenis "Cruor innocuus me tinxerit?" inquit
et "Quo forte modo gladius potis est inimicos
sternere, tam fidae si nunc non parcit amicae? 550
Absit quod rogitas, mentis depone pavorem.
Qui me de variis eduxit saepe periclis,
hic valet hic hostes, credo, confundere nostros."
Haec ait atque oculos tollens effatur ad ipsam
"Non assunt Avares hic, sed Franci nebulones, 555
cultores regionis," et en galeam Haganonis
aspicit et noscens iniunxit talia ridens
"Et meus hic socius Hagano collega veternus."
Hoc heros dicto introitum stationis adibat,

inferius stanti praedicens sic mulieri 560
"Hac coram porta verbum modo iacto superbum.
Hinc nullus rediens uxori dicere Francus
praesumet se impune gazae quid tollere tantae."
Necdum sermonem complevit, humotenus ecce
corruit et veniam petiit quia talia dixit. 565

Postquam surrexit, contemplans cautius omnes
"Horum quos video nullum Haganone remoto
suspicio; namque ille meos per proelia mores
iam didicit, tenet hic etiam sat callidus artem;
quam si forte volente deo intercepero solam, 570
tunc" ait "ex pugna tibi, Hiltgunt sponsa, reservor."
Ast ubi Waltharium tali statione receptum
conspexit Hagano, satrapae mox ista superbo
suggerit "O senior, desiste lacessere bello
hunc hominem! Pergant primum, qui cuncta requirant, 575
et genus et patriam nomenque locumque relictum,

Espied men coming by the dust that they had raised
And with a gentle touch warned Walter to awaken.
He lifts his head and asks if someone is approaching. 535
She tells him that a force is speeding from the distance.
And as he rubbed his eyes free of the veil of sleep,
Then gradually he garbed his still stiff limbs in iron;
And then he grasped once more his hefty shield and spear,
And leaping, with his sword he stabbed the empty air, 540
With weapons practiced keenly for a bitter fight.
The woman, standing next to him, sees flashing spears
And badly stunned by fear cries out, "The Huns are here!"
Then falling to the ground in sorrow says these words:
"I beg you lord, by your sword let my throat be slit, 545
That I, who could not be allied with you in marriage,
Not suffer carnal use by any other man."
The young man says, "Shall I be stained by guiltless blood?
And how shall my sword have the power to destroy
My foes, if now it does not spare so true a friend? 550
Withdraw your plea, put off the fear within your mind!
That which has often rescued me from many dangers
Here too, I trust, has strength to rout our enemies."
He spoke, then lifting up his eyes he says to her,
"These are not Avars here, but Frankish Nibelungs, 555
The people of this land." Then he sees Hagen's helmet,
And recognizing it, he laughs and adds these words,
"And here is my companion Hagen, my old friend."
The hero with this word approached the stronghold's
    entrance,
Addressing thus the woman who stood just behind: 560
"Before this gate I now declare in boastful words:
No Frank, returning from this place, will dare to tell
His wife that he, unharmed, took any of this treasure."
And so he fell to earth before he finished speaking
And begged forgiveness for the words which he had
    uttered 565
Arising, he then carefully appraised them all:
"Of these I see I am concerned with none but Hagen;
For that one has already learned my practices
In battle, and he is quite skillful in that art.
God willing, if I thwart his skill alone," he said, 570
"Then from the battle I'll be saved for you, my bride."
When Hagen saw that Walter was ensconced in such
A stronghold, to his haughty lord he said these words
At once: "My lord, desist from challenging this man
In war! First have men go and find out everything, 575
His lineage, his home, his name, the place he left.

vel si forte petat pacem sine sanguine praebens
thesaurum. Per responsum cognoscere homonem
possumus, et si Waltharius remoratur ibidem,
— est sapiens — forsan vestro concedet honori." 580
Praecipit ire virum cognomine rex Camalonem,
inclita Mettensi quem Francia miserat urbi
praefectum, qui dona ferens devenerat illo
anteriore die quam princeps noverit ista.
Qui dans frena volat rapidoque simillimus euro 585
transcurrit spatium campi iuvenique propinquat
ac sic obstantem compellat "dic, homo, quisnam
sis. Aut unde venis? Quo pergere tendis?"

Heros magnanimus respondit talia dicens
"Sponte tua venias an huc te miserit ullus, 590
scire velim." Camalo tunc reddidit ore superbo
"Noris Guntharium regem tellure potentem
me misisse tuas quaesitum pergere causas."

His auscultatis suggesserat hoc adolescens
"Ignoro penitus, quid opus sit forte viantis 595

scrutari causas, sed promere non trepidamus.
Waltharius vocor, ex Aquitanis sum generatus.
A genitore meo modicus puer obsidis ergo
sum datus ad Hunos, ibi vixi nuncque recessi
concupiens patriam dulcemque revisere gentem." 600
Missus ad haec "Tibi iam dictus per me iubet heros,
ut cum scriniolis equitem des atque puellam.
Quod si promptus agis, vitam concedet et artus."
Waltharius contra fidenter protulit ista
"Stultius effatum me non audisse sophistam 605
arbitror. En memoras, quod princeps nescio vel quis
promittat, quod non retinet nec fors retinebit.
An deus est, ut iure mihi concedere possit
vitam? Num manibus tetigit? Num carcere trusit
vel post terga meas torsit per vincula palmas? 610
At tamen ausculta: si me certamine laxat,
— aspicio, ferratus adest, ad proelia venit —
armillas centum de rubro quippe metallo
Factas transmittam, quo nomen regis honorem."
Tali responso discesserat ille recepto, 615
principibus narrat, quod protulit atque resumpsit.
Tunc Hagano ad regem "Porrectam suscipe gazam,
hac potis es decorare, pater, tecum comitantes,
et modo de pugna palmam revocare memento.

Perhaps he may seek peace by giving gold without
Bloodshed; by his response we can identify
The man. If Walter is the one who tarries there—
He is a prudent man—he may yield to your rank." 580
The king commands a man named Gamalo to go,
Whom glorious France had sent as prefect to the town
Of Metz, and who had just arrived there, bearing gifts,
The day before the prince had heard about this matter.
With slackened reins he flew and like the flowing wind 585
He crossed the distance of the field, drew near the youth
And thus addressed him as he stood his ground: "Say, who
Are you, man? Where do you come from? Where are you
    heading?"
The great-souled hero answers, saying this: "I wish
To know, do you come on your own, or did someone 590
Dispatch you here?" Gamalo states with haughty tongue,
"Then know that Gunther, mighty king within the land,
Sent me to come and to inquire about your business."
When he had heard these words, the young man made this
    statement:
"I am completely ignorant what need there is
To pry into the business of a traveler; 595
However, we are not afraid to make it known.
My name is Walter. I was born in Aquitaine.
My father sent me, still a little boy, to be
A hostage of the Huns. I lived there; now I have
Returned, and wish to see my homeland and dear people." 600
Then he: "Through me the forenamed hero orders you
That you give up the horse and coffers and the girl.
If you comply at once, he grants you life and limb."
But Walter in his confidence made this reply:
"I do not think that I have heard a smart man speak 605
More stupidly. You claim some prince or other offers
What he does not possess and likely never will.
Is he a god, that he can by his power grant
Me life? Has he laid hands on me? Thrust me in prison?
Or has he bound my hands behind my back with ropes? 610
But listen; if he nonetheless spares me this fight
(I see that he is here in arms, and comes for battle),
A hundred arm-rings made of bright red metal I
Will send, to honor thus the title of the king."
Receiving this reply, the other man departed; 615
He told the lords what he has offered and brought back.
Then Hagen to the king: "Accept that offered treasure,
With which you can reward your band of men, dear father.
Remember only to withdraw your hand from battle!

Ignotus tibi Waltharius et maxima virtus. 620
Ut mihi praeterita portendit visio nocte,
non, si conserimus, nos prospera cuncta sequentur.
Visum quippe mihi te colluctarier urso,
qui post conflictus longos tibi mordicus unum
crus cum poplite ad usque femur decerpserat omne 625
et mox auxilio subeuntem ac tela ferentem
me petit atque oculum cum dentibus eruit unum."
His animadversis clamat rex ille superbus
"Ut video, genitorem imitaris Hagathien ipse.
Hic quoque perpavidam gelido sub pectore mentem 630
gesserat et multis fastidit proelia verbis."
Tunc heros magnam iuste conceperat iram,
si tamen in dominum licitum est irascier ulli.
"En" ait "in vestris consistant omnia telis.
Est in conspectu, quem vultis. Dimicet omnis. 635
Comminus astatis nec iam timor impedit ullum;
eventum videam nec consors sim spoliorum."
Dixerat et collem petiit mox ipse propinquum
descendensque ab equo consedit et aspicit illo.
Post haec Guntharius Camaloni praecipit aiens 640
"Perge et thesaurum reddi mihi praecipe totum.
Quodsi cunctetur — scio tu vir fortis et audax —
congredere et bello devictum mox spoliato."
Ibat Mettensis Camalo metropolitanus,
vertice fulva micat cassis, de pectore thorax, 645
et procul acclamans "Heus! audi" dixit "amice!
Regi Francorum totum transmitte metallum,
si vis ulterius vitam vel habere salutem!"
Conticuit paulum verbo fortissimus heros,
opperiens propius hostem adventare ferocem. 650
Advolitans missus vocem repetiverat istam. 651
Tum iuvenis constans responsum protulit istud 653
"Quid quaeris? Vel quid reddi, importune, coartas?
Numquid Gunthario furabar talia regi? 655

Aut mihi pro lucro quicquam donaverat ille,
ut merito usuram me cogat solvere tantam?
Num pergens ego damna tuli vestrae regioni,
ut vel hinc iuste videar spoliarier a te?
Si tantam invidiam cunctis gens exhibet ista, 660
ut calcare solum nulli concedat eunti,
ecce viam mercor, regi transmitto ducentas
armillas. Pacem donet modo bella remittens."
Haec postquam Camalo percepit corde ferino,
"Amplificabis" ait "donum, dum scrinia pandis. 665

Unknown to you are Walter and his mighty valor;   620
But, as a dream revealed to me last night, if we
Join battle, all will not turn out successfully.
It seemed to me that you were wrestling with a bear
Which, after lengthy struggles, with a bite tore off
From you one whole leg with the knee up to the thigh.   625
As I rushed up to help while bearing arms, it turned
On me and gouged my eye out, with some of my teeth."
That haughty king, when he heard these remarks, exclaims,
"As I observe, you are the image of your father;
Hagathie also bore a timid heart inside   630
A frigid chest, avoiding war with many words."
The hero rightly then became extremely angered,
If to be angry with one's lord is ever right.
He says, "On your arms, then, let everything depend.
The one you want is in your sight. Let each man fight.   635
You stand quite close, and fear is holding no one back.
Let me observe the outcome and not share the spoils."
He spoke, and went immediately to a nearby hill;
Dismounting from his horse, he sat and watched from there.
Then Gunther speaks to Gamalo and gives his orders: 640
"Go, command all the treasure to be returned to me.
If he objects—I know that you are strong and brave—
Attack, despoil him once you conquer him in battle."
Then Gamalo, prefect of Metz, advanced; his helmet
Shines golden on his head, his byrnie on his chest.   645
And shouting from afar he said, "Hey! Listen, friend!
Hand over all your treasure to the Frankish king,
If you wish to have life and safety any more."
The valiant hero stood in silence for a moment,
Awaiting his fierce enemy to come still closer.   650
The legate, speeding on, repeated that demand . . .   651
The young man, unperturbed, then offered this reply: 653
"What do you say, churl? What do you demand returned?
Do you suggest that I stole such things from King
    Gunther?   655
Or did he ever give me anything on loan
That he justly can now force me to pay such interest?
While traveling did I do some damage to your land?
And for this reason seem fit to be robbed by you?
If that race shows so great a hatred for all men   660
That it allows no traveler to tread its soil,
I buy my way; I send your king two hundred arm-rings!
And let him merely offer peace, rejecting battle."
When Gamalo heard this within his brutish heart,
He said: "You'll raise your gift by opening those
    coffers   665

Consummare etenim sermones nunc volo cunctos.
Aut quaesita dabis aut vitam sanguine fundes."
Sic ait et triplicem clipeum collegit in ulnam
et crispans hastile micans vi nititur omni
ac iacit. At iuvenis devitat cautior ictum. 670
Hasta volans casso tellurem vulnere mordit.
Waltharius tandem "Si sic placet" inquit "agamus!"
Et simul in dictis hastam transmisit. At illa
per laevum latus umbonis transivit, et ecce

palmam, qua Camalo mucronem educere coepit, 675
confixit femori transpungens terga caballi.
Nec mora, dum vulnus sentit sonipes, furit atque
excutiens dorsum sessorem sternere temptat;
et forsan faceret, ni lancea fixa teneret.
Interea parmam Camalo dimisit et, hastam 680

complexus laeva, satagit divellere dextram.
Quod mox perspiciens currit celeberrimus heros
et pede compresso capulo tenus ingerit ensem;
quem simul educens hastam de vulnere traxit.
Tunc equus et dominus hora cecidere sub una. 685
Et dum forte nepos conspexerat hoc Camalonis,
filius ipsius Kimo cognomine fratris,
quem referunt quidam Scaramundum nomine dictum,
ingemit et lacrimis compellat tristior omnes
"Haec me prae cunctis heu respicit actio rerum. 690
Nunc aut commoriar vel carum ulciscar amicum."
Namque angusta loci solum concurrere soli
cogebant, nec quisquam alii succurrere quivit.
Advolat infelix Scaramundus iam moriturus,
bina manu lato crispans hastilia ferro. 695

Qui dum Waltharium nullo terrore videret
permotum fixumque loco consistere in ipso,
sic ait infrendens et equinam vertice caudam

concutiens "In quo fidis? Vel quae tua spes est?
Non ego iam gazam nec rerum quidque tuarum 700
appeto, sed vitam cognati quaero perempti."
Ille dehinc "Si convincar quod proelia primus
temptarim, seu quid merui quod talia possim
iure pati, absque mora tua me transverberet hasta."
Necdum sermonem concluserat, en Scaramundus 705
unum de binis hastile retorsit in illum

For now I wish to end all talk, and you will give
The things I seek or pour your life out with your blood."
He speaks and places on his arm his three-plyed shield,
And brandishing his flashing spear hurls it with all
His might. But warily the youth avoids the blow.   670
The flying weapon with a vain wound bites the dirt.
Then Walter says, "Let us proceed, if so you wish."
As he was speaking, Walter threw his spear, and it
Went through the left side of the shield and pinned his
    hand,
With which Gamalo had begun to draw his sword,   675
Against his thigh, while puncturing the horse's back.
At once the stallion, when it feels the wound, rears up
And shakes its back as it attempts to throw its rider,
And might have done so had the spear not held him pinned.
Meanwhile Gamalo dropped his shield; he grasped the
    spear   680
In his left hand, and tried to pry his right hand loose.
Observing this, the famous hero ran at once
And grabbed his foot and plunged his sword in to the hilt.
As he removed the sword, he wrenched the spear out from
The wound. In the same instant horse and rider fell.   685
And when by chance the nephew of that Gamalo
Saw this (he was the son of that man's brother Kimo,
Who some say was known by the name of Scaramund)
He groaned and, sorrowing, called out in tears to all,
"Alas! These troubles fall on me above all others!   690
Let me avenge my dear friend's death or die myself."
So narrow was the place that it forced single combat,
Nor could another offer help to anyone.
About to die, the luckless Scaramund advances
While shaking in his hand two spears tipped with broad
    iron.   695
But when he saw that Walter, utterly unmoved
By any fear, was standing firmly in his place,
He gnashed his teeth and shook his horsehair crest and
    cried,
"In what do you place confidence? What is your hope?
Now I do not seek gold or anything you have;   700
But I demand a life for that of my slain kinsman."
Then he: "If I am shown that I was first to start
The fight, or can be proved to suffer as I have
Deserved, without delay may your spear pierce through me."
He had not finished speaking when, look, Scaramund   705
Hurled one of his two spears at him and then at once

confestimque aliud. Quorum celeberrimus heros
unum devitat, quatit ex umbone secundum.
Tunc aciem gladii promens Scaramundus acuti
proruit in iuvenem cupiens praescindere frontem, 710

effrenique in equo propius devectus ad illum
non valuit capiti libratum infindere vulnus,
sed capulum galeae impegit; dedit illa resultans
tinnitus ignemque simul transfudit ad auras.
Sed non cornipedem potuit girare superbum, 715
donec Waltharius sub mentum cuspidis ictum
fixerat et sella moribundum sustulit alta.
Qui caput orantis proprio mucrone recidens
fecit cognatum pariter fluitare cruorem.
Hunc ubi Guntharius conspexit obisse superbus, 720
hortatur socios pugnam renovare furentes
"Aggrediamur eum nec respirare sinamus,
donec deficiens lassescat; et inde revinctus
thesauros reddet luet et pro sanguine poenas."
Tertius en Werinhardus abit bellumque lacessit, 725
quamlibet ex longa generatus stirpe nepotum,
o vir clare, tuus cognatus et artis amator,
Pandare, qui quondam iussus confundere foedus
in medios telum torsisti primus Achivos.
Hic spernens hastam pharetram gestavit et arcum, 730
eminus emissis haud aequo Marte sagittis
Waltharium turbans. Contra tamen ille virilis
constitit opponens clipei septemplicis orbem,
saepius eludens venientes providus ictus.
Nam modo dissiluit, parmam modo vergit in austrum 735
telaque discussit, nullum tamen attigit illum.
Postquam Pandarides se consumpsisse sagittas
incassum videt, iratus mox exerit ensem
et demum advolitans has iactitat ore loquelas
"O si ventosos lusisti callide iactus, 740
forsan vibrantis dextrae iam percipis ictum."
Olli Waltharius ridenti pectore adorsus
"Iamque diu satis expecto certamina iusto
pondere agi. Festina, in me mora non erit ulla."
Dixerat et toto conixus corpore ferrum 745
conicit. Hasta volans pectus reseravit equinum;
tollit se arrectum quadrupes et calcibus auras
verberat effundensque equitem cecidit super illum.
Accurrit iuvenis et ei vi diripit ensem.
Casside discussa crines complectitur albos 750
multiplicesque preces nectenti dixerat heros,

The other one. The celebrated hero dodged
The first of these; he shook the second from his shield.
Then Scaramund unsheathed the blade of his sharp sword
And rushed the youth, his wish to split the other's
    skull,   710
But carried close to him on his unbridled horse
Could not inflict the blow he aimed at Walter's head
But struck the helmet's boss; and this, resounding, rang
And also sent forth fiery sparks into the sky.
But he could not make his proud charger wheel about   715
Before a thrust from Walter's spear caught him beneath
The chin and raised him, dying, from his lofty saddle;
Then Walter, with the suppliant's own sword, cut off
His head, and once more caused familial blood to flow.
When haughty Gunther saw this man had died, he roused   720
His comrades, who were eager to renew the fight:
"Let us attack, give him no chance to catch his breath
Until he loses strength, exhausted; then, tied up,
He will return the treasure and pay for his bloodshed."
The third who went and joined the fight was Werinhard, 725
Descended from a lengthy line of your descendants,
Your kinsman, lover of your craft, O famous man,
Pandarus, who, once ordered to confound the treaty,
Were first to shoot an arrow into the Achaeans.
Rejecting spears, he bore a quiver and a bow,   730
Harassing Walter in unequal war with shafts
Shot from a distance; but that virile man stood firm,
And raised the circle of his seven-plated shield,
Adroitly dodging frequent arrows as they came.
And now he jumped aside or with his tilted shield   735
He knocked the shafts away; and not one touched that man.
When Werinhard saw he had used up all his arrows
In vain, enraged he drew his sword immediately;
Then, rushing forward, hurled these statements from his
"If you have skillfully avoided airborne shafts,   740
Perhaps now you will feel a blow my right arm wields."
Then Walter answered him with laughing heart, "Now have
I waited long enough for this fight to be waged
On equal terms. Make haste! You'll not find me delaying."
He spoke, then straining his entire body hurled   745
His spear. The flying shaft laid bare the horse's breast.
The charger reared upright and with its hooves it flailed
The air, then bucking off its rider, fell on him.
The youth runs up and wrests his sword away by force;
He rips his helmet off and grabs his light blond hair. 750
The hero told him as he made repeated pleas,

"Talia non dudum iactabas dicta per auras."
Haec ait et truncum secta cervice reliquit.
Sed non dementem tria visa cadavera terrent
Guntharium: iubet ad mortem properare vicissim. 755
En a Saxonicis oris Ekivrid generatus
quartus temptavit bellum, qui pro nece facta
cuiusdam primatis eo diffugerat exul.
Quem spadix gestabat equus maculis variatus.
Hic ubi Waltharium promptum videt esse duello, 760
"Dic" ait "an corpus vegetet tractabile temet
sive per aerias fallas, maledicte, figuras.
Saltibus assuetus faunus mihi quippe videris."
Illeque sublato dedit haec responsa cachinno
"Celtica lingua probat te ex illa gente creatum, 765
cui natura dedit reliquas ludendo praeire.
At si te propius venientem dextera nostra
attingat, post Saxonibus memorare valebis,
te nunc in Vosago fauni fantasma videre."
"Attemptabo quidem quid sis" Ekivrid ait ac mox 770
ferratam cornum graviter iacit. Illa retorto
emicat amento quam durus fregerat umbo.
Waltharius contra respondit cuspide missa
"Haec tibi silvanus transponit munera faunus.
Aspice, num mage sit telum penetrabile nostrum." 775
Lancea taurino contextum tergore lignum
diffidit ac tunicam scindens pulmone resedit.
Volvitur infelix Ekivrid rivumque cruoris
evomit. En mortem fugiens incurrit eandem.
Cuius equum iuvenis post tergum in gramen abegit. 780
Tunc a Gunthario clipeum sibi postulat ipsum
quintus ab inflato Hadawardus pectore lusus.
Qui pergens hastam sociis dimisit habendam,
audax in solum confisus inaniter ensem.
Et dum conspiceret deiecta cadavera totam 785

conclusisse viam nec equum transire valere,
dissiliens parat ire pedes. Stetit acer in armis
Waltharius laudatque virum, qui praebuit aequam
pugnandi sortem. Hadawart tum dixit ad illum
"O versute dolis ac fraudis conscie serpens, 790
occultare artus squamoso tegmine suetus
ac veluti coluber girum collectus in unum
tela tot evitas tenui sine vulneris ictu
atque venenatas ludis sine more sagittas.
Numquid et iste putas astu vitabitur ictus, 795
quem propius stantis certo libramine mittit

"Just now you were not shouting words like these aloud."
He spoke, and left a body with its head cut off.
The sight of three dead bodies did not scare mad Gunther.
Instead, his order is to hasten on toward death.   755
See now how Ekivrid, produced from Saxon lands,
Was fourth to try the fight; he had been forced, because
He killed some chieftain in that place, to flee in exile.
He rode upon a dappled chestnut horse; and when
He saw that Walter chafed for single combat, said: 760
"Now tell me, is your body solid, living flesh?
Or, devil, are you tricking us with airy phantoms?
Indeed, you seem just like a woodland sprite to me."
With raucous laughter that man gave his answer thus:
"Your Celtic accent shows you are descended from   765
That race whom nature made supreme in verbal play;
But if our right hand touches you as you come closer,
You will be able afterward to tell the Saxons
That now you see a woodsprite's phantom in the Vosges."
"I will test what you are," called Ekivrid at once.   770
He roughly threw his iron-pointed spear, which flew
Propelled by twisted thongs but broke on Walter's shield.
Then Walter said in answer as he threw his spear,
"The woodsprite sends this silvan gift across to you;
See whether our shaft may implant itself more deeply." 775
The missile shuddered through the bull's-hide-covered wood
And piercing through his corselet lodged within his lung.
The luckless Ekivrid collapses, vomits out
A stream of blood; in fleeing death, he ran to it.
The young man led his horse behind him to a pasture. 780
Deceived by his inflated spirit, Hadaward,
The fifth, claimed Walter's shield from Gunther for himself.
He gave his comrades, as he left, his spear to hold,
A bold man vainly trusting in his sword alone.
Seeing scattered corpses having blocked the path
        completely,   785
Nor could his horse pass through, dismounting, he prepared
To go on foot. There, fierce in arms, stood Walter, and
He praised the man who offered him an equal chance
In fighting. Hadaward at that point said to him:
"You serpent versed in tricks and skillful in deceit: 790
Accustomed to conceal your limbs with scaly hide
And coiled into a single spiral like a snake,
You dodge so many shots without the slightest wound,
Defiantly eluding even poisoned arrows!
By craft you think this blow will be avoided which   795
The right hand of a man delivers close by with

dextera manus? Neque enim is teli seu vulneris auctor.
Audi consilium, parmam deponito pictam.
Hanc mea sors quaerit, regis quoque sponsio praestat;
nolo quidem laedas, oculis quia complacet istis. 800
Sin alias, licet et lucem mihi dempseris almam,
assunt hic plures socii carnisque propinqui,
qui, quamvis volucrem simules pennasque capessas,
te tamen immunem numquam patientur abire."
Belliger at contra nil territus intulit ista 805
"De reliquis taceo, clipeum defendere curo.
Pro meritis, mihi crede, bonis sum debitor illi.
Hostibus iste meis se opponere saepe solebat
et pro vulneribus suscepit vulnera nostris.
Quam sit oportunus hodie mihi, cernis, et ipse 810
non cum Walthario loquereris forsan, abesset.
Viribus o summis hostem depellere cures,
dextera, ne rapiat tibi propugnacula muri!
Tu clavum umbonis studeas retinere, sinistra,
atque ebori digitos circumfer glutine fixos! 815
Istic ne ponas pondus, quod tanta viarum
portasti spatia ex Avarum nam sedibus altis!"
Ille dehinc "Invitus agis, si sponte recusas.
Nec solum parmam, sed equum cum virgine et auro
reddes. Tum demum scelerum cruciamina pendes." 820
Haec ait et notum vagina diripit ensem.
Inter se variis terrarum partibus orti
concurrunt. Stupuit Vosegus haec fulmina et ictus.
Olli sublimes animis ac grandibus armis,
hic gladio fidens, hic acer et arduus hasta, 825

inter se multa et valida vi proelia miscent.
Non sic nigra sonat percussa securibus ilex
ut dant tinnitus galeae clipeique resultant.
Mirantur Franci, quod non lassesceret heros
Waltharius, cui nulla quies spatiumve dabatur. 830
Emicat hic impune putans iam Wormatiensis
alte et sublato consurgit fervidus ense,
hoc ictu memorans semet finire duellum.
Providus at iuvenis ferientem cuspide adacta
intercepit et ignarum dimittere ferrum 835
cogebat. Procul in dumis resplenduit ensis.
Hic ubi se gladio spoliatum vidit amico,
accelerare fugam fruticesque volebat adire.
Alpharides fretus pedibus viridique iuventa
insequitur dicens "Quonam fugis? Accipe scutum!" 840

Sure aim? This spear and wound are not from such a man.
Take my advice; lay down your painted shield. My lot
Claims this as mine. The king's pledge guarantees it too.
I don't want you to hurt it; it delights my eyes.   800
If not, and you should rob me of the gracious light,
My many friends and relatives are present who,
Though you assume the form and feathers of a bird,
Still never will allow you to escape unharmed."
In turn, the warrior whom nothing frightened answered,   805
"The rest I do not mention; I wish to defend
My shield. I owe it much, believe me, for good service,
For often it was wont to set itself against
My foes, and suffered blows that would have wounded me.
You see how useful I find it today; were it   810
Not here, you might not be conversing now with Walter.
With all your strength strive to repel this enemy,
Right hand; prevent the theft of your defending bulwark!
You, left hand, strive to grip the handle of the shield,
Wrap fingers stuck like glue around the ivory.   815
Do not put down the burden here that you have borne
So great a distance from the Huns' high citadels!"
Then he: "If you resist, you'll act against your good.
You will return not just the shield, but horse and girl
And gold, and then will suffer punishment for crimes."   820
He says these words and then unsheathes his trusty blade.
The two men born in different lands attack each other.
The Vosges was astonished by the sparks and blows.
Distinguished by their courage and their mighty weapons,
One trusts his sword; the other, fierce and hard, his
    spear.   825
With fearsome force, they traded blows between themselves.
The crash of ax blades on a dark oak tree resounds
Less loudly than the ringing of their shields and helmets.
The Franks were stunned that Walter, to whom neither rest
Nor respite had been given, did not grow exhausted.   830
The man from Worms, believing he was safe, sprang forward
And with his blade raised high stood up impulsively,
Believing that with this stroke he would end the fight.
As it was striking, though, the cautious youth held out
His spear and blocked it, forcing his unwary foe   835
To lose his sword, which glittered back from distant brambles.
When he saw that he had been stripped of his dear sword,
He wished to speed his flight and reach the underbrush;
Relying on his feet and fresh youth, Alphere's son
Pursued: "Where do you flee?" he called; "Pick up your
    shield!"   840

Sic ait atque hastam manibus levat ocius ambis
et ferit. Ille cadit, clipeus superintonat ingens.
Nec tardat iuvenis, pede collum pressit et hasta
divellens parmam telluri infixerat illum.
Ipse oculos vertens animam sufflavit in auram.   845

Sextus erat Patavrid. Soror hunc germana Haganonis
protulit ad lucem. Quem dum procedere vidit,
vocibus et precibus conatur avunculus inde
flectere proclamans "Quonam ruis? Aspice mortem,
qualiter arridet! Desiste! En ultima Parcae   850
fila legunt. O care nepos, te mens tua fallit.
Desine! Waltharii tu denique viribus impar."
Infelix tamen ille means haec omnia sprevit,
arsit enim venis laudem captare cupiscens.
Tristatusque Hagano suspiria pectore longa   855
traxit et has imo fudit de corde loquelas
"O vortex mundi, fames insatiatus habendi,
gurges avaritiae, cunctorum fibra malorum!
O utinam solum gluttires dira metallum
divitiasque alias, homines impune remittens!   860
Sed tu nunc homines perverso numine perflans
incendis nullique suum iam sufficit. Ecce
non trepidant mortem pro lucro incurrere turpem.
Quanto plus retinent, tanto sitis ardet habendi.
Externis modo vi modo furtive potiuntur   865
et, quod plus renovat gemitus lacrimasque ciebit,
caeligenas animas Erebi fornace retrudunt.
Ecce ego dilectum nequeo revocare nepotem,
instimulatus enim de te est, o saeva cupido.
En caecus mortem properat gustare nefandam   870
et vili pro laude cupit descendere ad umbras.
Heu, mihi care nepos, quid matri, perdite, mandas?
Quis nuper ductam refovebit, care, maritam,

cui nec, rapte spei, pueri ludicra dedisti?
Quis tibi nam furor est? Unde haec dementia venit?" 875
Sic ait et gremium lacrimis conspersit obortis,
et longum "formose, vale" singultibus edit.
Waltharius, licet alonge, socium fore maestum
attendit, clamorque simul pervenit ad aures.
Unde incursantem sic est affatus equestrem   880
"Accipe consilium, iuvenis clarissime, nostrum
et te conservans melioribus utere fatis.
Desine, nam tua te fervens fiducia fallit!
Heroum tot cerne neces et cede duello

Then quickly raised his spear in both his hands and struck.
The other fell, his great shield crashing down on him.
Without delay, the youth stepped on his neck, removed
His shield, and with his spear then pinned him to the ground.
He rolled his eyes, breathed out his life into the
   breeze.   845
The sixth was Batavrid, whom Hagen's sister brought
Into the world; but when he saw the boy step forward,
His uncle tried to change his mind with shouts and pleas:
"Where are you rushing to?" he called out, "Look at Death,
How it is grinning! Stop! The Fates are drawing out   850
Your final threads. Your mind deceives you, darling nephew!
Desist! You are in fact no match for Walter's strength."
And still the luckless boy, advancing, spurned all this,
For in his veins he burned and longed to capture fame.
And Hagen mournfully drew long sighs from his breast   855
And poured out these complaints from deep within his heart:
"O whirlpool of the world, voracious lust of having!
Abyss of avarice, the root of every evil!
O dreadful one, if you would gulp down only gold
And other riches, letting men escape unharmed!   860
You kindle men, inspiring them with evil power;
And now for no one is his own enough. Behold!
For profit's sake undaunted they risk shameful death;
The more they have, the more the thirst for having burns.
They take another's goods by force now, now by theft;   865
And what provokes more sighs again and summons tears,
They thrust god-given souls into Erebus' furnace.
I am not able to recall my darling nephew;
For he is prodded on by you, O savage greed,
And blindly rushes on to taste repulsive death,   870
And for cheap praise he would descend among the shades.
What message for your mother, ah, my dear lost nephew?
Dear boy, who'll love your newly wedded bride, whom you,
Bereft of hope, gave not the pleasure of a child?
What is this rage of yours? Whence has this madness
   come?"   875
He spoke, and sprinkled welling tears upon his lap,
And sobbing choked out a prolonged "Farewell, fair boy."
Now Walter, although far away, sensed that his friend
Was sad, and at the same time heard his lamentation.
He spoke thus to the horseman who was charging forward: 880
"Accept this good advice of ours, most handsome youth.
Go and preserve your life. Enjoy a better fate.
Now halt! for your rash confidence is tricking you.
Behold so many heroes' corpses! Quit this fight,

ne suprema videns hostes facias mihi plures." 885
"Quid de morte mea curas" ait ille "Tyranne?
Est modo pugnandum tibimet, non sermocinandum."
Dixit et in verbo nodosam destinat hastam,
cuspide quam propria divertens transtulit heros.
Quae subvecta choris ac viribus acta furentis 890
in castrum venit atque pedes stetit ante puellae.
Ipsa metu perculsa sonum prompsit muliebrem.
At postquam tenuis redit in praecordia sanguis,
paulum suspiciens spectat num viveret heros.
Tum quoque vir fortis Francum discedere bello 895
iussit. At ille furens gladium nudavit et ipsum

incurrens petiit vulnusque a vertice librat.
Alpharides parmam demum concusserat aptam
et spumantis apri frendens de more tacebat.
Ille ferire volens se pronior omnis ad ictum 900
exposuit, sed Waltharius sub tegmine flexus

delituit corpusque suum contraxit, et ecce
vulnere delusus iuvenis recidebat ineptus.
Finis erat, nisi quod genibus tellure refixis
belliger accubuit calibemque sub orbe cavebat. 905

Hic dum consurgit, pariter se subrigit ille
ac citius scutum trepidus sibi praetulit atque
frustra certamen renovare parabat. At illum
Alpharides fixa gladio petit ocius hasta
et mediam clipei dempsit vasto impete partem, 910
hamatam resecans loricam atque ilia nudans.

Labitur infelix Patavrid sua viscera cernens
silvestrique ferae corpus, animam dedit Orco.
Hunc sese ulturum spondens Gerwitus adivit,
qui forti subvectus equo supra volat omnem 915
stragem, quae angustam concluserat obvia callem.
Et dum bellipotens recidisset colla iacentis,
venit et ancipitem vibravit in ora bipennem.
(Istius ergo modi Francis tunc arma fuere.)
Vir celer obiecit peltam frustravit et ictum, 920
ac retro saliens hastam rapiebat amicam
sanguineumque ulva viridi dimiserat ensem.
Hic vero metuenda virum tum bella videres.
Sermo quidem nullus fuit inter Martia tela.
Sic erat adverso mens horum intenta duello. 925
Is furit ut caesos mundet vindicta sodales,

So your death will not make more enemies for me." 885
Then he: "What do you care about my death, you tyrant?
The time demands a fight and not a conversation."
He spoke and with that word he threw his knotted spear,
Which Walter parried, blocking it with his own spear.
Propelled by breezes and the raging warrior's strength, 890
It reached the stronghold, landing at the maiden's feet.
Her fear provoked her to give out a woman's cry;
But when a little blood had come back to her heart,
She peeked out to see if the hero still was living.
That brave man even then commanded that the Frank 895
Stop fighting; but, enraged, he bared his sword and,
 charging,
Attacked and aimed a blow from high above his head.
The son of Alphere thrust his shield to the right place
In time, and gnashing like a foaming boar, kept silent.
The other, all intent upon a blow, leaned forward. 900
He wished to strike, but Walter, crouched beneath his
 shield,
Concealed himself and drew his body in, and lo!
The awkward boy, tricked into a wild blow, fell down.
This would have been the end, had not the warrior knelt
Down on the ground and shunned the steel beneath his
 shield. 905
When he stood up, the other likewise rose; at once
The frightened boy held out his shield in front of him,
Prepared, in vain, to fight again. But Alphere's son,
His spear stuck in the ground, attacked him with his sword
And with one mighty stroke sliced half his shield away, 910
And driving through the chain-linked byrnie bared his
 entrails.
While falling, luckless Batavrid gazed on his bowels.
He gave his body to wild beasts, his soul to Orcus.
Then Gerwit, vowing to avenge this man, advanced,
And borne upon his robust steed, vaulted all the carnage 915
Which, lying in the way, had blocked the narrow path;
And as the warlike man cut through the corpse's neck,
He came and swung a double-bladed ax straight at
His face (The Franks in those days had this kind of weapon).
The agile man staved off this blow by holding up 920
His shield, then jumping back he grabbed his trusty spear
And dropped his bloody sword there on the blooming sedge.
Here then indeed you would see heroes' fearsome struggles.
There was no talking while their warring weapons clashed;
Their minds were utterly absorbed in single combat. 925
One rages to atone for fallen friends by vengeance;

ille studet vitam toto defendere nisu
et, si fors dederit, palmam retinere triumphi.
Hic ferit, ille cavet, petit ille, reflectitur iste.
Ad studium fors et virtus miscentur in unum. 930
Longa tamen cuspis breviori depulit hostem
armatum telo, girat sed et ille caballum
atque fatigatum cupiebat fallere homonem.
Iam magis atque magis irarum mole gravatus
Waltharius clipeum Gerwiti sustulit imum, 935

Transmissoque femur penetraverat inguine ferrum.
Qui post terga ruens clamorem prodidit atrum
exitiumque dolens pulsabat calcibus arvum.
Hunc etiam truncum caesa cervice reliquit.
Idem Wormatiae campis comes extitit ante. 940

Tum primum Franci coeperunt forte morari
et magnis precibus dominum decedere pugna

deposcunt. Furit ille miser caecusque profatur
"Quaeso, viri fortes et pectora saepe probata,
ne fors haec cuicumque metum, sed conferat iram. 945
Quid mihi, si Vosago sic sic inglorius ibo?
Mentem quisque meam sibi vindicet. En ego partus
ante mori sum, Wormatiam quam talibus actis
ingrediar. Petat hic patriam sine sanguine victor?
Hactenus arsistis hominem spoliare metallis, 950

nunc ardete, viri, fusum mundare cruorem
ut mors abstergat mortem, sanguis quoque sanguem,
soleturque necem sociorum plaga necantis."
His animum dictis demens incendit et omnes
Fecerat immemores vitae simul atque salutis. 955
Ac velut in ludis alium praecurrere quisque
ad mortem studuit, sed semita, ut antea dixi,
cogebat binos bello decernere solos.
Vir tamen illustris dum cunctari videt illos,
vertice distractas suspendit in arbore cristas 960
et ventum captans sudorem tersit anhelus.
Ecce repentino Randolf athleta caballo
praevertens reliquos hunc importunus adivit
ac mox ferrato petiit sub pectore conto.
Et nisi duratis Wielandia fabrica giris 965

obstaret, spisso penetraverit ilia ligno.
Ille tamen subito stupefactus corda pavore

One strives with all his effort to defend his life,
And to retain, if luck allows, the palm of triumph.
Attack and parry: one advances, one retreats;
There chance and courage mingle into one endeavor.   930
The long spear, nonetheless, repelled the man armed with
The shorter weapon; but he wheeled his horse around
Attempting to deceive the man who had grown tired.
Now Walter, more and more oppressed by the weight of
His wrath, cut through the lower part of Gerwit's
    shield;   935
The weapon, piercing Gerwit's groin, lodged in his thigh:
He gasped a gloomy sound as he fell back and mourned
His death while with his heels he beat upon the earth.
And Walter left him, too, a trunk, its head cut off.
That same trunk once had been, in lands near Worms, a
    count.   940
The Franks now for the first time started to hold back,
And they beseeched their lord, with heartfelt prayers, to
    end
The fight. Enraged, that wretched blinded man proclaims:
"Brave men and often tested hearts, I ask that this
Misfortune not cause fear in anyone, but anger.   945
If thus, thus shamed I leave the Vosges—what of me?
Let each adopt my attitude. I am prepared
To die before I enter Worms on such conditions.
Shall he, the victor, reach his home with no blood shed?
Up to this point you burned to strip the man of
    treasures.   950
Now, men, burn to avenge the blood that has been spilled,
So that death may atone for death, and blood for blood,
The killer's death console us for the loss of comrades!"
The madman with these words inflamed them all, and made
Them all forgetful of their lives, as well as safety.   955
Just as in games, each strived to best another in
The race to Death. However, as I said before,
The path compelled two men—no more—to meet in battle.
The famous man, when he saw they were hesitating,
Took his plumed helmet off and hung it on a tree,   960
Then caught his breath and, gasping, wiped away the sweat.
Behold! One athlete, Randalf, on his rapid horse,
Outstripping all the rest, attacked him violently,
And quickly aimed an iron pike beneath his chest.
Had Wieland's work not stopped its flight with tempered
    rings,   965
It would have punctured Walter's bowels with its thick wood.
Though stunned by sudden fear within his heart, he held

munimen clipei obiecit mentemque recepit;
nec tamen et galeam fuerat sumpsisse facultas.
Francus at emissa gladium nudaverat hasta 970
et feriens binos Aquitani vertice crines
abrasit, sed forte cutem praestringere summam
non licuit, rursumque alium vibraverat ictum
et praeceps animi directo obstamine scuti
impegit calibem, nec quivit viribus ullis 975
elicere. Alpharides retro, se fulminis instar
excutiens, Francum valida vi fudit ad arvum
et super assistens pectus conculcat et inquit
"En pro calvitio capitis te vertice fraudo
ne fiat ista tuae de me iactantia sponsae." 980
Vix effatus haec truncavit colla precantis.
At nonus pugnae Helmnod successit, et ipse
insertum triplici gestabat fune tridentem,
quem post terga quidem socii stantes tenuerunt,
consiliumque fuit, dum cuspis missa sederet 985

in clipeo, cuncti pariter traxisse studerent,
ut vel sic hominem deiecissent furibundum;
atque sub hac certum sibi spe posuere triumphum.
Nec mora, dux totas fundens in brachia vires
misit in adversum magna cum voce tridentem 990

edicens "Ferro tibi finis, calve, sub isto!"
Qui ventos penetrans iaculorum more coruscat,
quod genus aspidis ex alta sese arbore tanto
turbine demittit, quo cuncta obstantia vincat.
Quid moror? Umbonem sciderat peltaque resedit. 995

Clamorem Franci tollunt saltusque resultat,
obnixique trahunt restim simul atque vicissim,
nec dubitat princeps tali se aptare labori.
Manarunt cunctis sudoris flumina membris.
Sed tamen haec inter velut aesculus astitit heros, 1000
quae non plus petit astra comis quam Tartara fibris,
contempnens omnes ventorum immota fragores.
Certabant hostes hortabanturque viritim
ut, si non quirent ipsum detrudere ad arvum,
munimen clipei saltem extorquere studerent, 1005
quo dempto vivus facile caperetur ab ipsis.
Nomina quae restant edicam iamque trahentum:
nonus Eleuthir erat, Helmnod cognomine dictus,

His shield in self-defense until his senses cleared;
However, Walter had no chance to don his helmet.
The Frank, since he had thrown his pike, unsheathed his
    sword,   970
And, slashing, shaved two locks of hair from Walter's head;
And yet by chance he could not even graze the scalp.
Again he aimed another blow and, rash of mind,
He plunged his steel into the shield held opposite,
And could not pull it out by any of his efforts.   975
The son of Alphere shaking free like lightning hurled
The Frank with awesome power backward on the ground;
Then, standing over him, stepped on his chest and said,
"I take your head from you as payment for my baldness,
So there can be no boast about me to your wife."   980
Just having spoken, he cut through the suppliant's neck.
The ninth who came to join the fight was Helmnot, and
He grasped a three-pronged spear fixed to a triple cord
Which his companions who stood back of him were holding.
This was their plan: that when the spear, once cast, had
    lodged   985
In Walter's shield, they all would strive to pull together
So that they might, in this way, throw the raging man.
And in this hope they pictured certain victory.
Straightway the leader, pouring all his strength into
His arms, released his trident at the foe, while
    shouting   990
"You, bald head! With this spear the end has come for you!"
It flashes as it cleaves the air, just like the breed
Of snakes, the javelin-snakes, which pounce down from the
    tops
Of trees so violently they smash all obstacles.
Why pause? It splits the boss and sticks in Walter's
    shield.   995
The Franks are raising up a shout; the grove resounds.
Together and in turns they tug the rope with vigor;
The king does not hold back from joining in such work.
From all their limbs the sweat was flowing down in streams,
Yet all the while the hero stood there like an oak   1000
That thrusts its roots to Tartarus, its branches to
The stars, and scorns unmoving all the stormy blasts.
His enemies, exhorting one another, sought,
If they could not drag Walter down onto the ground,
At least to try and wrest from him his stalwart shield.   1005
With this gone, they could easily take him alive.
I will reveal the names of those left and still pulling:
Eleuthir (his name also Helmnot) was the ninth;

argentina quidem decimum dant oppida Trogum,
extulit undecimum pollens urbs Spira Tanastum, 1010
absque Haganone locum rex supplevit duodenum.
Quattuor hi adversum summis conatibus unum
contendunt pariter multo varioque tumultu.
Interea Alpharidi vanus labor incutit iram,
et qui iam pridem nudarat casside frontem, 1015
in framea tunicaque simul confisus aena
omisit parmam primumque invasit Eleuthrin.
Huic galeam findens cerebrum diffudit et ipsam
cervicem resecans pectus patefecit, at aegrum
cor pulsans animam liquit mox atque calorem. 1020
Inde petit Trogum haerentem in fune nefando.
Qui subito attonitus recidentis morte sodalis
horribilique hostis conspectu coeperat acrem
nequiquam temptare fugam voluitque relicta
arma recolligere ut rursum repararet agonem. 1025
(Nam cuncti funem tracturi deposuerunt
hastas cum clipeis.) Sed quanto maximus heros
fortior extiterat, tanto fuit ocior, olli
et cursu capto suras mucrone recidit

ac sic tardatum praevenit et abstulit eius 1030
scutum. Sed Trogus, quamvis de vulnere lassus,
mente tamen fervens saxum circumspicit ingens,
quod rapiens subito obnixum contorsit in hostem
et proprium a summo clipeum fidit usque deorsum.
Sed retinet fractum pellis superaddita lignum. 1035

Moxque genu posito viridem vacuaverat aedem
atque ardens animis vibratu terruit auras,
et si non quivit virtutem ostendere factis,
corde tamen habitum patefecit et ore virilem.
Nec manes ridere videns audaciter infit 1040

"O mihi si clipeus vel sic modo adesset amicus!
Fors tibi victoriam de me, non inclita virtus
contulit. Ad scutum mucronem hic tollito nostrum!"
Tum quoque subridens "Venio iam" dixerat heros
et cursu advolitans dextram ferientis ademit. 1045

Sed cum athleta ictum libraret ab aure secundum
pergentique animae valvas aperire studeret,
ecce Tanastus adest telis cum rege resumptis
et socium obiecta protexit vulnere pelta.
Hinc indignatus iram convertit in ipsum 1050

Indeed, the town of Strassburg sent the tenth, named Trogus;
And wealthy Speyer sent Tanastus, the eleventh;   1010
Not counting Hagen, Gunther occupied twelfth place.
Exerting all their strength, these four together wage
An indecisive struggle with a single foe.
Their useless efforts, meanwhile, angered Alphere's son,
Who had long since removed his helmet from his head   1015
And was relying on his sword and his bronze byrnie.
He threw away his shield, then charged Eleuthir first
And hacking through his helmet halved his brains; next he
Cut off his head and left the breast exposed; the hurt
And throbbing heart at once gave up its life and warmth. 1020
He then sought Trogus, clinging to the hateful rope;
That man, stunned by his fallen comrade's sudden death
And by the awful visage of his foe, began
In vain to try swift flight and wished to pick up his
Abandoned arms in order to resume the struggle.   1025
(To pull the rope, they all had laid aside their spears
And shields.) But Walter, best of heroes, by as much
As he was stronger was superior in speed;
When he caught him, he slashed his hamstrings with his
    sword.
Then overtaking Trogus, thus slowed down, he grabbed   1030
His shield; but Trogus, though exhausted by his wound,
Still raging in his mind, caught sight of a huge rock;
At once he seized it, threw it at his steadfast foe.
It split the shield from top to bottom, but the hide
That covered it still held the shattered frame
    together.   1035
Though kneeling down, he quickly emptied his green sheath,
And burning in his spirit scared the winds with slashing.
And if he could not show his courage in his deeds,
His spirit and his words revealed his manliness.
He boldly speaks, but does not see the shades are
    laughing: 1040
"Oh, if I only had my trusty shield here now!
For Chance, not wondrous valor, gave you victory.
You took our shield; come here and take our sword as well!"
Then, smiling also, "Here I come," the hero said,
And charging hacked his right hand off as he was
    striking;   1045
But when he poised a second blow above his ear,
And tried to forge an exit for his soul's departure,
Tanastus, with the king, was there (their arms retrieved),
And kept his friend from harm by holding out his shield.
Enraged because of this, then Walter turned his wrath 1050

Waltharius humerumque eius de cardine vellit
perque latus ducto suffudit viscera ferro.
"Ave!" procumbens submurmurat ore Tanastus.
Quo recidente preces contempsit promere Trogus
conviciisque sui victorem incendit amaris, 1055
seu virtute animi, seu desperaverat. Exin
Alpharides "Morere" inquit "et haec sub Tartara transfer
enarrans sociis, quod tu sis ultus eosdem."
His dictis torquem collo circumdedit aureum.
Ecce simul caesi volvuntur pulvere amici, 1060
crebris foedatum ferientes calcibus arvum.
His rex infelix visis suspirat et omni

aufugiens studio falerati terga caballi
scandit et ad maestum citius Haganona volavit
omnimodisque illum precibus flexisse sategit, 1065
ut secum pergens pugnam repararet. At ille
"Me genus infandum prohibet bellare parentum,
et gelidus sanguis mentem mihi ademit in armis.
Tabescebat enim genitor, dum tela videret,
et timidus multis renuebat proelia verbis. 1070
Haec dum iactasses, rex, inter te comitantes,
extitit indignum nostri tibi quippe iuvamen."
Ille recusanti precibus nihilominus instans
talibus aversum satagit revocare loquelis
"deprecor ob superos, conceptum pone furorem. 1075
Iram de nostra contractam decute culpa,
quam vita comitante, domum si venero tecum,
impensis tibimet benefactis diluo multis.
Nonne pudet sociis tot cognatisque peremptis
dissimulare virum? Magis, ut mihi quippe videtur, 1080
verba valent animum quam facta nefanda movere.
Iustius in saevum tumuisses mente tyrannum,
qui solus hodie caput infamaverat orbis.
Non modicum patimur damnum de caede virorum,
dedecus at tantum superabit Francia numquam. 1085
Antea quis fuimus suspecti, sibila dantes
"Francorum" dicent "exercitus omnis ab uno,
proh pudor ignotum vel quo, est impune necatus!"
Cunctabatur adhuc Haganon et pectore sponsam
Walthario plerumque fidem volvebat et ipsum 1090
eventum gestae recolebat in ordine causae.
Supplicius tamen infelix rex institit illi.
Cuius subnixe rogitantis acumine motus
erubuit domini vultum, replicabat honorem
virtutis propriae, qui fors vilesceret inde, 1095

On him; he wrenched Tanastus' shoulder from its socket.
With naked blade he probed his entrails through his side.
"Farewell," Tanastus muttered from his lips while falling.
His comrade fallen, Trogus scorns to beg for mercy,
And he inflames the victor with his bitter taunts,   1055
From courage or from desperation. Alphere's son
Replies "Now die, and take beneath the earth this message,
Recounting to your friends that you avenged them all."
This said, he gave a bright-red necklace to his neck.
Behold! Together slaughtered friends roll in the dust,   1060
While with their heels they often beat the bloodied ground.
The luckless king, when he saw these things, sighs; and,
    fleeing
With all his effort mounts his richly furbished horse
And quickly flies to mournful Hagen. And he tried
With every kind of prayer to persuade that man   1065
That he, going with him, should renew the fight. But he:
"My shameful ancestry prohibits me from warring,
And chill blood has deprived me of resolve in arms.
My father used to faint whenever he saw weapons—
That coward who avoided fights with many words.   1070
When you spoke thus, my king, among your followers,
Our service was of course disgraceful to you then."
But still beseeching the reluctant man with pleas,
He tries to win back his estranged man with such words:
"I beg you by the gods, give up the rage you have   1075
Conceived! Our fault has caused it. Cast away your wrath,
Which, if we live and if I reach my home with you,
I will redeem for you with many lavish gifts.
Are you not shamed to disavow your manhood, with
So many friends and kinsmen killed? It seems to me   1080
That words can rouse your spirit more than evil deeds.
More justly should you swell with rage at that cruel tyrant
Who by himself today disgraced the world's prime lord.
We suffer no small loss from slaughtered warriors;
But France will never overcome so great a shame,   1085
For those by whom we formerly were feared will hiss
And say, "The Franks' entire army has been slain
By one man unscathed (for shame!) whom nobody knows."
Still Hagen wavered and considered in his breast
The faith so often pledged to Walter, and he pondered   1090
The outcome of the matter as it had transpired.
But now the luckless king begged more insistently.
Moved by the fervor of his pleading, he avoided
His sovereign's gaze, and thought about his reputation
For valor, that it might be sullied if he should   1095

si quocumque modo in rebus sibi parceret istis.
Erupit tandem et clara sic voce respondit
"Quo me, domne, vocas? Quo te sequar, inclite princeps?
Quae nequeunt fieri, spondet fiducia cordi.
Quis tam desipiens quandoque fuisse probatur,   1100
qui saltu baratrum sponte attemptarit apertum?
Nam scio Waltharium per campos sic fore acerbum
ut tali castro nec non statione locatus
ingentem cuneum velut unum temnat homullum.
Et licet huc cunctos equites simul atque pedestres   1105

Francia misisset, sic his ceu fecerat istis.
Sed quia conspicio te plus doluisse pudore
quam caedis damno nec sic discedere velle,
compatior propriusque dolor succumbit honori
regis; et ecce viam conor reperire salutis,   1110
quae tamen aut nusquam ostendit se sive coacte.
Nam propter carum (fateor tibi, domne) nepotem
promissam fidei normam corrumpere nollem.
Ecce in non dubium pro te, rex, ibo periclum.
Ast hic me penitus conflictu cedere noris.   1115
Secedamus eique locum praestemus eundi
et positi in speculis tondamus prata caballis,
donec iam castrum securus deserat artum,
nos abiisse ratus. Campos ubi calcet apertos,
insurgamus et attonitum post terga sequamur;   1120
sic aliquod virtutis opus temptare valemus.
Haec mihi in ambiguis spes est certissima rebus.
Tum pugnare potes, belli si, rex, tibi mens est.
Quippe fugam nobis numquam dabit ille duobus,
at nos aut fugere aut acrum bellare necesse est."   1125
Laudat consilium satrapa et complectitur illum
oscilloque virum demulcet; et ecce recedunt
insidiisque locum circumspexere sat aptum
demissique ligant animalia gramine laeto.
Interea occiduas vergebat Phoebus in oras,   1130
ultima per notam signans vestigia Thilen,
et cum Scottigenis post terga reliquit Hiberos.
Hic postquam oceanas sensim calefecerat undas,
Hesperos Ausonidis obvertit cornua terris,
tum secum sapiens coepit tractare satelles,   1135
utrum sub tuto per densa silentia castro
sisteret, an vastis heremi committeret arvis.
Aestuat immensis curarum fluctibus, et quid
iam faceret, sollers arguta indagine quaerit.
Solus enim Hagano fuerat suspectus et illud   1140

In any manner spare himself in this affair.
At length he broke the silence and responded clearly,
"Where do you call me, lord? Where shall I follow you,
Famed prince? Self-confidence vows the impossible.
But who has ever shown himself so stupid that   1100
He willingly tried jumping in a gaping pit?
I know that Walter is so fierce in open fields
That placed in such a stronghold or encampment he
Would scorn a mighty force just as a single man.
And although France should send here all its
    foot-soldiers   1105
And knights, he would dispose of those as he did these.
But since I see that you are pained more by disgrace
Than by your loss through slaughter, and opposed to leaving,
I sympathize: my own distress yields to your rank
As king; yes, I will try to find a path to safety   1110
Which will reveal itself—if not at once, then never.
No, even for my darling nephew (lord, I say
To you) I would not want to break my plighted faith.
Look then! For you, king, I will enter certain danger;
But know that I am leaving from this place of battle. 1115
Let us depart, give him a chance to go away,
Then hide in caves and let our horses graze the meadows
Until, believing we have gone, now safe, he quits
His narrow stronghold. When he treads on open fields,
We rise up from behind, pursue the startled man,   1120
And in this way we can attempt some task of valor.
This seems the surest hope in our uncertain plight.
Then you can fight, king, if you have a mind for war;
That man will never give us two a chance for flight;
but we must either flee or face a bitter fight."   1125
The king approves the plan, then he embraces him
And with a kiss he soothes the man. They then withdrew
And found a place well suited for an ambush, then
Dismounting, tied their horses in the pleasant grass.
And Phoebus meanwhile was inclining toward the west   1130
While shedding his last rays on famous Thule, and
He left behind his back the Spaniards with the Irish.
Then, after he had slowly warmed the ocean waves
And Hesperus turned its horns toward the Ausonian lands,
The clever warrior began to ponder whether   1135
He should remain in his safe fortress in the dense
Recess, or risk the open stretch of wilderness.
Great waves of care surged over him as he with keen
Intelligence intently sought a course of action.
For only Hagen was a threat to Walter—and   1140

oscillum regis subter complexibus actum.
Ambierat prorsus, quae sit sententia menti
hostis et an urbem vellent remeare relictam,
pluribus ut sociis per noctem forte coactis
primo mane parent bellum recreare nefandum   1145
an soli insidias facerent propiusque laterent.
Terret ad haec triviis ignoti silva meatus,
ne loca fortassis incurreret aspera spinis,
immo quippe feris, sponsamque amitteret illis.
His ita provisis exploratisque profatur   1150
"En quocumque modo res pergant, hic recubabo,
donec circuiens lumen spera reddat amatum,
ne patriae fines dicat rex ille superbus
evasisse fuga furis de more per umbras."
Dixit et ecce viam vallo praemuniit artam   1155
undique praecisis spinis simul et paliuris.
Quo facto ad truncos sese convertit amaro
cum gemitu et cuicumque suum caput applicat atque
contra orientalem prostratus corpore partem
ac nudum retinens ensem hac voce precatur   1160

"Rerum factori, sed et omnia facta regenti,
nil sine permisso cuius vel denique iusso
constat, ago grates quod me defendit iniquis
hostilis turmae telis nec non quoque probris.
Deprecor at dominum contrita mente benignum,   1165
ut qui peccantes non vult sed perdere culpas,
hos in caelesti praestet mihi sede videri."
Qui postquam orandi finem dedit, ilico surgens
sex giravit equos et virgis rite retortis
vinciit. Hi tantum remanebant, nempe duobus   1170
per tela absumptis ternos rex Gunthere abegit.
His ita compositis procinctum solvit et alte
ingenti fumans leviabat pondere corpus.
Tum maestam laeto solans affamine sponsam
moxque cibum capiens aegros recreaverat artus,   1175
oppido enim lassus fuerat, clipeoque recumbens
primi custodem somni iubet esse puellam,
ipse matutinam disponens tollere curam,
quae fuerat suspecta magis, tandemque quievit.
Ad cuius caput illa sedens solito vigilavit   1180
et dormitantes cantu patefecit ocellos.
Ast ubi vir primum iam expergiscendo soporem
ruperat, absque mora surgens dormire puellam
iussit et arrepta se fulciit impiger hasta.
Sic reliquum noctis duxit, modo quippe caballos   1185

That kiss the king gave him along with an embrace.
He was in doubt what plan his foe had in his mind:
Did they intend to go back to the town they'd left
And, mustering more soldiers overnight, prepare
To recommence the evil combat in the morning?   1145
Or did they lurk nearby, alone, and plan an ambush?
He feared the forest, with its unknown winding trails,
Perhaps would lead him into places filled with thorns
Or even beasts, and he might lose his bride to them.
When he had weighed and contemplated this, he said: 1150
"Whatever way things may turn out, I will rest here
Until the circling sphere returns its cherished light.
That haughty king will not proclaim that I have left
His borders fleeing like some robber in the dark."
He spoke, then barricaded up the narrow path   1155
By placing hawthorn and cut brambles all around.
When this was done, he turned back to the trunks and with
A bitter sigh attached the proper head to each.
Then bowing down, his body facing toward the east,
And clenching his bared sword he makes this prayer
    aloud: 1160
"To the Creator who rules all created things,
Without whose nod or bidding nothing has existence,
I give thanks for defending me from unjust weapons
Hurled by the hostile troop and also from dishonor.
With a repentant mind I pray my kindly Lord   1165
That He who would destroy not sinners but their sins
May grant that I might see these men in Paradise."
When he had finished praying, he stood up at once;
He gathered six steeds which he bound with twisted withes.
These were the only horses left: two had been killed 1170
By weapons, and King Gunther led three more away.
With these things thus attended to, he loosed his belt
And freed his steaming body of the massive weight.
While he consoled his sad betrothed with pleasant talk,
And took some food, he soon refreshed his aching limbs. 1175
Reclining on his shield, for he was very tired,
He told the girl to stand guard at the first night-watch,
For he was planning to assume the morning watch,
Which was more dangerous; and then at last he rested.
She sat, as was her custom, by his head, and watched, 1180
And by her singing kept her drowsy eyes alert.
But when the man, awaking, cut the first sleep short,
He rose up right away and told the girl to sleep.
Once he had grasped his spear, he leaned on it unwearied,
And thus spent the remaining night. Now checking on   1185

circuit, interdum auscultans vallo propiavit,
exoptans orbi species ac lumina reddi.
Lucifer interea praeco scandebat Olympo
dicens "Taprobane clarum videt insula solem."
Hora fuit gelidus qua terram irrorat Eous.   1190
Aggreditur iuvenis caesos spoliarier armis
armorumque habitu, tunicas et cetera linquens.
Armillas tantum cum bullis baltea et enses,

loricas quoque cum galeis detraxerat ollis.
Quattuor his oneravit equos sponsamque vocatam   1195
imposuit quinto, sextum conscenderat ipse
et primus vallo perrexerat ipse revulso.
At dum constricti penetratur semita callis,
circumquaque oculis explorans omnia puris
auribus arrectis, ventos captavit et auras,   1200
si vel mussantes sentiret vel gradientes
sive superborum crepitantia frena virorum,
seu saltim ferrata sonum daret ungula equorum.
Postquam cuncta silere videt, praevortit onustas
quadrupedes, mulierem etiam praecedere iussit.   1205
Scrinia gestantem comprendens ipse caballum
audet inire viam consueto cinctus amictu.
Mille fere passus transcendit, et ecce puella
(sexus enim fragilis animo trepidare coegit)
respiciens post terga videt descendere binos   1210
quodam colle viros raptim et sine more meantes
exanguisque virum compellat voce sequentem
"Dilatus iam finis adest. Fuge, domne, propinquant!"

Qui mox conversus visos cognovit et inquit
"Incassum multos mea dextera fuderat hostes,   1215
si modo supremis laus desit, dedecus assit.
Est satius pulchram per vulnera quaerere mortem
quam solum amissis palando evadere rebus.
Verum non adeo sunt desperanda salutis
commoda cernenti quondam maiora pericla.   1220
Aurum gestantis tute accipe lora Leonis
et citius pergens luco succede propinquo.
Ast ego in ascensu montis subsistere malo,
eventum opperiens adventantesque salutans."
Obsequitur dictis virguncula clara iubentis.   1225
Ille celer scutum collegit et excutit hastam,
ignoti mores equitis temptando sub armis.
Hunc rex incursans comitante satellite demens

The steeds, now going to the barricade, he listened,
Awaiting the orb and light to be returned to earth.
The herald Lucifer said, as he climbed Olympus,
"The island Taprobane now sees the brilliant sun."
It was the hour when chill Eos moistens earth.   1190
The young man went to strip the slaughtered of their arms
And byrnies, leaving tunics and the rest behind.
He took from them just arm-rings, belts with studs, and
    swords;
Their corselets also, these together with their helmets.
Four horses he weighed down with these, and his
    betrothed,   1195
Whom he had called, he placed upon the fifth; he rode
The sixth. He moved the barricade, then led the way.
While they rode on the pathway of the narrow gorge,
Surveying everything around with his sharp eyes,
With his keen ears he strained at every breath of wind 1200
If he could hear men whispering or on the march,
Or if the jingling bridles of proud warriors
Or maybe horses' iron hooves were making noise.
When he saw all was calm, he placed the loaded steeds
In front, and bade the woman also ride ahead.   1205
He led the horse that bore the treasure-coffers, and
Clad in his usual armor dared to venture forth.
He had traversed almost a mile. But look! The girl,
Whose weaker sex forced her to have a timid spirit,
While glancing back saw two men coming rapidly   1210
Down from a hill who were advancing without pause.
She blanches and calls to the man who rides behind,
"Our end, delayed, is here. Lord, flee! They are
    approaching."
He, turning quickly, knew the man he saw, and said,
"In vain my right hand would have conquered many foes, 1215
If in the end dishonor and not praise is mine.
To seek a noble death by wounds is better than,
My wealth lost, to survive, a lonely wanderer.
But I, who formerly was facing greater dangers,
Must not despair so of our chances for salvation.   1220
You, take the reins of Lion carrying the gold
And walking quickly go into the grove nearby.
But I prefer to make my stand here on the hillside,
Both greeting those who come and waiting for the outcome."
The lovely girl obeys his words as he commands.   1225
He quickly grasps his shield and brandishes his spear,
While trying out how the strange horse responds in combat.
The mad king, charging with his vassal next to him

eminus affatu compellat valde superbo
"Hostis atrox, nisu deluderis! Ecce latebrae   1230
protinus absistunt, ex quis de more liciscae
dentibus infrendens rabidis latrare solebas.
En in propatulo, si vis, confligito campo,
experiens, finis si fors queat aequiperari
principio. Scio, Fortunam mercede vocasti   1235
idcircoque fugam tempnis seu deditionem."
Alpharides contra regi non reddidit ulla,
sed velut hinc surdus alio convertitur aiens
"Ad te sermo mihi, Hagano, subsiste parumper!
Quid, rogo, tam fidum subito mutavit amicum,   1240
ut, discessurus nuper vix posse revelli
qui nostris visus fuerat complexibus, ultro,
nullis nempe malis laesus, nos appetat armis?
Sperabam, fateor de te — sed denique fallor —
quod si de exilio redeuntem nosse valeres,   1245
ipse salutatum mihimet mox obvius ires
et licet invitum hospitii requiete foveres
pacificeque in regna patris deducere velles;
sollicitusque fui, quorsum tua munera ferrem.
Namque per ignotas dixi pergens regiones   1250
'Francorum vereor Haganone superstite nullum.'
Obsecro per ludos, resipiscito iam, pueriles,
unanimes quibus assueti fuimusque periti
et quorum cultu primos attrivimus annos.
Inclita quonam migravit concordia nobis   1255
semper in hoste domique manens nec scandala noscens?
Quippe tui facies patris obliviscier egit,
tecum degenti mihi patria viluit ampla.
Numquid mente fidem abradis saepissime pactam?
Deprecor, hoc abscide nefas neu bella lacessas   1260
sitque inconvulsum nobis per tempora foedus.
Quod si consentis, iam nunc ditatus abibis
eulogiis, rutilo umbonem complebo metallo."

Contra quae Hagano vultu haec affamina torvo
edidit atque iram sic insinuavit apertam,   1265
"Vim prius exerces, Walthari, postque sopharis.
tute fidem abscideras, cum memet adesse videres
et tot stravisses socios immoque propinquos.
excusare nequis, quin me tunc affore nosses.
Cuius si facies latuit, tamen arma videbas   1270
nota satis habituque virum rescire valebas.
Cetera fors tulerim, si vel dolor unus abesset.
Unice enim carum rutilum blandum pretiosum

From out of weapon's reach bellows most haughtily,
"Cruel foe! You are deluded in your effort! Yes,   1230
Your hiding place is far away, from which, just like
A bitch, you used to gnash your rabid teeth and bark.
Now, if you wish, come fight on open ground. See if
By chance the end can be compared to the beginning.
I know that you have summoned Fortune with a bribe,   1235
And therefore you now scorn surrender or retreat."
The son of Alphere made no answer to the king,
But as if deaf turned from him to the other, saying,
"My words are meant for you now, Hagen. Stay a moment!
I ask, what changed my faithful friend so suddenly,   1240
Who, when he was about to leave not long ago,
Seemed scarcely able to be torn from our embrace,
That now, harmed by no crimes, he looks for us with arms?
I hoped, I will confess, of you (but I was wrong),
If you could recognize me coming back from exile,   1245
You would come out at once yourself to greet me, and
Would honor me with hospitality (though I
Demurred), and offer peaceful escort to my homeland;
And I was anxious as to where to bring your presents.
I said, while passing through the unfamiliar regions, 1250
'If Hagen is alive, I fear none of the Franks.'
Be reasonable, I pray now, by the childhood games
In which we friends passed time and honed our skills, and in
The exercise of which we spent our early years.
Where has the famous harmony between us gone,   1255
Which lasted both in battle and at home, nor knew
Dissent? Indeed, your face made me forget my father.
My spacious homeland palled when I spent time with you.
Are you erasing from your mind the faith you pledged
So often? Stop, I pray, this crime. Do not provoke   1260
A fight. From now on let our pact be undisturbed.
If you agree to this, then you will leave enriched
With gifts, for I will fill your shield with red-gold
    metal."
In answer to this statement Hagen spoke these words,
And showed his anger clearly in his grim expression: 1265
"First, Walter, you use force, then turn to sophistry.
For you yourself broke faith, because you saw me there,
And still you killed so many friends and even kinsmen.
You cannot plead you did not know that I was there.
You saw familiar arms (although the face was hidden), 1270
And could identify the man from his equipment.
The rest I might have borne, if this grief were not present;
For you have cut down with the curved blade of your sword

carpsisti florem mucronis falce tenellum.
Haec res est, pactum qua irritasti prior almum, 1275

iccircoque gazam cupio pro foedere nullam.
Sitne tibi soli virtus, volo discere in armis,
deque tuis manibus caedem perquiro nepotis.
En aut oppeto sive aliquid memorabile faxo."
Dixit et a tergo saltu se iecit equino, 1280
hoc et Guntharius nec segnior egerat heros
Waltharius, cuncti pedites bellare parati.
Stabat quisque ac venturo se providus ictu
praestruxit. Trepidant sub peltis Martia membra.

Hora secunda fuit, qua tres hi congrediuntur, 1285
adversus solum conspirant arma duorum.
Primus maligeram collectis viribus hastam
direxit Hagano disrupta pace; sed illam

turbine terribilem tanto et stridore volantem
Alpharides semet cernens tolerare nequire, 1290
sollers obliqui delusit tegmine scuti.
Nam veniens clipeo sic est ceu marmore levi
excussa et collem vehementer sauciat usque
ad clavos infixa solo; tunc pectore magno,
sed modica vi fraxineum hastile superbus 1295

iecit Guntharius, volitans quod adhaesit in ima
Waltharii parma, quam mox dum concutit ipse,
excidit ignavum de ligni vulnere ferrum.
Omine quo maesti confuso pectore Franci
mox stringunt acies, dolor est conversus ad iras, 1300

et tecti clipeis Aquitanum invadere certant.
Strennuus ille tamen vi cuspidis expulit illos
atque incursantes vultu terrebat et armis.
Hic rex Guntharius coeptum meditatur ineptum,
scilicet ut iactam frustra terraeque relapsam, 1305
— ante pedes herois enim divulsa iacebat —
accedens tacite furtim sustolleret hastam,
quandoquidem brevibus gladiorum denique telis
armati nequeunt accedere comminus illi,
qui tam porrectum torquebat cuspidis ictum. 1310
Innuit ergo oculis vassum praecedere suadens,
cuius defensu causam supplere valeret.
Nec mora, progreditur Haganon ac provocat hostem,
rex quoque gemmatum vaginae condidit ensem,

The darling, ruddy, charming, precious, tender flower.
This was the deed by which you first marred our fair
    contract.   1275
And so I wish no treasure for a settlement.
I wish to learn in arms if you, alone, have courage,
And from your hands seek vengeance for my nephew's death.
Lo, I will die or else do something memorable!"
He spoke, then with a leap swung from his horse's back; 1280
Next Gunther; and the hero Walter was not slow
To do the same—all three prepared to fight on foot.
Each stood there warily preparing for the blows
To come; behind their shields the warriors' limbs were
    trembling.
It was the second hour when these three men clashed: 1285
The arms of two unite against a single foe.
Now that the peace was broken, Hagen was the first
To hurl his baleful spear with all his strength. But
    Walter,
When he saw he could not withstand the shaft, which hissed
And flew with vicious twisting force, deflected it   1290
Adroitly with the cover of his tilted shield.
For speeding on and glancing from the shield as from
Smooth marble, it then roughly stabbed the hill, sunk in
The ground up to its socket. With a mighty heart
But little strength, at that point haughty Gunther
    hurled   1295
His ash-wood shaft, which, flying, became stuck low down
In Walter's shield. As soon as he had shaken it,
The sluggish spear dropped from the fissure in the wood.
The Franks, confused in heart and saddened by this omen,
At once unsheathed their blades—their sorrow turned to
    wrath—   1300
And covered by their shields they vied in charging Walter.
But still that robust man repelled them with spear-thrusts,
With glare and weapons terrifying his attackers.
King Gunther here was thinking up a foolish venture—
To wit, approaching silently, to grab by stealth   1305
The spear which, cast in vain, had fallen on the ground
(Discarded, it was lying at the hero's feet).
Because they were armed with the shorter blades of swords,
They could not venture close enough to that man who
Was stabbing spear thrusts out so far; he motioned with 1310
His eyes, thus signalling his vassal to advance
So he, with his protection, could perform the deed.
Advancing quickly, Hagen challenges his foe
While Gunther now has placed his jewelled sword in its sheath,

expediens dextram furto actutum faciendo. 1315
Sed quid plura? Manum pronus transmisit in hastam
et iam comprensam sensim subtraxerat illam
fortunae maiora petens. Sed maximus heros,
utpote qui bello semper sat providus esset
praeter et unius punctum cautissimus horae, 1320
hunc inclinari cernens persenserat actum
nec tulit, obstantem sed mox Haganona revellens,
denique sublato qui divertebat ab ictu,
insilit et planta direptum hastile retentat
ac regem furto captum sic increpitavit, 1325
ut iam perculso sub cuspide genua labarent.
Quem quoque continuo esurienti porgeret Orco,
ni Hagano armipotens citius succurreret atque
obiecto dominum scuto muniret et hosti
nudam aciem saevi mucronis in ora tulisset. 1330
Sic, dum Waltharius vulnus cavet, ille resurgit
atque tremens stupidusque stetit, vix morte reversus.
Nec mora nec requies, bellum instauratur amarum.
Incurrunt hominem nunc ambo nuncque vicissim;
et dum progresso se impenderet acrius uni, 1335
en de parte alia subit alter et impedit ictum.
Haud aliter Numidus quam dum venabitur ursus
et canibus circumdatus astat et artubus horret
et caput occultans submurmurat ac propiantes
amplexans Umbros miserum mutire coartat, 1340
tum rabidi circumlatrant hinc inde Molossi
comminus ac dirae metuunt accedere belvae
taliter in nonam conflictus fluxerat horam,
et triplex cunctis inerat maceratio: leti
terror et ipse labor bellandi solis et ardor. 1345
Interea herois coepit subrepere menti
quiddam, qui tacito premit has sub corde loquelas:
"Si Fortuna viam non commutaverit, isti
vana fatigatum memet per ludicra fallent."
Ilico et elata Haganoni voce profatur 1350
"O paliure, vires foliis, ut pungere possis;
tu saltando iocans astu me ludere temptas.
Sed iam faxo locum, propius ne accedere tardes.
Ecce tuas — scio, praegrandes — ostendito vires!
Me piget incassum tanto sufferre labores." 1355
Dixit et exiliens contum contorsit in ipsum,
qui pergens onerat clipeum dirimitque aliquantum
loricae ac magno modicum de corpore stringit;
denique praecipuis praecinctus fulserat armis.
At vir Waltharius missa cum cuspide currens 1360

Thus freeing his right hand to make the theft at once.   1315
In short, he stooped, then reached his hand out for the spear
And once he had it drew it slowly back to him,
But thereby asked too much of luck. The best of heroes,
Because he always kept alert enough in battle—
And very cautious too, except for one brief instant—   1320
Saw Gunther bending down. Perceiving his plan, he
Does not allow it, but at once repelling Hagen—
Though in the way, he jumped back from the threatened blow—
He leaps and slams his foot down on the stolen shaft.
So fiercely did he taunt the king, caught in the theft,   1325
The coward's knees began to shake beneath the spear.
Him too he would have sent straightway to hungry Orcus
If Hagen, strong in arms, had not rushed in to help
And used his shield to guard his lord while jabbing with
The naked edge of his cruel blade at Walter's face.   1330
While Walter warded off the blow, the king arose,
And stood, afraid and senseless, barely saved from death.
No pause or rest, the bitter fighting is resumed.
They press the man, now both at once, now each in turn.
While he is fiercely occupied with one attacker,   1335
One charges from another side and checks the blow.
Not otherwise when a Numidian bear is hunted,
It stands, surrounded by the hounds, and bares its claws,
And lowering its head it growls, and grabs the dogs
That come too near and makes them yelp in misery.   1340
Here, there, on every side the raging hounds are barking,
But fear to move in to attack the awful beast.
Just so the battle wavered into the ninth hour.
Threefold distress oppresses all three men—the fear
Of death, the task of fighting, and the burning sun.   1345
A thought begins to steal into the hero's mind,
Who silently is keeping these thoughts to himself:
"If Fortune does not change her course, those men will catch
Me with their empty tricks, exhausted as I am."
Immediately, his voice raised, he addresses Hagen,   1350
"O hawthorn, flourishing with leaves so you can prick,
You jump and feint and try to fool me with your cunning.
But now I'll make a move to hurry your attack.
Now then, display your strength, which I know is enormous;
For I am tired of suffering such work in vain."   1355
He spoke, then with a leap he hurled his spear at him.
The speeding shaft bursts through the shield and rips away
Part of his byrnie, grazing his tremendous body
(He was of course resplendent, clad in finest armor).
Now Walter, having thrown his spear, unsheathes his
    sword   1360

evaginato regem importunior ense
impetit et scuto dextra de parte revulso
ictum praevalidum ac mirandum fecit eique
crus cum poplite adusque femur decerpserat omne.
Ille super parmam ante pedes mox concidit huius.   1365
Palluit exanguis domino recidente satelles.
Alpharides spatam tollens iterato cruentam
ardebat lapso postremum infligere vulnus.
Immemor at proprii Hagano vir forte doloris
aeratum caput inclinans obiecit ad ictum.   1370
Extensam cohibere manum non quiverat heros,
sed cassis fabrefacta diu meliusque peracta
excipit assultum mox et scintillat in altum.
Cuius duritia stupefactus dissilit ensis,
proh dolor! Et crepitans partim micat aere et herbis.   1375
Belliger ut frameae murcatae fragmina vidit,
indigne tulit ac nimia furit efferus ira
impatiensque sui capulum sine pondere ferri,
quamlibet eximio praestaret et arte metallo,
protinus abiecit monimentaque tristia sprevit.   1380
Qui dum forte manum iam enormiter exeruisset,
abstulit hanc Hagano sat laetus vulnere prompto.
In medio iactus recidebat dextera fortis
gentibus ac populis multis suspecta, tyrannis,
innumerabilibus quae fulserat ante trophaeis.   1385
Sed vir praecipuus nec laevis cedere gnarus,
sana mente potens carnis superare dolores,
non desperavit neque vultus concidit eius,
verum vulnigeram clipeo insertaverat ulnam
incolomique manu mox eripuit semispatam,   1390
qua dextrum cinxisse latus memoravimus illum,
ilico vindictam capiens ex hoste severam.
Nam feriens dextrum Haganoni effodit ocellum
ac tempus resecans pariterque labella revellens
olli bis ternos discussit ab ore molares.   1395
Tali negotio dirimuntur proelia facto.
Quemque suum vulnus atque aeger anhelitus arma
ponere persuasit. Quisnam hinc immunis abiret,
qua duo magnanimi heroes tam viribus aequi
quam fervore animi steterant in fulmine belli?   1400
Postquam finis adest, insignia quemque notabant:
illic Guntharii regis pes, palma iacebat
Waltharii nec non tremulus Haganonis ocellus.
sic sic armillas partiti sunt Avarenses!
Consedere duo, nam tertius ille iacebat,   1405

And running forward savagely attacks the king.
He forced the shield away from his right side, then struck
A blow of unimagined power, hacking off
From him one whole leg with the knee up to the thigh.
At once he fell down on his shield at Walter's feet.   1365
The vassal blanched and paled when he saw his lord fall.
The son of Alphere raised his bloody sword again
And burned to deal the fallen man a final blow.
The vassal Hagen, heedless of his own distress,
By sticking out his bronze-clad head then intercepted   1370
The blow. The hero could not check his outstretched hand;
But now the helmet, strongly forged and finely made,
Receives the blow at once and fills the air with sparks.
The sword, astounded by the hardness, splinters, and
The clattering pieces glitter in the air and grass.   1375
The warrior, seeing fragments of his shattered blade,
Grew angry and, wild with excessive wrath, he raged.
Impatient with a hilt that lacked its weight of iron,
Despite the worth of its choice metal and design,
He threw it far away and spurned the wretched pieces.   1380
Now, while by chance he had stretched out his hand so far,
This Hagen—quite pleased by the easy blow—hacked off.
In mid-stroke fell that powerful right hand, which had
Been feared by tribes, by many peoples, and by tyrants,
Which in the past had shone with countless victories.   1385
The noble man, unskilled in yielding to misfortunes,
Who with his sound mind could surmount pains of the flesh,
Did not despair, nor did his countenance fall; instead,
He slipped his mutilated forearm in the shield
And quickly grabbed, with his uninjured hand, a dagger   1390
(Which, as we mentioned, he had strapped to his right side),
At once exacting dreadful vengeance on his foe.
For, striking, he dug Hagen's right eye from its socket
Then slashing at his temple, in that instant tore
His lips away, and from his mouth knocked out six teeth. 1395
And with such business done, the fights are broken off.
His wound and grave exhaustion prompted each to lay
His weapons down. Who might have left that place unscathed,
Where two great-hearted heroes, equal in both strength
And passion, stood among the lightning-bolts of battle?   1400
The fight is ended; marks of honor branded each.
King Gunther's foot was lying there, and Walter's hand
Was lying there, and also Hagen's twitching eye.
Thus, thus the men have shared the treasure of the Avars!
Two sat, because the third of them was lying down,   1405

sanguinis undantem tergentes floribus amnem.
Haec inter timidam revocat clamore puellam
Alpharides, veniens quae saucia quaeque ligavit.
His ita compositis sponsus praecepit eidem
"Iam misceto merum Haganoni et porrige primum.   1410
Est athleta bonus, fidei si iura reservet.
Tum praebeto mihi, reliquis qui plus toleravi.
Postremum volo Guntharius bibat utpote segnis
inter magnanimum qui paruit arma virorum
et qui Martis opus tepide atque enerviter egit."   1415
Obsequitur cunctis Heririci filia verbis.
Francus at oblato licet arens pectore vino

"Defer" ait "prius Alpharidi sponso ac seniori,
virgo, tuo, quoniam, fateor, me fortior ille
nec solum me, sed cunctos supereminet armis."   1420
Hic tandem Hagano spinosus et ipse Aquitanus,
mentibus invicti, licet omni corpore lassi,
post varios pugnae strepitus ictusque tremendos
inter pocula scurrili certamine ludunt.
Francus ait "Iam dehinc cervos agitabis, amice,   1425

quorum de corio wantis sine fine fruaris.
At dextrum, moneo, tenera lanugine comple,
ut causae ignaros palmae sub imagine fallas.
Wah! sed quid dicis, quod ritum infringere gentis
ac dextro femori gladium agglomerare videris   1430

uxorique tuae, si quando ea cura subintrat,
perverso amplexu circumdabis euge sinistram?
Iam quid demoror? En posthac tibi quicquid agendum est,
laeva manus faciet." Cui Walthare talia reddit
"Cur tam prosilias, admiror, lusce Sicamber.   1435
Si venor cervos, carnem vitabis aprinam.
Ex hoc iam famulis tu suspectando iubebis
heroum turbas transversa tuendo salutans.
Sed fidei memor antiquae tibi consiliabor.
Iam si quando domum venias laribusque propinques,   1440

effice lardatam de multra farreque pultam.
Haec pariter victum tibi conferet atque medelam.
His dictis pactum renovant iterato coactum
atque simul regem tollentes valde dolentem
imponunt equiti et sic disiecti redierunt   1445
Franci Wormatiam patriamque Aquitanus adivit.
Illic gratifice magno susceptus honore

While wiping up with herbs the surging flow of blood.
Meanwhile the son of Alphere summoned with a cry
The timid girl, who came and bandaged each man's wounds.
When this was finished, her betrothed commanded her,
"Now mix some wine and offer it to Hagen first,   1410
A worthy champion, if he keeps the laws of faith.
And then serve me: I suffered more than both of them.
And I want Gunther to drink last of all, since he
Was sluggish in a battle of great-hearted men;
Lukewarm and nerveless he performed the work of Mars."   1415
Hereric's daughter follows all of his commands.
When offered wine, the Frank, though parched with thirst,
    instructs,
"First serve the son of Alphere, your betrothed and master;
For I say, girl, he is a stronger man than I,
Surpassing not just me but every man in arms."   1420
Here thorny Hagen and the man from Aquitaine,
Fatigued throughout their bodies but in minds undaunted,
After the crashing tide and awesome blows of battle,
Amid their drinking play a game of taunting jokes.
The Frank: "From now on, friend, you will go hunting
    stags   1425
To make gloves without number fashioned from their hides.
But my advice is, stuff the right glove with soft down,
And use this phantom hand to fool the ignorant.
Ah! How will you explain your breach of social custom
When you are seen to gird your sword on your right
    thigh.   1430
Or when the wish comes over you, will you then hug
Your wife—good Lord!—with a perverse embrace, left-handed?
But why go on? Henceforth, whatever you must do,
Your left hand will perform!" Walter gives him this answer:
"And why do you poke so much fun, I wonder, one-eye?   1435
If I go hunting stags, you will avoid boar meat,
And you will squint when giving orders to your servants,
While welcoming the throngs of heroes, looking sideways.
But, mindful of old loyalty, I'll give you this
Advice: when you come home now and approach your
    hearth,   1440
Prepare a gruel of milk and grain, and cooked in grease.
This will give you both nourishment and medicine."
When this was said, the men renew again their pledge;
Together lifting up the king, who suffered gravely,
They put him on a horse, then went their separate ways: 1445
The Franks to Worms, the man from Aquitaine back home.
There, joyously received with lavish honors, he

publica Hiltgundi fecit sponsalia rite
omnibus et carus post mortem obitumque parentis
ter denis populum rexit feliciter annis. 1450
Qualia bella dehinc vel quantos saepe triumphos
ceperit, ecce stilus renuit signare retunsus.
Haec quicunque legis, stridenti ignosce cicadae
raucellam nec adhuc vocem perpende, sed aevum,
utpote quae nidis nondum petit alta relictis. 1455
Haec est Waltharii poesis. Vos salvet Iesus.

Declared in public he would marry Hildegund.
Upon his father's death and loss, beloved by all,
He ruled his people happily for thirty years.   1450
What wars he fought and what great triumphs often gained,
Behold, my blunted stylus now declines to write.
Whoever read this work, forgive a chirping cricket.
Consider not its voice, still strident, but its age;
For, not yet seeking lofty heights, it has just left   1455
The nest. This is the poem of Walter. Christ save you.

Ruodlieb

I.

Quidam prosapia vir progenitus generosa
moribus ingenitam decorabat nobilitatem,
qui dominos plures habuisse datur locupletes,
saepius ad libitum quibus is famulans et honor[um
nil deservisse potuit, putat ut meruisse.   5
Quicquid et illorum sibi quis commisit herorum
aut ulciscendum causaeque suae peragendum
non prolongabat, quam strennuiter peragebat.
Saepius in mortem se pro dominis dat eisdem
seu bello seu venatu seu quolibet actu.   10
Nil sibi fortuna prohibente dabant male fida.
Semper promittunt promissaque dissimulabant.
Ast inimicicias horum causa sibi nactas
cum superare nequit, super hoc quid agat, neque dic[it,
nusquam secure se sperans vivere posse,   15
rebus dispositis cunctis matrique subactis,
tandem de patria pergens petit extera reg[na.
Nullus et hunc alius sequitur nisi scutifer e[ius,
qui vehat enthecam rebus variis oneratam,

a puero sibi quem docuit sufferre labore[m.   20

Balenam dextrim parmam vehit atque sinistri[m;
dextra lanceolam sub scuto fertque pharetra[m,
annonae saccum modicum sub se satis aptu[m.
Ast loricatus dominus super et tunicatus
pro] mitra galeam rutilam gestat chalibinam,   25
a]ccinctus gladio compto capulo tenus auro.
Pen]det et a niveo sibimet gripis ungula collo,
un]gula non tota, medii cubiti modo longa,
qua]e post ad latum vel prae decoratur ad artum
ob]rizo mundo cervino cinctaque loro,   30
no]n ut nix alba tamen ut translucida gemma
qu]am dum perflabat, tuba quam melius reboabat,
ul]time dans matri domuique vale simul omni.
St]at niger ut corvus equus et ceu smigmate lotus,
un]dique punctatus hac sub nigredine totus.   35
Ad] laevam colli complexa iuba iacet illi,
qu]i faleratus erat ceu summum quemque decebat,
ad] cuius sellam nil cernitur esse ligatum,

I.

A certain man, born of a noble family,
Graced his inherited nobility with his
Behavior. They say he had many wealthy lords,
Whom he served very often at their bidding, but
Could gain none of the honors he thought he deserved.   5
Whatever any of those heroes gave to him
To do—seek vengeance or transact a business matter—
He did not put it off but acted forcefully.
For those same lords he very often risked his life,
Whether in war or hunting or some other action.   10
Since faithless Fortune was opposed, they gave him nothing.
They always promised, but they broke their promises.
When he can not surmount the enmities incurred
In their employ, he does not know what he should do
About it; thinking he could live nowhere securely,   15
All his affairs set and entrusted to his mother,
At length he leaves his homeland, seeking foreign kingdoms.
No other person follows him except his squire,
Who bears his pack weighed down with different goods, whom he
Had trained to work for him since childhood. The squire bears   20
The pack on his right shoulder; on the left, a shield.
His right hand holds a lance; beneath the shield, a quiver.
He has a very adequate small sack of food.
The master, though, was clad in chain mail and a coat.
He wears a glittering steel helmet as a headdress,   25
While girded with a sword adorned with gold up to
The hilt. A griffin's claw hung from his snow-white neck—
Not a whole claw, one only half a cubit long:
In back, where wide, and front, where thin, it is adorned
With solid gold and fastened with a deer-skin strap,   30
Not white like snow but more like a translucent gem.
When he blew this, it sounded better than a horn.
At last he bids his mother and whole house farewell.
Black as a raven stands his horse, and as if washed
With soap, its black was speckled everywhere with white. 35
The mane lay covering the left side of its neck.
The horse's trappings would have suited any noble;
Tied to the saddle nothing can be seen except

e] corio sutum ni vas mastice perunctum,
du]lcius ut sapiat potus, qui fusus in id sit, 40
ex] ostro factum vel cervical modicellum.
Qu]em super ut saluit, equus altius ipse salivit,
ceu gau]dens domino residenti fortiter illo.
Praes]ilit hunc post mox canis in cursu bene velox,
inv]estigator, quo non melior fuit alter, 45
prae] quo bestiola vel grandis sive minuta
non abscondere quit se, quin hanc mox reperire[t.
Ultime fando vale matri famulisque valete
perfusa lacrimis facie dabat oscula cunctis.
Arrepto freno, monito calcare poledro 50

cursitat in campo, cita ceu volitaret hirund[o.
Ast per cancellos post hunc pascebat ocellos
mater, at in saepes conscendens eius omnis plebs
post hunc prospiciunt, singultant, flendo gem[iscunt,
cum plus non cernunt hunc, planctum multiplicar[unt. 55
Detersis lacrimis qui tunc lotis faciebus

consolaturi dominam subeunt cito cuncti,
quae simulando spem premit altum corde dolor[em.
Consolatur eos, male dum se cernit habere.
Non minor interea natum premit utique cura 60
inque via secum perpendit plurima rerum,
deservire domi quod nil valet emolumenti
et propter faidas sibi multas undique nactas
a patria dulci quod debuit exiliari.
Secum volvebat, se sicubi vile clientet, 65
si fortuna vetus infestaretur ei plus,
esse novercales omnes inibi sibi fratres,
non meliorasse res sed peius reperisse.
Intime suspirans rogat obnixe dominum flens,
ut non deseruisset se nolitve perire, 70
sed sibi succurrat, aerumnas quo superaret.
Intranti regnum maerenti sic alienum
venator regis subito tunc fit comes eius
isque salutat eum resalutaturque per ipsum.
Exul erat fortis membris facieque virilis 75
voceque grandiloquus, in responso seriosus.
Quem rogat indigena, quis et unde sit, ire velit quo.
Quo sibi non dicto dedignanterque sileto,
inquisisse piget, velut est res, menteque tractat
"Est si legatus, minor est eius comitatus; 80
dum venit ad curtem, quis munera, quis gerit ensem?
Pauperis est posse, reor, aut virtutis opimae."

A vessel, sewn from leather, that was smeared with resin
To make a drink that was poured into it taste sweeter;   40
And also a small pillow made of purple cloth.
When he jumped on the horse, the horse itself jumped higher,
As if rejoicing that its master sat there boldly.
A dog, quite swift at running, soon is bounding front
And back of him—a hunting dog, and none was better.   45
No beast, not big or small, could hide itself when it
Was near, and keep that dog from quickly finding it.
Then he bids farewell to his mother and the servants,
And as he kissed them all his face was moist with tears.
Once he has seized the rein, he spurs his horse and
    speeds   50
Across the plain as swiftly as a swallow flies.
But through the grating his mother fed her eyes on him;
But all the household servants, climbing on a fence,
Peer after him. They sigh and weep and groan. When they
No longer see him, they increase their lamentation.   55
And then, when they had dried their tears and washed their
    faces,
They all ran quickly to console their mistress, who,
While feigning hope, suppressed the pain deep in her heart,
Consoling them because she saw that they were sad.
Surely, however, no less care oppressed her son,   60
And on his way he pondered very many things:
That he was able to earn no rewards at home,
And on account of many feuds he had incurred
He must depart from his dear land and go in exile.
He thought if he served somewhere else for little pay,   65
And if his former luck continued plaguing him,
Then all his comrades there would soon become his foes,
And he would find conditions not improved, but worse.
Then sighing deeply, weeping, earnestly he prayed
The Lord not to desert him or to let him die,   70
But help him so that he might overcome his hardships.
Thus grieving, he was entering a foreign kingdom,
When suddenly the hunter for the king became
His comrade. He greets him, is greeted by him in
Return. The exile was well built and manly looking,   75
Both eloquent in speech and sober in reply.
The native asked him who he was, from where he came,
His destination. He, aloofly silent, gave
No answer. Sorry he had asked his situation,
He thought: "His retinue is too small if he's an envoy.   80
If he heads to the court, who bears his gifts, his sword?
I think he is, though poor in means, a man of virtue."

Dum satis obticuit, demum sibi denuo dixit:
"Non irascaris, de me si plus rogiteris!
Nam tibi prodesse volo, si possum, nec obesse. 85
Venator regis sibi carus sumque fidelis,
nec solet audire quemquam clementius ac me.
Pro faida grandi patriam si deseruisti
vis et in hac terra mihi ceu tibimet peregrina
quid deservire causasque tuas superare, 90
utile consilium tibi tunc do, non renuendum.
Usum venandi quoniam bene si didicisti,
o quam felicis huc ominis exiliaris!
Diligit hanc artem rex et in arte peritum.
....
quisquis habet, dare quit, qui non habet, hic dare, dic 95
                                                                                                                                          quid?
Si non cottidie, tamen assidue dabit ille;
numquam sollicitus victus fueris vel amictus.
Cum donantur ei pulchri celeresque caballi,
nobis praestantur, cursu quo more probentur,
qui celer et facilis est nec gyrando rebellis; 100
est cui maxime tunc opus, illi donat et illum.
Propter et annonam numquam nummum dabis unum;
nam sine mensura dabitur tibi, cum cupis, illa.
Ad mensam comites superexaltans locupletes,
dum convivatur, nobiscum fando iocatur. 105
Appositum quidquid melioris erit sibi, mittit,
id faciens nobis plus quam mercedis honoris.
Si libeat cum me te fidum foedus inire,
dando fidem nostras iungamus foedere dextras,
separet ut nil nos, dumtaxat amara nisi mors. 110
Simus ubicumque, res alterutrius uterque
sic agat ut proprias, melius si quid queat illas."
Exul tum demum fidens sibi dixit ad illum
"Sat mihi, domne, tuum demonstras velle benignum,
consiliumque tuum non aestimo transgrediendum; 115
namque meas causas, ut sunt, tu coniciebas.
Hinc pactum fidei placet inter nos stabiliri."
Dando sibi dextras ibi fiunt moxque sodales
....
oscula dando sibi firmi statuuntur amici 120
alterutris dominis famulantes cordibus unis.
Dum satis inter se de rebus disposuere,
regni metropoli coeperunt appropiare,
in qua rex genti legem dedit advenienti.
Castris ingressis, pueris et equis stabulatis, 125

When he kept silent for a while, he said again
To him: "Do not be angry if you hear more questions.
I want to help, not hurt you, if I can. I am   85
The king's beloved faithful hunter; he is wont
To listen to no man more graciously than me.
If you have left your land because of some great feud,
And wish to earn a living and improve your lot
In this land where I am a foreigner like you,   90
I offer good advice to you which you should heed!
Because, if you have learned the art of hunting well,
O what a lucky chance brought you here into exile!
The king adores this art and loves those skilled in it.
....
Who has, can give; who has not, say what can he give?   95
That man will give gifts often, if not every day.
There you will never be concerned with food and clothes.
When beautiful swift steeds are given to that man,
He puts them in our charge, to test by riding which
Is fast and easy to control and not rebellious.   100
He gives the horse to him whose need for it is greatest.
And you will never spend a cent to purchase fodder,
Which he will give you lavishly when you desire.
And at the table he ignores the wealthy counts,
But when he dines he talks and jokes with us instead.   105
The better food that he is served he sends to us,
And does this more to honor us than as a payment.
If you would like to make a bond of loyalty
With me, let us clasp right hands in alliance, pledging
That nothing will divide us two but bitter death.   110
Let each pursue the other's business as his own,
Wherever we may be, if he can better it."
The exile, trusting him at last, then said to him,
"Sir, you show me sufficiently your good intentions.   115
I think that I must not ignore your good advice;
Since you have guessed the state of my affairs, I wish
To strike a pact of loyalty between us two."
They clasp right hands there and at once become
    companions . . .
....

Exchanging kisses, they are settled as firm friends,   120
Who will serve one another's lords in harmony.
When they arranged things between them sufficiently,
They started to approach the kingdom's capital,
In which the king imposed his law upon the people
Arriving there. Inside the castle, when they had   125

insimul ad curtem properabant visere regem.
Ut venatorem rex vidit, dixit ad illum
"Unde venis, quid rumoris fers, dicito nobis.
Investigasti, per silvam quando measti,
ursum sive suem, libeat nos pergere post quem?" 130
Qui non ut domino sed ceu respondit amico
"Illorum neutrum sed eorundem domitorem
investigavi, reperi, mecum tibi duxi,
scilicet hunc iuvenem tibimet servire decentem,
arte satis catum venandi satque beatum, 135
ut reor utque suo mihi cernitur in comitatu;
et cum dignaris, illum satis ipse probabis.
Is sua fert dona tibi parva nec abicienda
inque clientelam quo suscipias, cupit, illum."
Qui praecursorem laeva tenuit bicolorem, 140
cui fuit aurata collo connexa catena.

Both lodged their squires and found stables for their
    horses,
They hurried to the court to see the king together.
The king then, when he saw the hunter, said to him,
"Where are you coming from? Tell us what news you bring.
When you went through the forest, did you track a bear
Or boar which it would give us pleasure to go hunt?"   130
He answered not as to a master but a friend,
"No, I tracked neither of those two, but I did find
Their conqueror, whom I have brought you here with me—
I mean this youth who is most worthy for your service,
Quite skillful in the art of hunting and quite lucky   135
(I think and so he seemed to me as his companion).
You, when you wish, will test him thoroughly yourself.
He brings to you his presents, small but not unworthy;
And he desires that you take him into your service."
With his left hand he held his dog of double color,   140
Around whose neck there was attached a golden chain.

II.

Illius herbae vim medici dicunt fore talem,
torridula trita cum parvo polline mixta,
hinc pilulae factae si fient more fabellae
et iaciantur aquis, quicunque comederet ex his
piscis, quod nequeat subtus supra sed aquam net. 5
Inter tres digitos pilulas tornando rotundas
dilapidat stagno, quo pisces agmine magno
conveniunt avide capiendo pilam sibi quisque,
quam qui gustabant, sub aqua plus nare nequibant
sed quasi ludendo saltus altos faciendo 10
undique diffugiunt nec mergere se potuerunt.
Ille sed in cimba percurrit remige stagna,
post pisces virga cogens ad littora sicca,
quos duo cum funda circumcinxere sub unda,
cum terram peterent ad aquam resalire nequirent. 15

Sic piscando sibi ludum fecitque sodali.
Tunc iussere cocos prunis assare minores,
maiores scuto regi portant ioculando
"Venari melius hodie nos non poteramus."
"Retibus aut hamis hos cepistis ve sagenis?" 20

"Non sic piscamur" ait incola "sed dominamur
piscibus, e fundo veniant ad nos sine grato,
et super stagnum saliendo iocum dare magnum;
dum sub aquam nequeunt satis et saltando fatiscunt,
hos tandem virga facimus requiescere terra." 25
"Hoc volo" rex dixit "speculari, copia dum fit."
Plinius herbarum vires scribens variarum
laudat buglossam res ad multas nimis aptam.
In validum potum, dicit, qui ponat eandem,
quantumcunque bibat, quod is ebrius haud fore possit. 30
P]ulveris eiusdem, describit Plinius idem,
q]ui serat in carnem, si forte cani det eandem,
tem]pore quod modico canis obcaecetur ab ipso,
e]t quidquid caecum fuerit sine lumine natum,
hu]ius si gustet quid, mox visum cito perdat. 35
H]erbae venator cuius studiosus amator
i]n silvam pergit, plures hirpos ubi rescit,

II.

(Ruodlieb has been accepted into the service of the king.
He is demonstrating his skill in fishing with an herb called
bugloss.)

The doctors say the power of this herb is such,
If it is roasted, ground, mixed with a little flour,
Then fashioned into pellets in the shape of beans,
And thrown into the water, fish that eat of these
Cannot swim under water, but will float on top.   5
To make the pellets round he rubbed them in three fingers,
Then sprinkled them upon the lake in which a school
Of fish swarmed eagerly, and each one snatched a pellet.
Those fish that swallowed one could swim no more beneath
The waves, but leaping high up as if they were playing,   10
Dispersed in all directions and could not submerge.
He, with his oarsman, crossed the water in a boat
While prodding fish in front toward dry land with a stick.
The two men trapped them with a net beneath the surface,
So going toward land they could not jump back in the
    water.   15
Thus he made fishing sport for him and his companion.
They told the cooks to bake the smaller fish on coals,
But took the king the bigger ones upon a shield,
And joked "This is the best that we could do today."
"Did you catch these with nets or hooks or seines?" "We
    do   20
Not fish that way," the native said, "but lure the fish
To come out of the deep to us against their will
And give great entertainment leaping on the lake.
When they cannot submerge and are tired out from leaping,
At length with sticks we make them come to rest on land."   25
The king said, "This I want to see when there's a chance."
Describing powers of the different herbs, that Pliny
Lauds bugloss as quite suitable for many things.
Whoever puts it into a strong drink, he says,
Cannot get drunk no matter how much he might drink.   30
And Pliny says if someone sprinkles some of this
Same powder over meat and he gives it to a dog,
The dog would in a short time be made blind by it;
And any animal that was born blind, if it
Tastes some of this, will very quickly lose its vision.   35
The most devoted lover of this herb, the hunter
Goes in the woods, where he knows there are many wolves,

c]apram cum fune secum ducente sodale;
q]uam caedunt inibi lato sub tegmine fagi
a]bstrahendo cutem caedunt per frustaque carnem, 40
qu]am super aspergunt cum pulvere, pelle recondunt
a]mboque scandebant super arbore vel residebant.
E]xul et horribiles hirporum dans ululatus
nun]c veterum grandes, iuvenum graciles modo voces
ex]primit, ut veros hirpos ululare putares. 45
Qu]o dum conveniunt hirpi, capram repererunt,
q]uam discerpebant in momentoque vorabant,
n]ec procul hinc abeunt, ambo quam lumina perdunt.
Ta]libus et paribus instat miles peregrinus
Af]fectans sese cunctis, valet ut, studiose, 50
in] magna pace regnum dum stat vel honore.
Al]terius regni marhmanni valde benigni
nostr]is, a nostris is amor servatur et ipsis.
al]terutrique meant emptum, quodcunque volebant,
ve]ctigal dantes vectigal et accipientes, 55
nu]bunt hinc illuc natasque suas dederant huc,
com]patres fiunt vel qui non sunt, vocitabant.
Hi]c amor inter eos per multos duruit annos,
do]nec peccatis sunt rupta ligamina pacis.
Ex]osor pacis nostri generalis et hostis 60
se]men zizaniae non cessat multiplicare,
e]st ubicunque fides, ut stet ea non ibi perpes;
q]uo succedente fit grandis vverra repente.
Q]uodam mercato multo populo glomerato,
pro] causa vili sunt occisi quia multi. 65

While his friend leads a she-goat on a rope; they kill
It there beneath the cover of a spreading beech;
Then, skinning it, they cut the flesh in pieces, and   40
They sprinkle these with powder, which they hide inside
The skin. The two then climbed a tree and sat there
    waiting.
The exile, making horrible wolf sounds, now feigns
Loud cries of old wolves, now the gentle howls made by
The young; and you would think that there were real wolves
    howling;   45
But when the wolves assembled there they found the goat,
Which they tore into pieces and devoured quickly.
They went not far from there before both eyes were blinded.
The foreign knight takes charge of such affairs, and he
Serves everyone as zealously as possible.   50
The kingdom, all the while, thrives in firm peace and honor.
The people bordering our realm were very well
Disposed to ours, and this love was preserved by ours.
They traveled back and forth to purchase what they wanted,
Sometimes collecting toll and sometimes paying it.   55
Our daughters wed their sons, their daughters married ours.
They were godparents (even those who were not were
Thus called). This love between them lasted many years,
Until the bonds of peace were torn apart by crimes.
The hater of our peace and common enemy   60
Is sowing without pause his crop of weeds where faith
Exists, so it cannot remain firm there forever.
They sprouted, and a great war suddenly erupted.
And at a certain market, where a large crowd had
Assembled, many men were killed for little reason.   65

III.

"Esse scio regem quia vestrum tam sapientem,
haec quod non iussit, tua stulta superbia suasit.
Hinc videas qualem nunc nanciscaris honorem.
rem peiorasti, cum te famare cupisti,
ramo suspendi per suras sat meruisti." 5
Acclamant cuncti, cur haec tardet celerari.
Princeps respondit "Rex noster non ita iussit,
aut se dedentem vel captum perdere quemquam,
sed si possemus, captivos erueremus
cum praeda pariter, quae fecimus ambo decenter. 10
Vincere victorem, maiorem vult quis honorem?
Sis leo pugnando par ulciscendo sed agno!
Non honor est vobis, ulcisci damna doloris.
Magnum vindictae genus est, si parcitis irae.
Hinc precor annuite, vestro quo fiat amore, 15
solus ut iste comes nobiscum vadat inermis,
seu vultis proprio seu quovis vile caballo,
ni placeat vobis, sibi serviat ut puer unus,
qui sibi prendat equum stabulans annonet et ipsum,
utque suam gentem vinctam prae se gradientem 20
cernat, in obprobrium duxit vel quale periclum,
ne quicquam temere praesumat tale patrare."
Tunc sibi dixere cuncti sua verba placere.
Et iubilo magno patriam repetunt properando
et quamvis videant, sua domata qualiter ardent, 25
non tristabantur, dum libertate fruuntur.
Signifer et proceres alii regisque fideles
finipolim subeunt ibi captivosque reservant
et numerant socios, sanos habuisseque cunctos
intime gaudebant laudemque deo tribuebant. 30
Missus dirigitur regi, qui cuncta loquatur,
quid velit ut faciant praedonibus, utque remandet.
Qui proper]ando suum poscit sibi ferre caballum;
scutifer] hunc dum fert, virgam de saepe simul dat.
Quam super] insedit, feriens volitare coegit, 35

III.

(After forces led by a count of the neighboring kingdom
attacked the land ruled by the Greater King, Ruodlieb was
appointed commander-in-chief of the army. The forces led by
him defeated the invaders and took the count prisoner. The
count has defended his actions on the ground that they were
the orders of his king. Ruodlieb is speaking.)

"I know that your king is so wise that he did not
Command this; but your foolish pride has prompted it.
Now you shall see what sort of honor you obtain
From this. You made the matter worse because you wished
To glorify yourself. You thoroughly deserve 4-5
To be suspended from a tree branch by your calves."
They all shout why he is so slow in doing this.
The leader answers, "Our king did not order us
To kill those who surrendered or were taken captive,
But, if we could, to rescue prisoners along
With loot; and we have rightly done both things. For who 10
Wants greater honor than to overcome the victor?
Fight like a lion; when avenging, be a lamb.
You gain no honor by avenging grievous losses.
The greatest kind of vengeance is to spare your wrath.
Therefore, I ask, approve, so this is done with your 15
Consent, that this count go with us—alone, unharmed—
On his own horse or on whatever nag you like;
Or, if it please you, let one squire serve him, who
Can take his horse and feed and stable it; and let
Him see his people walk in front of him in chains, 20
What shame and peril he has led them to, so that
He will not rashly dare commit so great a crime
Again." Then they all said that his words pleased them, and
With great rejoicing quickly went back to their homeland.
And even though they saw their homes were burning, they 25
Were not dismayed, since they enjoyed their liberty.
The leader, chiefs, and other vassals of the king
Went to a border town where they secured their captives.
They count their comrades and they mightily rejoice
That all are healthy; and they then gave praise to God. 30
A messenger was sent the king to tell all, and
Report how he would have them treat the plunderers.
He, hurrying, asks them to bring his horse to him.
His squire brings it, and gives him a thorny stick;
He mounts the horse and, striking it, he makes it fly, 35

coepit c]alcare latus obmaculare cruore.
Prospicien]s s[axo] regis speculator ab alto
exclama]t "iuvenem video nimium properantem,
parva, qu]o narret, non ab re sic pavitabit."
Obveniu]nt illi multi rumoris avari 40
comprendu]nt et equum, quid narret eumque requirunt.
Dicens] omne bonum nec plus modicum neque multum,
dans pue]ro gladium regem properavit ad ipsum
dixit et] "Aeternum columen regale tuorum,
laete vi]ve, vale, gaude, dignissime laude." 45
Cui rex] "Dic sodes, nostri sunt ergo fideles
incolum]es aut qui sunt in pugnando perempti?
Nobis abl]ata, dic, si sit praeda redempta."
Nuntius] inmensa circumdatus undique turba
inclina]ns dixit "Rex, a te tale quid absit! 50
Gaude, g]ratorum periit quia nemo tuorum,
cunctaque nunc] praeda redit integra non temerata.
Nunc socii quae]runt hoc per me vel petierunt,
de capti]s quid agant, in vincula quos redigebant.
Trans hoc] commissum nil est mihi, rex, tibi dictum." 55
Tres marc]as tribui legato rex iubet auri,
dicit don]ato misso nimis exhilarato:
"Care, red]i propere vel ai sociis ita de me:
Rex gra]tes dictis vobis demandat et actis;

cum vestri]s vinctis sibi quam propere veniatis." 60
Inclina]ns ad equum iuvenis citat ad remeandum,
hora qu]ae bina prius iverat, ibat id una;
ad cele]randas res est pernimium bona merces.
Ut redi]it, socios, veniant, iubet, insimul omnes.
Illi co]nveniunt et in ampla curte steterunt. 65
Tunc] per cancellos legatus dixit ad illos
"Vobis in]manes rex iussit dicere grates
non so]lum dictis sed dicta sequentibus actis.
Rex vult], visatis hunc quam citius valeatis,
mandan]s, praedonum nec dimittatis ut ullum." 70

And with his spurs he stains the horse's flanks with blood.
From a high rock the watchman of the king sees him
And shouts, "I see a young man coming in great haste,
Atremble for no small reason to report his message."
Then many rush to him in eagerness for news.   40
They take his horse and ask what news he has to tell.
While telling them "hello" (no more or less than this),
He gave a boy his sword and hurried to the king,
And said: "Eternal royal pillar of your people,
Rejoice, live happily, most worthy to be praised!"   45
The king to him: "Please tell us, are our loyal men
Unharmed, my friend? And who are those men slain in battle?
And tell me, was the loot they stole from us regained?"
Surrounded by a large crowd on all sides, the envoy
Then bowed and said, "My king, do not think such a thing! 50
Be glad! For not one of your servants has been killed,
And all the booty is returned intact, unharmed.
My comrades now have asked and sought through me what they
Should do about the captives they have bound in chains.
I was empowered to tell you no more than this."   55
The king commands three marks of gold be paid the envoy,
And to him, very gladdened by the gift, he said,
"My friend, return in haste and tell your comrades this
From me: your king sends thanks to you with words and
    deeds.
Return as quickly as you can with those you captured."   60
The youth bowed, then rushed to his stallion to return.
A trip that took two hours now he makes in one.
Good pay is quite effective to make things go faster.
Returning, he tells all his comrades to assemble.
They gathered and were standing in a spacious courtyard,   65
And then the envoy said to them in that enclosure,
"The king bade me to say to you not just in words
But in deeds that will follow words his deepest thanks.
He says to come to him as quickly as you can,
Commanding that you not release a single culprit."   70

IV.

"Nunc est consilio nobis opus inveniendo,
qualiter illius pietati gratificemus,
non solis verbis, quorum satis inveniemus,
sed quid donorum mittamus ei variorum,
est ut equis frenis auro compte faleratis, 5
pelliciis crisis varicosis sive crusennis,
ad quod quid mihi quis dicat, velit auxiliari."
Respondent pariter, quod agant id valde libenter.
Grates egit eis rex et post haec ait illis
"Quid respondendum sit missis, dicite primum!" 10
Est ibi philosophus cunctis sapientior unus,
quem timor aut amor a recto divertere quoquo
non in iudicio faciendo praevalet ullo,
dicere quem pro se dicunt debere petuntque.
In regis velle qui dicens maxime stare 15
eius consilium solum monet esse sequendum.
Rex "Mihi consilium quoniam sinitis tribuendum,
restat, ut huc veniant legati dictaque dicant
utque sciatis ab his, si credere neve velitis."
Post hos direxit. Veniunt quando, sibi dixit 20
"En regis, vestri domini nostri vel amici,
dulcia narravi fidei legamina plena,
quam pie tractavit, merito quos perdere quivit,
reddere vel sanos mihi contra se nece dignos;

clementer nobis demandavit sat honoris. 25
Quod deservire communiter hos decet et me,
si sic persolvet, per vos velut ipse spopondit."
Dixit legatus "Non est sic morigeratus,
ut quid verborum soleat mutare suorum.
Est quod ait verum, dictum sibi vult fore verum." 30
Rex ait "Id quando vel ubi fore possit, ai tu."
"Hoc" ait "est vestri iuris, rex, induciari."

"Tu tamen inque locum, quo conveniamus in unum,
ut pax inter nos firmetur mille per annos."
Missus ait "Si vis dominis et si placet istis, 35

IV.

(The Greater King has treated the prisoners captured by his forces with extraordinary kindness. He has sent Ruodlieb to the court of the Lesser King to act as his agent in setting up peace negotiations. The Lesser King is discussing with his advisers what he should respond to the Greater King.)

"Now there is need for us to seek advice how we
May find a way to thank him for his piety,
Not just by words, of which we soon will find enough.
What different kinds of gifts should we dispatch to him—
Fine stallions elegantly decked with reins of gold,   5
Coats of gray pelts or made from varicolored furs?
Let each one state to me how he can help in this."
They said together they would do this very gladly.
The king expressed his thanks to them, then to them said,
"Say first what answer I should give the messengers."   10
And one philosopher, most prudent of them all,
Was present there, whom neither fear nor love could sway
At all from what was right when he made a decision.
They said that he should speak for them and asked him to.
He, stating that the king's wish was the best, advised   15
That they should follow only what the king suggested.
The king: "Since you allow me to make this decision,
Then let the messengers come here and make their statement,
To know from them if you wish to trust them or not."
He summoned them, and when they came, he said to them,   20
"Behold, I have announced those sweet words full of faith
Sent by your king, who is your sovereign and our friend.
How piously the king has treated those whom he
Could justly kill, and sent them back to me unharmed,
Although deserving death for their attack on him.
And out of mercy he has offered us much honor.   25
Both I and all my people ought to earn this mercy,
If he will carry out what he has vowed through you."
The envoy said, "He is not so disposed that he
Is wont to alter any of his words; for what
He says is true; he wants his word to be the truth."   30
The king: "Say when and where this meeting will take
   place."
He said, "King, it is your right to determine this."
"You name the place where we should gather so that peace
May be secured between us for a thousand years."
The envoy said, "If you so wish and if it suits   35

non tam nosco locum vestris conventibus aptum,
campus ut est ille, quo nos pugnavimus ante,
inter clausuras nostri vestrique gemellas,
sunt ut ubi victi vestri nostrique redempti,
dimittantur ibi nobiscum pacificati." 40
Omnibus ille locus est visus ad hoc satis aptus,
regibus ambobus conventuris spaciosus,
induciasque trium laudant ad id ebdomadarum.
Post haec rex surgit sic conciliumque diremit
inque caminatam cum paucis it requietum. 45
Missis valde bona dantur regalia dona,
qui regem repetunt dignas gratesque sibi dant,
quis miscere iubet summi vini quod habebat.
Legati surgunt deturque licentia poscunt.
Rex ait "Audite mihi dilectique notate 50
quae vobis dico, quae dicite non ut amico
sed veluti patri meliora malis referenti
'Qualis es in corde, te talem prodis in ore,
quae nobis venit, tua quod legatio pandit,
quae spondendo reis veniam, spem dando salutis 55
mirum velle satis docet ultroneae pietatis,

contra quae grates non sufficimus dare dignas;
sed tibi subiecti sumus in pugnando subacti
semper et omnigeni serviminis intime prompti;
ut demandasti, quo vis, sumus ire parati, 60
est quod laudatum ternarum septimanarum
ad spacium (vestris est visum sic uti nostris)
in campo, primus es quo tu consiliatus.'
Oblitus si quid sum, vestra fides at id implet."
Respondent pariter "Meruisti sufficienter, 65
nos servire tibi semper cum corde fideli."
Tunc inclinabant, cum rite "valete" recedunt.
Inde petunt summum, velut est dignum, vicedomnum,
a quo donati sunt valde, "vale" benefacti.
Ex iussu regis provisorem dedit illis, 70
qui procuraret, quod opus sit eis, ut haberent,
quod studio summo complevit cordeque fido,
donec pacifice vel eos perduxit honeste
extra clausuram fines regni dirimentem.
Quem bene donatum vel verbis gratificatum 75
poscunt, inclinet regi, "faciam" quibus inquit.
A se divisi sunt ad patriamque reversi.
Utque domum redeunt, regem properando revisunt.
Ut primum videt bene quos suscepit et inquit
"Dicite, rumoris nunc quid nobis referatis!" 80

Your lords, I know no place more suitable for you
To meet than on that field where formerly we fought,
Between the double borders of our realm and yours
There where your people were defeated, ours released,
That yours may be released and reconciled with us."   40
The place seemed very suitable for this to all,
And with sufficient space for both the kings to meet.
They set negotiations for three weeks from then.
At this the king arose, dismissed his counsellors,
And with a few men went into his room to rest.   45
Then quite good royal gifts were given to the envoys,
Who went back to the king and gave due thanks to him.
Some of the finest wine he had he ordered poured
For them. The envoys rose and asked that leave be granted.
The king said, "Listen to me, friends, and note the words 50
I say. Report them not as to a friend, but more
As to a father who is giving good for evil:
Your mouth reveals you as you are within your heart,
As your legation which has come to us disclosed.
By pledging pardon to the guilty and by giving   55
Hope of salvation it taught well your wonderful
Intention to be pious voluntarily,
For which we cannot offer you sufficient thanks.
Subdued by you in battle, we are in your power
And always wholly ready for all kinds of service,
Prepared to go, as you required, where you wish.   60
It seemed best to your people, as it did to ours,
To hold the meeting, as agreed, three weeks from now
There on the battlefield which you suggested first.
If I forget something, your faith will fill its place."
Together they replied, "You have sufficiently   65
Deserved that we serve you with faithful hearts forever."
And then they bowed, and left with suitable farewells;
Then, as was proper, they sought out the vice-regent,
By whom they were rewarded amply, blessed "farewell."
By order of the king he gave a scout to them   70
Who would procure whatever they might need to have.
He discharged this both zealously and faithfully
Until he led them peacefully and loyally
Beyond the border marking off the kingdom's limits.
The scout, whom they rewarded well and thanked with words,75
They asked to bow to his king. "I'll do that," he said.
Departing from him, they returned to their own land.
When they reached home, they quickly went to see the king.
When he saw them, he offered cordial welcome, saying,
"Now tell me any piece of news you bring to me."   80

Respondit missus "Quia clemens est tibi Christus,
quod reges alii nisi grandi non superant vi,
dat deus id sponte tibi clemens absque labore.
Nam per contigua tibi quae sunt undique regna
crederis esse leo vigilanti semper ocello; 85
quin agnellina pietate tuaque sophia
tu vincis melius, gladius quam vincat alius.
Namque deo teste, quo mittebar modo de te,
nescio, plus ab eis adameris seu verearis.
Cum rex audisset (summatum grex et adesset), 90
quae demandasti sibi vel plebi simul omni,
primo servimen post fidi cordis amorem,
sublata cydare surgens inclinat honeste.
Tunc residens tacuit, donec rem pleniter audit,
quantum nostrates disceptabantque suates 95
atque sui nostros offendentes inopinos
occidunt spoliant captivatosque cremabant,
qualiter et nostri sunt illorum dominati,
captivos redimunt captivantesque ligabant;
quos tibi cum referunt perituros seque putarent, 100

quam clementer eis adimendo metum misereris,
illos absolvens consolans et bene tractans
praesulibus ducibus locupletibus [abbatibusque
ipsos servandum dederis vel equos ad alendum;
non, ut sunt meriti, sub carcere compedis aut vi 105
nec tractent illos, deceat quam regis amicos,
ut, dum reddantur, super his ne forte querantur.
'Quin ipsum comitem scelus hoc inmane patrantem
nulli conmisit, super hunc nulli bene fidit,
sed sibimet servit gladium persaepeque portat, 110
ut nullus noceat, quem rex sic glorificabat.'
Nolle recordari te, sed postquam sibi dixi,
dedecus inmensum vel inedicibile damnum,
quod tibi fecerunt, sub iure tuo modo qui sunt,
quos inpunitos, quamvis meritos inimicos, 115
reddere laudares in nulla re nichilatos,
si velit, in plebe pax ut reparetur utrimque—
sic dicens silui vel rege nuente resedi.
In cras induciat, his ut responsa rependat.
In summo mane curtem cuncti petiere 120
(plures rumoris cupidi quam regis honoris);
intromittuntur, qui quid prodesse videntur,
regi consilium pro tali re tribuendum;
valvae clauduntur, nescitur quid loquerentur.
Est breve colloquium pro consensu sapientum. 125

The envoy said, "Since Christ is well disposed to you,
What other kings do not achieve except by force,
God freely in His mercy grants you without labor.
Throughout the lands that touch yours on all sides you are
Believed a lion with an ever watchful eye.   85
Indeed, with wisdom and your lamb-like piety,
You conquer better than another with a sword.
God be my witness, where I was just sent by you
I know not if you are more loved or feared by them.
When that king heard (a group of nobles was there too)   90
What you have offered him and with him all his people,
First service, afterward the love of a faithful heart,
He stood, first taking off his crown, and bowed politely,
Then, silent, sat until he heard the matter fully:
How his men were involved in a dispute with ours,   95
And his, attacking our men unexpectedly,
Had killed, despoiled and even burned their prisoners;
How our men then emerged victorious over them,
Released the prisoners, and then bound up the captors.
When they were brought to you, they thought that they would
    die;   100
How mercifully you pitied them, removed their fear;
Absolving, cheering them, and justly treating them,
You gave them to the bishops, wealthy dukes and abbots
So that they might take care of them and feed their horses.
We did not shackle or imprison them, as they   105
Deserved, but treated them as suits friends of the king,
So, when returned, they would perhaps have no complaints.
Indeed, you handed that count who committed this
Foul crime to no one (fully trusting no one to
Watch him). No, he serves him and often wears a sword,   110
That no one harm a man the king thus glorified.
And then I told him you did not want to recall
Your massive shame or the unutterable loss inflicted
On you by men who now are under your control;
If he wished, you agreed to send them back unpunished   115
(Although deserving hostile treatment) and uninjured,
That mutual peace might be restored between your peoples.
So speaking, I was silent; at the king's command,
I sat. He put off his reply until tomorrow.
And first thing in the morning all went to the court.   120
They came for news more than for honoring the king.
Those who seemed somehow useful were admitted so
That they might give the king advice in this affair.
The doors were closed, and it is not known what was said.
A brief discussion sought the agreement of the wise.   125

nobis interea data prandia sunt sat opima.
Dum pranderemus et adhuc vinum biberemus,
mittitur et post nos tres, omnes ut veniamus.
Fecimus, ut iussit. Cum prae se venimus, inquit
'O nostri domini missi summique patroni,   130
si respondere bene sciremus vel honeste
demandaminibus clementibus atque paternis,
est ut promeritus nimium, prompte faceremus.
Dicite nunc illi de me de plebe vel omni,
(de summis mediis imis mihi iure subactis)   135
fidum vel promptum subiectorum famulamen.
Virtus mira tua, pietas tua magna, sophia,
intus ut adimplent te sic foris undique comunt.
Scimus inaequales re militibusque tibi nos,
si velles, posse nos pro meritis nichilasse.   140
Reddere pro pravis bona stat satis ultio grandis;
nam quo rescitur faciens plus inde timetur.
Grande tuum posse vel inaequiparabile velle
sunt tibi pro muro per nullum deiciendo.
Laesum laedenti veniam miserendo precari!   145

Nonne deizare nobis merito videare
indulgens sponte peccantibus absque petente?
Econtra nil nos simile praebere valemus,
retribuat sed ut is rex post, quem sic imitaris,
nos exorare debemus corde vel ore;   150
utque diu vivas valeas regnes et abundes,
nobis et cunctis affinibus undique regnis
est exoptandum communiter atque precandum.
Nam columen nostri tu solus es in vice Christi
atque superstite te bene possumus imperitare   155
sub vestrae fidei scuto diutissime tuti.
Et nunc, o domine, non dedignare venire
ad loca laudata, quando sunt induciata;
vobis congredimur de nostris ac famulamur.'
Sic ait et donis ditavit nos sat opimis,   160
pelliciis vel equis faleratis sive chrusennis,
post poscit vinum, Gerdrudis amore quod haustum
participat nos tres; postremo basia figens,
Quando vale dixit, post nos gemit et benedixit.
Hinc rediebamus vicedomnum postque videmus,   165
qui nos condonans provisorem simul et dans
oscula fert more, grandi nos liquit amore,
tam tibi devotum mandans, ut hero, famulatum.

Sic datur a cunctis sat amica licentia nobis.

Meanwhile a very sumptuous lunch was served to us.
While we were eating and still drinking wine, a man
Was sent to us to tell the three of us to come.
We did as he commanded; when we came before
Him, he said, 'Envoys of our lord and highest patron,   130
If we knew how to answer well and honorably
The merciful paternal messages as they
Assuredly deserve, we would do so at once.
Report now to that man from me and all my people
(My noblest, middle, and my humblest lawful subjects)   135
The ready and the faithful service of his subjects.
Your awesome virtue, piety and wisdom so
Adorn you outside just as they fill you within.
We know we cannot equal you in wealth or knights;
You could destroy us, if you wish, as we deserve.   140
Returning good for evil is a very great
Revenge: a man who acts as he is known is feared
The more for that; for like a wall for you that none
Can breach are your great power and incomparable will.
To think, an injured man takes pity on the one   145
Who injured him and even prays for his forgiveness!
Do you not rightly seem like God to us when you
Forgive the sinners on your own, without their asking?
Though we can offer nothing like that in return,
May that King whom you imitate reward you later—
We ought to ask this with our mouth and with our heart.   150
Both we and all the lands that touch ours on both sides
Desire earnestly and seek by prayer together
That you live long, be well, and rule and prosper; for
Alone you are our pillar in the place of Christ.
As long as you are living, we can govern well,   155
Beneath the shield of your faith safe for a long time.
And now, my lord, do not disdain to come to that
Place we agreed upon at the appointed time;
For we will come to you from our folk and serve you.'
So speaking, he enriched us with some splendid gifts: 160
With cloaks, fur coats, and richly decorated steeds.
He asked for wine and with a toast to Saint Gertrude
He shared it with the three of us; then giving kisses
Sighed after us and blessed us when he said farewell.
We left that place and went to visit the viceregent;   165
Presenting gifts, he gave a guide to us as well,
Kissed us (as was the custom) and dismissed us with
Much love, while pledging you—as lord—his faithful
    service.
Thus very friendly leave was taken by us all.

Disciplinate noster ductor vel honeste 170
servivit nobis in simplicitateque cordis,
huius dum regni confinia vidimus ampli."
Talis rumoris rex talis ovans et honoris
subridens modicum nil protulit ore superbum;
susspiciens laudat dominum, quo dante triumphat, 175

nil reputando sibi sed ei dans omnia dixit
"Induciae quo sunt laudatae quandove, dic, sunt?"

"Ebdomadae cum praetereunt tres, induciae sunt

hac in planicie, qua concertavimus ante
solventes nostros in vincla redegimus hostes, 180
sunt ubi tristati quo fiant laetificati.
Sic de te regi tunc induciando spopondi."
Rex ait "Hoc laudo promissorum neque fraudo.
Dum fueras at ibi, quid agendum, dic, habuisti?"
Respondit "Summus mihi clemens fit vicedomnus 185
procurans multum, defectum ne paterer quem;
scachorum ludo temptat me vincere crebro
nec potuit, ludo ni sponte dato sibi solo.
Quinque dies sic me non siverat ante venire;
explorare cupit, meus adventus quid eo sit. 190
Investigare nulla quod dum valet arte,
post me rex misit, sibi quae dixi satis audit,
in cras responso, dixi velut, induciato.
Rex poscens tabulam iubet opponi sibi sellam
et me contra se iubet in fulchro residere, 195
ut secum ludam, quod ego nimium renuebam
dicens 'Terribile miserum conludere rege';
et dum me vidi sibi non audere reniti,
ludere laudavi cupiens ab eo superari,
'Vinci de rege' dicens 'quid obest miserum me? 200
Sed timeo, domine, quod mox irasceris in me,
si fortuna iuvet, mihi quod victoria constet.'
Rex subridendo dixit velut atque iocando
'Non opus est, care, super hac re quid vereare;
si nunquam vincam, commocior haut ego fiam, 205
sed quam districte noscas ludas volo cum me;
nam quos ignotos facies volo discere tractus.'
Statim rex et ego studiose traximus ambo,
et, sibi gratia sit, mihi ter victoria cessit,
multis principibus nimis id mirantibus eius. 210
Is mihi deponit, sibi me deponere nil vult
et dat quae posuit, pisa quod non una remansit.

Our guide performed his service to us skillfully   170
And honorably, and with straightforwardness of spirit,
Until we saw the boundaries of this ample realm."
The king, rejoicing in such news and in such honor,
Though he was smiling slightly, uttered no proud word
But looking up praised God by whose gift he has
    triumphed;   175
And giving God all credit, taking none himself,
He spoke, "Say where and when the peace talks have been
    set."
"When three weeks have elapsed, the talks have been
    arranged,
There on that field where earlier we fought and freed
Our men while we reduced our enemies to chains,   180
That they may be made happy where they once were saddened.
I made the king this promise acting as your agent."
The king: "This promise I approve and will not break.
Tell me, while you were there, what did you have to do?"
He said, "The highest viceregent was kind to me;   185
He gave much, so I never suffered any want.
He often tried to beat me at the game of chess,
But he could not unless I let him win a game.
For five days thus he kept me from an audience.
He wished to learn the reason for my coming there.   190
When he could not find this by any means, the king
Then summoned me and listened closely to my words.
His answer, as I said, was set for the next day.
The king called for a board, and had a chair brought him,
And made me sit down on a stool opposing him   195
To play with him, but I objected strongly, saying
'It's dreadful for a lesser man to play a king.'
But when I saw that I dare not refuse him, I
Agreed to play, in hopes that I would lose to him.
'What harm for lowly me in losing to a king?'   200
I said; 'but, lord, I fear that soon you will be angry
At me, if Fortune helps to make the triumph mine.'
The king said with a smile as if he spoke in jest,
'No need, my friend, for any fear in this affair.
For if I never win, I will not be upset.   205
Please play with me as skillfully as you know how.
I want to learn the unfamiliar moves you'll make.'
At once the king and I both played intently, and—
Thanks be to her—three times the victory was mine,
With many of his nobles marveling at this.   210
He bet with me, but let me wager nothing back,
And paid his bets off until not one coin remained.

Plures succedunt, hunc ulcisci voluerunt
pignora praebentes mea pignora despicientes,
perdere nil certi, dubiae fisi bene sorti. 215
Alterutrumque iuvant nimiumque iuvando nocebant.
Praepediebantur, varie dum consiliantur,
inter litigium cito vincebam quod eorum
hoc tribus et vicibus, volui nam ludere non plus.
Quae deponebant, mihi mox donare volebant. 220
Primo respueram, vitiosum namque putabam,
sic me ditari vel eos per me tenuari.
Dixi 'Non suevi quicquam ludendo lucrari.'
Dicunt 'Inter nos cum sis, tu vive velut nos;
quando domum venias, ibi vivere quis veluti vis.' 225
Cum sat lorifregi, quae porrexere recepi,
commoda cum laude mihi fortuna tribuente."
Rex ait "Hunc ludum tibi censeo semper amandum,
quo sunt sarcita tua tam bene calciamenta.
Nunc grates habeas, causas quod agis bene nostras." 230
Misit et ad quosque, qui captivos habuere,
hos ut vestirent ad honorem vel sibi reddant,
ipsis quos pedites misit, reddant ut equestres,
insuper armatos velut ad nova bella paratos.
Vestivit comitem velut ex summatibus unum 235

binis pelliciis preciosis totque chrusennis;
coccineam tunicam gemmis auroque micantem
dat sibi, qua regi praeberet pocula vini;
dat vel equum fortem celerem nimis aequipedantem,
auratum frenum pulchram faleramque gerentem; 240
et dat loricam, tutus valeat fore per quam
in quovis bello communi sive duello;
ensem vel galeam sibi lanceolam dat acutam.
Qui famulantur ei, donantur utrique clienti
vestes valde bonae semperque domi sibi rarae; 245
insuper ad bella sibi congrua praestitit arma.
Misit praecones satrapas comitesque vocandos,
ad curtem veniant quo regis, quam bene possint,
et secum ferrent, sibi quae vel equis opus essent
ad tres ebdomadas secum seu plus remanendas. 250

Illuc pontifices invitantur sapientes
abbatesque pii scioli bene consiliari.

Then many followed, eager to avenge this man:
They offered wagers, but would not take mine, convinced
They would lose nothing (fully trusting fickle luck);   215
They helped each other, and by helping did much harm,
Because conflicting strategies would trip them up,
And I won easily amid their arguments.
Three times this happened, for I wanted no more games.
They wished to pay me right away what they had bet;   220
First I refused, because I thought it wrong that I
Be thus enriched and those impoverished by me.
I said, 'I am not wont to profit by my playing.'
And they said, 'When you are among us, live like us.
When you go home, there you can live just as you wish.'   225
When I resisted them enough, I then took what
They offered—Fortune granting me both praise and profit!"
The king said, "I think you should always love this game
By means of which your shoes have been well heeled indeed.
Accept my thanks now, for you do our business well."   230
Then he sent word to all those holding prisoners,
To clothe them honorably and send them back to him.
Those he sent them as foot soldiers should be returned
As cavalry, armed as if ready for new battles.
He clothed the count just as if one of his own
    chieftains,   235
With two expensive cloaks and just as many furs.
He gave to him a scarlet tunic bright with jewels
And gold, in which to serve his own king cups of wine.
He gave a horse—strong, swift and very steady-gaited—
Which bears a golden bridle and exquisite trappings.   240
He gave a suit of armor so that he could be
Protected when in any mass combat or duel.
He gave to him a helmet, sword and a' sharp lance.
To both the servants who attend the count he gave
Fine garments which were always rare in their own land,   245
And also furnished them with weapons fit for war.
He dispatched heralds then to call his counts and satraps
To come to their king's court as well dressed as they could
And bring with them whatever they would need themselves
And for their mounts to stay with him three weeks or
    more.   250
Wise clergymen and pious abbots, men well skilled
At counselling were summoned to that place as well.

V.

Hic regis lata] curtis fuit amphiprehensa
in me]dio vacua scenis foris undique saepta,
qua cum praesulibus abbatibus et duodenis
posset prandere cenareve sat spaciose.
Curti contiguum stat tentorium satis amplum 5
solis ad exortum, de quo posuere podismum,
cuius ad extremum fixerunt papilionem,
in quo stans mensa vestita fuit velut ara,
quam super est posita regis crux et diadema;
qua missae regi solet officium celebrari, 10
matutinalis et vespertina sinaxis
cursibus inmixtis aliis de more diurnis.
Quo dum rex venit, missam properantius audit
et per legatum regi demandat eundem,
qui fuerat rerum prius internuncius harum, 15
primitus ut videant sese quam prandia sumant.
Quem rex, ut vidit, bene subridendo recepit
oscula datque sibi "Quid narras?" Post ait illi
"Omne bonum dici tibi de me, sat meruisti."
"Ad te me misit rex et tibi dicere iussit, 20
ne prandere velis prius illum quam tuearis.
Obvius ad pontem venit is tibi nos dirimentem,
pax ibi firmatur res omnis et adbreviatur,
capti redduntur captos se neve queruntur,
nam meliorati redeunt, non attenuati." 25
Rex "ita fiat" ait. Ad herum missus remeavit.
Dum convenerunt reges ubi constituerunt,
nil penitus dicunt sibi quam prius oscula figunt.
Noster pontifices, ut idem facerent, iubet omnes,
et post abbates ex ordine basiat omnes; 30
eius praesulibus tunc praebitus est amor ipsus.
Reges pontifices abbates clerus et omnis
assumptis ducibus vel summis alterutrius
dum resident pariter, rex maior ait sapienter
"O nimium nobis rex dilectissime cunctis, 35
sicut laudavi tibi demandansque spopondi,
quicquid stulticiae plebs nostra patravit utrimque,
hoc dimittamus et eosdem pacificemus,
ut sint inter se concordantes sine fraude.

V.

(The Greater King, accompanied by his retinue and all the
prisoners, has arrived at the battlefield to engage in the
peace negotiations.)

And here the broad court of the king had been enclosed,
The middle bare, but on the outside ringed with lodges.
In this place with twelve bishops and twelve abbots he
Had room enough to eat his lunch or have his dinner.
Adjacent to the court a very large tent stood, 5
Which faced the rising sun; from this they built a walkway;
And at the end of that they had set up a tent
In which there stood a table covered as an altar.
On top of this were placed the great king's cross and crown;
And here the mass was celebrated for the king, 10
And matins, vespers and the other services
Occurring in the daily order set by custom.
When he arrived, the king immediately heard mass,
Then told the lesser king through that same envoy who
Had earlier served as their agent in these matters 15
To come to him before they ate their lunch. When he
Saw him, the king received him with a kindly smile;
Then kissing him, to him he said: "What is your message?
You well deserve that I give you my fondest greeting."
"My king sent me to you and ordered me to say 20
That you should not have lunch until you visit him.
And he will meet you at the bridge dividing us.
There peace will be confirmed, and every matter settled.
The prisoners who are returned do not complain,
For they return enriched and not impoverished." 25
The king: "Agreed." The envoy went back to his lord.
The kings, when they assembled where they had agreed,
Said nothing to each other until they had kissed.
Our king commanded all the clergy that they do
The same; then he kissed all the abbots in succession. 30
The same affection was displayed then to the bishops.
When they sat down together—kings, the bishops, abbots,
And all the clergy, once the dukes and nobles on
Both sides were seated—then the greater king spoke wisely:
"O king, extremely well beloved by all of us, 35
As I agreed and in my summons pledged to you,
Let us forget whatever foolish things our folk
On either side have done, and reconcile them, that
They may have peace among themselves without deceit.

Nemo recordetur, adversi quid pateretur, 40
obliviscatur ulcisci nec meditetur.
Nam mala malo bono quam reddere vincere pravo."
Alter rex surgens huic dignas dicere grates.
A nostro vetitus residet, tamen est ita fatus
"Pro tot vel tantis impensis nos benefactis 45
reddere condignas non sufficimus tibi grates.
In cuius parma victricia tu geris arma,
ille tibi laudis sat praestat et omnis honoris;
non opus est hinc te laudare vel amplificare.
Virtus et pietas nimis et tua larga voluntas 50
omnibus invitis cumulant tibi praemia laudis.
Ipsemet atque mei tibi debemus famulari
ut bello victi sub vexilloque subacti."
Rex ait "Hoc absit, ego dum vivam neque fiet,
ut tibi quid iuris aut adminuatur honoris; 55
es rex sicut ego, tibi me praeponere nolo,
eiusdem iuris es, cuius sum, vel honoris.
Ob quod venimus huc, modo perficiamus id istic
tuque tuos recipe, sed non sine quovis honore."
Sic dicens comitem regali veste nitentem 60
reddidit armatum veluti bellare paratum;
sic nongentorum nullum reddebat eorum,
quin foret armatus vel veste decenter amictus.
Post ait "Hi, rex, sunt, quos vivere fata sinebant,
Qui non humane, dum nobis praevaluere, 65

Nos tractant igne praeda vel caede maligne.
Qualiter econtra tractarem quos vice versa,
praecipe, quo dicant tibi, quando domum remearint.
Nunc se concordent et sint, velut ante fuerunt,
firmi compatres posthac fidique sodales." 70
Quo facto nempe pax firmabatur utrimque
per iuramentum neutrim penitus temerandum.
Tunc ambo reges redeunt ad papiliones

cumque suis prandent; ibi grandia gaudia fiunt.
Gaudet quisque, suus salvus rediit quod amicus. 75
Mensa sublata disponit plurima dona,
quae regi dentur vel eis, hunc qui comitentur:
auri quingenta regi donanda talenta,
insuper argentum multum vel pallia centum,
centum loricae, totidem galeae chalibinae, 80
inter equos muli decapenta bis falerati
et bis quindeni onagri totidemque cameli
atque leopardi gemini binique leones

Let none recall whatever damage he incurred;   40
Let each forget revenge and think no more of that.
I would give good for bad, and not crush bad with evil."
The other king rose up to state his fitting thanks;
Forbidden by our king, he sat, but spoke as follows:
"For the so many profound favors you have done   45
We cannot offer fitting gratitude to you.
He under whose shield you wield your victorious arms
Holds out to you sufficient fame and every honor.
You have therefore no need of praise or celebration.
Your virtue, piety and generosity   50
Would win for you the prize of fame, though all objected.
I and my people owe to you our service, since
We are subdued in war and subject to your standard."
The king said, "No, it will not happen while I live
That any of your rights or honor be diminished.   55
You are a king like me. I will not place myself
Above you, who share in the selfsame rights and honor.
Let us now do what we came to this place to do.
Take back your men, but not deprived of any honor."
Thus speaking, he gave back the count resplendent in   60
His royal clothing, armed as if prepared for war.
Thus he returned not one of those nine hundred men
Unless he was well armed and suitably attired.
He said, "These are the men, king, fate allowed to live.
While they prevailed, they did not treat our side
    humanely,   65
But brutally, with conflagration, looting, murder.
And yet how differently I dealt with them in turn
Direct them to tell you when they reach home again.
Now let them come to terms and be as they once were,
Both constant friends and faithful allies after this."   70
This done, peace was indeed established on both sides
By oaths that both groups absolutely could not break.
Both kings then went back to their tents and ate their
    lunch
With their own people; in that place great joy prevailed.
Each man rejoiced because his friend had come back safely.75
The table cleared away, each brought out many gifts
To be presented to the king and his retainers:
Five hundred golden talents to be given him;
Much silver in addition, and a hundred cloaks,
A hundred helmets made of steel, a hundred corselets;   80
Among the horses, there were thirty spangled mules,
And two times fifteen asses, just as many camels;
There were two leopards also, and two lions, and

et pariles ursi, qui fratres sunt uterini,
omnino nivei gambis pedibusque nigelli, 85

qui vas tollebant, ut homo, bipedesque gerebant;
mimi quando fides digitis tangunt modulantes,
illi saltabant neumas pedibus variabant;
interdum saliunt seseque superiaciebant,
alterutrum dorso se portabant residendo, 90
amplexando se luctando deiciunt se;
cum plebs altisonam fecit girando choream,
accurrunt et se mulieribus applicuere,
quae gracili voce cecinerunt deliciose,
inse]rtisque suis harum manibus speciosis 95
erecti calcant pedetemptim, murmure trinsant,
ut mirarentur, ibi circum qui graderentur,
non irascantur, quodcunque mali paterentur.
Insuper et lincum de vulpe lupoque creatum
addiderat donis, expers quod non sit honoris, 100
eius ab urina quia crescit lucida gemma,
ardens ligurius carbunculus ut preciosus.
Qualiter is fiat, libeat quem discere, discat!
Ex ferro clavos tibi fac fabricare quaternos,

in lata butina, quos fige bis in loca bina 105
fortiter inpellens, evellere quis queat haut quos,
in medio butinae terebello facque foramen;
in quam pone feram licet invitam ve rebellem
ad clavosque pedes vincire sibi bene cures
et circa collum nexam suspende catenam 110
inclinando caput, ne vincula solvere possit!
Ad manducandum sibi sat da sive bibendum,
quod bibat at vinum validum sit, dulce bibendum!
Ebrius exinde, dum vult, nequeat retinere,
exeat urina, sed ut ignorante retenta, 115
et fluat in pelvim cito per butinam terebratam,

quam dum non poterit dispergere, vivere claudit.
Si non emittat tamen hanc moriensque retentet,
abstracta pelle vel aperto cautius alvo
tollito vesicam vel acu transpunge minutim 120
et sic urinam nimis in puram preme pelvim
inque modum pisae per cuprea vascula funde
maiorisve nucis ad grossum fundito vasis.
Suffodiens terra quae vasa dies decapenta
esse sinas, post effodiens exinde resumas 125
guttas in gemmas concretas cernis et omnes,

Two bears that were identical twin brothers (these
Completely white, although their legs and paws were
    black);   85
They picked up vessels and, like men, walked on two legs.
And when the mimes played on the strings of instruments,
They danced around and kept the rhythm with their paws.
Sometimes they leaped about and even somersaulted;
They carried one another on their backs, sat down,   90
Embraced each other, wrestled, threw each other down.
When people started dancing loudly in a circle,
The bears advanced and even joined up with the women,
Who with their gentle voices sang most pleasingly.
Then with their paws placed in the women's lovely hands,   95
The bears, upright, danced step-for-step and softly growled,
So that the people dancing round them were amazed
And were not angry for whatever hurt they suffered.
He also added to the gifts a lynx (born of
A fox and wolf)—this was a gift not lacking honor,   100
Since from its urine there is formed a brilliant gem,
The gleaming ligure, that is precious as carbuncle.
Let him who wants to learn, learn how it is created!
First, have formed for yourself four spikes made out of
    iron;
Attach them in a broad vat in four places and   105
Drive them so strongly that no one can pull them out.
Then use a drill to make a hole in that tub's center,
And put the beast inside, though it rebels and fights.
Take care to bind its paws securely to the spikes
And hang a woven chain around its neck (and bend   110
Its head so that it cannot break loose from its bonds).
Give it enough to eat and drink; however, what
It drinks must be a potent wine, sweet to the taste.
Thence drunk, it cannot, though it wants to, hold its urine.
Then let the urine drip away (but as from one   115
Who wrongly thinks it is retained) and quickly flow
Into a basin through the hole drilled in the vat.
And when it cannot void this, it will cease to live.
If it does not pass this, retaining it in death,
Draw back its skin and with care open up its belly;
Remove the bladder, prick it slightly with a needle;   120
In this way press the urine in a spotless basin,
And pour it into copper vessels shaped like peas
Or into cups about the size of larger nuts.
These vessels bury in the ground for fifteen days,
Then dig them up from there, remove the contents and   125
You'll see that all the drops have hardened into jewels

quae similes prunis lucent caligine noctis,
quas decet imponi reginarum digitali,
regis at impone magnas aptando coronae.
Adduntur donis, licet illis nil sit honoris, 130
simia nare brevi nate nuda murcaque cauda,
voceque milvina cute crisa catta marina,
in quibus ambabus nil cernitur utilitatis.
Ex genealogia vol[ucrum] regalia dona
auxit cum psitachis binis corvisque gemellis 135
monedulis sturnis doctis garrire loquelis,
quicquid et audierint imi[tari q]uae studuerunt.
Pontifici cuique sua dona reponit honeste.
Loricis galeis ducibus scutis retalatis
munerat atque tubis auro prae post decoratis, 140
praesidibus pulchris madris crisisve poledris,
militibus summis seu pelliciisve chrusennis.
His ita dispositis modicum requiescere vult is.
Explorare iubet, alter rex quando resurgat.
Post vigilans surgit mulum falerareque iussit 145
cumque quibus voluit ad regem tunc equitavit.
Plures occurrunt et ei servire studebant.
Quem bene suscepit rex atque sedere rogavit,
qui dixit "Domine, mecum dignare venire
et non abnuito quae munera parva tibi do, 150
quicquid summatum sit et hic, veniant, rogo, tecum."
Rex ait "Id fiat." —Rex alter doma revisat.
Convocat iste suos summates conveniendos.
Qui dum conveniunt vel coram rege sederunt,
ut mos eius erat semper, rogitando iubebat, 155
quo suus esset honor cuivis quam munera maior
et nihil acciperet, sibi si quae rex dare vellet,
"Ne sit opus census vobis videatur ut eius;
mecum nunc ite, quod ego faciam facitote."
Ibant cum rege suscepti sunt et honeste. 160
Dum consederunt ter miscendoque biberunt,
rex regem duxit secum quos ireque iussit
in curtem latam [canc]ellis amphiprehensam,
in qua stant mensae vario censu cumulatae,
in qua stant et equi, decet ut regem, falerati, 165
stant etiam muli stant enormesque cameli
stant et ter deni mites onagri domitique

stant et terribiles leopardi sive leones;
stas et inaurata connexus, lince, catena,
simia cum catta stat ibique marina ligata, 170

Which sparkle in the dark of night like glowing coals;
Some are deserving to be set in rings of queens,
But mount and set the large ones in the king's own crown.
Some other presents, though of little worth, were added: 130
A snub-nosed, bare-rumped ape with a truncated tail;
A long-tailed gray-skinned monkey with a hawk-like voice.
No usefulness at all was seen in either brute.
He added royal presents from the race of birds:
Together with two parrots and a pair of ravens,   135
Jackdaws and starlings trained for chattering in words
And eager to repeat whatever sounds they heard.
He suitably provided gifts for every pontiff.
Then he presented the dukes with corselets, helmets, shields
And horns adorned with gold on both the front and back. 140
He gave the counts gray steeds and handsome marten coats;
The highest knights were given cloaks and coats of fur.
When this was done, he wished to rest a little while.
He bade them find out when the other king would rise;
When he awoke, he rose and ordered his mule saddled;   145
Then with those whom he wished he rode to the great king.
There many met him and were eager to be helpful.
The king received him cordially and asked him to
Sit down. He said, "My lord, please deign to come with me
And not refuse the small gifts that I give to you.   150
I ask that all your highest lords come here with you."
The king said, "So be it." The other king went home.
The great king summoned all his highest chiefs together.
When they assembled and sat down before the king,
As always was his custom he commanded them
That each one value his own honor more than gifts,   155
Accepting nothing that king wished to give to them.
"Do not let it appear that you need that man's wealth;
Now come with me and do whatever I shall do."
They went with their king and were honorably received. 160
When they sat down and had prepared and drunk three toasts,
The one king led the other (and those whom he told
To come with him) into the courtyard bound by railings,
In which stood tables heaped with many kinds of treasures:
In which stood horses decked out as befits a king;   165
And there stood mules and even some enormous camels;
And there stood three times ten wild asses, tamed and
    gentle;
And there stood terrifying leopards, also lions;
And, lynx, you stand there fastened to your golden chain;
The ape and long-tailed monkey, tied up, stand there
    too;   170

stant ursi gemini multo variamine ludi;
quin ibi sunt et aves hominum sermone fruentes,
psitachus et corvus monedula picave sturnus.
Tunc ait "Haec dona tua sint, rex optime, cuncta,
praesulibus sint haec horumque fidelibus istaec." 175

Auri ter denas uni placuit dare libras
inque capellanos quinquaginta tribuendas
argenti libras totidemque per officiales,
inter scutiferos vilesque ministeriales
viginti libras nummorum distribuendas; 180
nec superexaltat lixas, quin hos quoque donet;
inter eos denas dispergendas quoque libras
det duodenorum tantundem cuivis eorum,
(post ducibus galeas loricas ponit et enses,
auratas parmas, lituos ad bella canoros 185
inque suos libras sexaginta tribuendas),
et post praesidibus det equos faleris redimitos

atque suis denas cunctis libras tribuendas;
postremo cunctis abbatibus his duodenis
se det in oramen spondendo suum famulamen, 190

illorum cuivis confratribus hosque secutis
libras triginta puerorum cuivis et unam;
mittat et ad claustra monachis libras decapenta.
Regis simnistis aliisque fidelibus eius,
eius servicio qui sunt in cottidiano, 195
qui veluti glandes semper flant regis ad aures
et pro mercedis succurrunt pondere cuivis,
bona dat eximia census ad mille talenta.
Inter quos illum venatorem peregrinum
munerat uberius, sic collegam facit eius, 200
missi qui fuerant ad se pacemque patrabant.
Munera dum vidit ea rex multumque probavit,
dixit ad aequivocum "Tua munera sunt bona multum;
ne tamen a nobis tantum donando graveris,
pro donis votum decernimus accipiendum. 205
Tam bene ludentes ursos hos tollo gemellos
atque meae natae picam sturnumque do de te
et grates habeas tantas, ceu cuncta dedisses;
nec volo presulibus ducibus quid praesidibus des.
Quod coenobitis dabis aut abbatibus istis, 210
non contra dico, quia redditur id tibi vero;
hi sunt assidui famulantes omnipotenti
orant et pro te studiose nocte dieque

There stand the twin bears which could do so many tricks;
And even birds that imitated human speech:
The parrot, raven, jackdaw, magpie, and the starling.
He said, "O best of kings, let these gifts all be yours;
Let these be for the bishops, those gifts for their
    faithful."   175
He wished to give to each one thirty pounds of gold,
With fifty pounds of silver to be given to
The chaplains, and for their attendants just as much;
And twenty pounds of coins to be distributed
Among the squires and the lesser household servants;   180
And he did not forget to give the waiters gifts;
He also gave ten pounds to be distributed
Among the twelve, with each to get the same amount.
His presents to the dukes were helmets, corselets, swords,
And gilded shields and deep-toned horns to sound in war,   185
And sixty pounds to be presented to their servants.
The counts then he gave gifts of steeds equipped with
    trappings,
And ten pounds to be given out to all their servants.
At last he gave himself to all twelve abbots for
Their prayers, and promised that he would give them his
    service;   190
To each of them and to the brothers following
Them he gave thirty pounds; and to each servant, one;
And for the monks he sent the cloister fifteen pounds.
The king's advisers and his other faithful men
(Those vassals who are in his service every day   195
And who, like seashells, always whisper in his ears
And, for a hefty payment, help out anyone)
He gave uncommon presents worth a thousand talents.
Among those people he rewards the foreign hunter
Abundantly, and treats his comrades just the same,   200
Who both were envoys to him and arranged the peace.
The king, when he had seen and scrutinized the presents,
Said to the other king, "Your gifts are very fine;
That you will not be burdened by us from such giving,
Our choice is to accept your vow in place of presents.   205
I will take these two bears which play so comically;
From you I'll give the magpie and the starling to
My daughter—thanking you as if you gave them all.
I wish that bishops, dukes and counts be given nothing;
But what you give the monks and abbots I do not   210
Gainsay; for that will truly be repaid to you.
These men serve God Almighty constantly, and they
Will pray for you with diligence both night and day;

et quod das illis, pariet tibi gaudia lucis.
Inter summates nolo plus muneris ut des."   215
gratis an oblitus reticeret is officiales,
hi bene donantur secretim sive beantur.
Hoc super edictum non ausus est dare cuiquam
grande vel exiguum nec desiderat quis eorum.
Reges inter se quando dixere "valete"   220
oscula dando sibi, placet his patriando reverti.
Cumque domum redeunt iuris propriique fiebant,

Ruodlieb dilectae matris cernens inopine
ad sese missum quendam bene suscipit illum.
Ad quem sic dixit "Mea mater sospes, ai, sit."   225
Respondit "Vivit valet et bene vel tibi misit
istas litterulas, melius quibus ac mihi credas,"
susceptaque dice sciolum facit hanc recitare.
Quam super ut legit, ait "Arbitror, haec brevis inquit
'ergo tui domini cuncti tibi valde benigni,   230
ut redeas, petimus; nam te caruisse dolemus
temporibus tantis, propter quos exiliaris
et faidas in te non cessabas cumulare,
donec e patria fugiens petis extera regna,
scimus ubi multos te sustinuisse labores.   235
Quod lamentamur nos, quandocumque gregamur
ad placitum vel ad inducias quacunque statutas;
tunc in consilio dando par est tibi nemo,
qui vel tam iuste ius dicat tam vel honeste
et qui sic viduas defendat sive pupillos,   240
propter avariciam cum damnabantur iniquam,
qui lamentantur nimium cum quando premuntur.
Ergo tui cuncti cum sunt hostes nihilati,
partim defuncti partim membris mutilati,
illorum nulli tibi quod plus sunt nocituri,   245
kare, redi citius, quia quo venias inhiamus,
inprimis ut nos bene tecum pacificemus
praestita dando tibi, saepissime quae meruisti
non parcens propriae pro nobis utique vitae.
Ast in fine brevis huius stat epistola matris: 250
Mi fili care, miserae matris memorare,
quam, sicut nosti, discedens deseruisti
inconsolatam, bina [causa] viduatam,
in genitore tuo, simul in te, nate, secundo.
Dum mecum fueras, mala cuncta mihi relevabas,   255
cum discessisti, gemitus mihi multiplicasti.
Sed tamen utcumque decernebam tolerare,
secure miseram dum posses ducere vitam

What you give them will win the joys of light for you.
I want you giving no more gifts among the nobles."   215
The servants he forgot (perhaps intentionally):
These were presented gifts in secret, and well treated.
He did not dare give anyone, against this edict,
A present great or small; and none desired this.
When they had kissed and said farewell to one another, 220
It pleased both kings to go back, each to his own land.
When they reached home, where they were under their own
    laws,
There Ruodlieb, surprised to see a messenger
From his dear mother, cordially received him and
Thus spoke to him: "Please tell me, is my mother well?" 225
He answered him, "She lives, is very well, and sent
To you this note which you should trust far more than me."
He took the letter, which he had a scholar read,
Who, when he read it over, said, "I think it says
'Now we, your lords, all very fond of you, beseech   230
You to return; we grieve that we so long have been
Without you, and because of us you went in exile
And never ceased to heap up feuds against yourself,
Until you fled your homeland seeking foreign realms,
And there we know that you have suffered many hardships. 235
This we lament whenever we assemble at
The court or at negotiations anywhere;
For no one is your equal in advising then,
Or makes decrees so justly or as honorably,
Or so protects the widows and the orphans, who,   240
Whenever they are harmed because of unjust greed
Or when they are oppressed, lament excessively.
Therefore, since all your enemies have been destroyed—
A few of them are dead, and some have lost their limbs—
And none of them will cause you any further harm,   245
Return at once, friend, since we long for you to come,
Above all to be fairly reconciled with you
By giving you rewards which you so often earned,
Not even sparing your own life on our behalf.'
But at the end there is a message from your mother: 250
'My darling son, remember your unhappy mother
Whom, as you know, when you departed you deserted
Both unconsoled and widowed by a double cause,
Once by your father, the second time by you, my son.
As long as you were with me, you eased all my woes;   255
When you departed, though, you multiplied my sighs.
However, I decided I could bear it somehow,
Provided you could live your wretched life safe from

prae tot tam validis tibi tam diris inimicis.
Qui quia sunt cuncti mutilati sive perempti, 260
fili kare, redi, luctus finem dato matri
adventuque tuo consanguineos hylarato
non solumque tuos sed omnes compatriotas.'"
Omnibus auditis miles nimis exhilaratur,
pro sola matre lacrimis perfunditur ore. 265
Id resciscente populi rumore sodale,
ultra credibile nimium fit mentis acerbae,
illeque non solum quin quod fuit apparitorum,
stant ubi vel resident simul, intime condoluerunt;
dicunt, quod nunquam vidissent huic similem quem 270
moris honestate fidei vel in integritate
quod nec obest ulli sed, ubi quit, profuit omni.
At qui servimen eius novere diurnum,
dicunt "Quid mirum, sibi si nunc est onerosum,
nil deservisse ni pauper vivere posse, 275
victum vel vestem, nullum plus emolumentum,
huius cum regni columen speciale sit omnis."
Qui sibi dilectum secum sumendo sodalem
ad regem graditur, prae quo sic fando precatur
"Si, rex, auderem tibi vel fore non grave scirem, 280
quod nimis angit me, tibi vellem notificare."
Rex ait "Eloquere, clemente potiris ad id me."
Ille pedes regis amplectitur oscula dans his
postque resurgendo vix protulit ista gemendo
"Quid mihi causae sit, melius rex ipse videbit." 285
Sic ait inque manus dat litterulas sibi missas.
Rex ait his lectis "Nunc compatior satis istis.

Quae tibi promittunt domini, si sic ea solvunt,
consilior videas, venias quin, neve relinquas.
Atque tuae matris nimis est legatio suavis; 290
hinc omnino tibi modo nolo reconsiliari,
quin vadas ad eam vel consoleris eandem
contribulesque tuos visendi te sat avaros.
Quando velis ito, nobiscum sed tamen esto
istius ebdomadae spacium; noli prius ire 295
quam pertractemus, quid mercedis tibi demus.
Nobis servisti quam devotissime scisti;
non oblivisci decet id nos sed reminisci,
et tibi prodesse, te saepe neci tribuisse
pro me pro populo pro cuncto denique regno." 300
Exul at inclinat regem meminisseque gaudet
eius servicii paucis respondit et illi
"Quod tibi servivi, mihi quam bene retribuisti.

So many enemies who were so strong and fearsome.
Because they all have now been maimed or killed, return, 260
Dear son, and bring your mother's grieving to an end.
By your arrival gladden all your relatives,
Not only yours but all your countrymen as well.'"
When he heard all these things, the knight was very pleased.
His face was wet with tears shed for his lonely mother. 265
And when his comrade learned of this from people talking,
His mind became extremely sad beyond belief.
Indeed, not only he but also all the squires
Expressed intense grief when they sat or stood together.
They say that they have never seen a man like him 270
In purity of faith or in integrity:
And that he harmed no one but helped each person when
He could; and those who knew his daily service say
"What wonder if it now is burdensome to him
To have gained nothing but to live in poverty, 275
To get his food and clothes but no more pay than that,
Although he is the special mainstay of all this realm."
But that man, taking his beloved friend with him,
Approached the king, and pled before him, speaking thus:
"King, if I dared and knew you would not be offended, 280
I would like to inform you what disturbs me deeply."
The king said, "Speak, you have me well disposed for this."
The man embraced his sovereign's feet and gave them kisses;
Then he arose and, sighing, barely spoke these words:
"The king himself will better see my situation." 285
He spoke and put the letter that was sent to him
Into his hands. When it was read, the king replied
"Now I am very sympathetic in this matter.
If your lords will pay these things which they promise you,
I counsel you to see them, nor delay in going.
The message from your mother is extremely pleasing, 290
So I do not at all wish to dissuade you now
From going to her or from consoling her and your
Relations who are very eager to see you.
Go when you wish, but nonetheless remain with us
The space of seven days, and do not leave before 295
We think about what payment we should give to you.
You served us as devotedly as you knew how.
And we should not forget this, but remember it,
And should reward you for so often risking death
For me, our people, truly our entire kingdom." 300
The exile bowed, rejoicing that the king recalled
His service, and he answered him with these few words:
"How well you have rewarded me for serving you!

Huc postquam veni, pie rex, tibi meque subegi,
Pascha fuit tecum mihi semper cottidianum, 305
semper habens multum vel honorum sive bonorum
a te non solum sed ab unoquoque tuorum."
Rex iubet, interea fiant argentea vasa,
ut grandes lances per circuitum cubitales,
non nisi bis bina duo plana tot atque profunda, 310
quando coaptentur, ceu panes sint videantur,
extra speltina si sint perfusa farina.
Quorum vasorum rex unum denariorum
replet, bizantes quos dicunt aurificantes,
et sic coniunctim, suppingere quod nequit unum 315
plus cum martello, ne clangant forte movendo.
Quando domum veniat, res inde suas meli[oret
atque suos dominos faciat sibi dando benignos,
ut sibi promissa dent praestita mente benigna.
Altera dividitur lanx in duo sicque repletur. 320
Ex una parte lancis nummos posuere
ex auro factos et in igne sat examinatos,
a pole Bizanto quibus agnomen tribuere,
est quibus insculpta graece circum titulata
istac maiestas illac regisque potestas, 325
inponendo manum stans quem signat bened[ictum,

quos det dilectis consanguineis et amicis
ad congaudendum, mos est velut, hunc fore sa[lvum
exilioque gravi non illum degenerasse
sed profecisse vel honore domum rediisse. 330
Citra mazeriam lancis nummis ita fartam
bis sex armillas imponit rex operosas,
ex quibus octonae solidae non sunt recavatae
plumbo repletae, ceu serpentes capitatae,

oscula quae sibi dant sic se nec amando noce[bant, 335
quarum quaeque meri grave pondus gesserat au[ri;
bis geminae reliquae gyrando fuere recur[vae
quaeque librans marcam velut epaticam sper[ulatam;
non in iis decori plus quam studet utilita[ti.
Et super additur his reginae fibula grandis, 340
in limo fusa, non malleolis fabricata
fabrili nullo compactave machinamento,
per totum solida non omninoque dolata,
in medio cuius aquilae stat imago volantis
eius et in rostro pila stat christallina su[mmo, 345
in qua motari visuntur tres volucelli,
essent ceu vivi, gestire volare[que prompti.

Since I came here, good king, and pledged myself to you,
Each day with you has always been for me an Easter;   305
For always I had many honors and good things,
Not just from you, but also from each of your people."
The king meanwhile commanded silver vessels made:
A cubit in circumference, in the shape of dishes,
Exactly four of them, two flat, two deep, so that   310
When joined together they would look like loaves of bread,
If they were sprinkled on the outside with spelt flour.
The king had one of these containers filled with coins,
The kind that goldsmiths call besants, so tightly packed
That with a hammer he could not force one more in: 315
He did this so they would not move around and rattle.
When he went home, he could improve his lot with these,
And win his lords' good will by generosity,
So they would graciously give him their promised gifts.
The other dish is split in two and filled as follows.   320
In one part of the dish they placed coins that were made
Of gold and had been tested thoroughly in fire:
Their name comes from the city of Byzantium.
One side had Christ in Majesty, surrounded by
A Greek inscription; the other had an image of   325
The power of the king; this figure stood and placed
Her hand upon the king to show that he was blessed.
He was to give these to dear relatives and friends,
As was the custom, to make them rejoice that he
Was safe and had not been made poor by his harsh exile,
But had succeeded and had come back home in honor.   330
The king placed in the bowl whose other half was crammed
So tight with coins twelve artfully made bracelets, eight
Of which were solid—neither hollowed out nor filled
With lead; their ends were shaped like serpents' heads that
    gave
Each other kisses but in loving caused no harm.   335
Each of them bore the heavy weight of solid gold.
The other four were twisted and were shaped like circles,
Just like hepatic veins, and each one weighed a mark.
In these he strived for beauty more than usefulness.
To these is added then a large brooch for a queen;   340
It had been cast in clay, not beaten out by mallets,
Nor had it been constructed with some craftsman's tool.
It was completely solid and had not been hammered.
The center has the image of a flying eagle,
And in its beak there is a crystal ball, in which   345
Three little balls were moving, so it seemed, as if
They were alive and ready to exult in flight.

Aureu]s hanc aqu[ilam] per girum circulus ambit,
quae t]am lata fuit, sibi pectus quod bene texit.
Lata fuit] merito sic, auri fusa talento. 350
Dat fibula]s alias in pensando leviores
quavis] et in quarum gemmarum multigenarum
fulgor] erat v[ar]ius, velut inspiceres ibi sydus,
quarum] quaeque librae quadrantem ponderat aequae.
Non gran]di boga gracili pendendo catena 355
addidit] his modicam, quam praetendendo diatim
interul]am cum qua configat, ne stet aperta
pectora] ne possint cerni maiuscula si sint.
Ex aur]o lunam solidam super addidit unam
pensan]tem libram, faber in qua protulit artem. 360
In cur]vatura sunt inque recircuitura
imposi]ti lapides generosi cuncticolores,
inventi] cocleis in maio mense marinis
rerum co]nmixtis auro de more reclusis.
Sunt in p]lanicie graciles sperulae variatae; 365

conser]itur vitro vitrum, discernitur auro,
compo]nens nodos vel folia vel volucellos.
Ignibus h]irsuta primo fiunt, tuberosa
cum sput]o vel aqua poliuntur cote scabrosa.
Id ge]nus electrum fabrile vocatur honestum. 370
Ast in sple]ndente post gemmas margine lunae
dant b]ullae dulcem se conlidendo fragorem.
Hanc lun]am lanci caute rex praecipit addi,
qui post] octonas in lancem ponit inaures.
quatt]uor ex illis comptae fulsere lapillis 375

et gemmis] variis ametistis atque berillis;
quatt]uor ast aliae non sunt gemmis redimitae,
nexus] delecti miris nodis variati,
sicut pincillo quis vitrum pingeret au[ro;
bullae cum bacis clangunt, cum se movet auri[s. 380
Tandem ter denos fabricare iubet digit[ales
ex auro puro, reperitur non melius quo.
In quorum quemque iubet includendo locare
ligurium vel iacinctum pulchrumve berillum,
quorum tres sponsae dandi sunt accipiendae, 385
non grandes, graciles, quos ferre decet m[ulieres.
Lancibus impletis his donis imperiosis
atque coaptatis clavis firme capitatis,
has iubet obduci rex glutine valde tena[ci,
polline commixto multo tribulamine [trito, 390
ut non abradi nec aqua queat hoc aboleri.

This eagle was encircled by a golden ring;
The brooch was so wide that it hid the wearer's breast:
With reason—it was cast from one whole golden talent.   350
He added other brooches that were less in weight—
On each there was the gleam of many kinds of jewels;
It was as if you saw a constellation there.
Each of these brooches weighed a quarter of a pound.
They hung from slender chains attached by tiny clasps.   355
He gave a graceful pin to use in front each day
With which to fasten shirts so they would not fall open,
To keep one's chest, if it were large, from being seen.
He gave him too a solid lune of gold which weighed
A pound, on which a goldsmith had displayed his skill.   360
On both the inside and the outside curvatures
Were set stones, precious and of many different colors,
Stones that are found in seashells in the month of May,
While gold was mixed among the stones, as was the custom,
And graceful spheres of different kinds were on the
    surface.   365
Since glass is joined to glass but is repelled by gold;
In this way it forms knots and leaves and little birds.
In fire first they are made rough; when full of bumps,
They then are rubbed, with spit and water, on a whetstone.
This noble product is what people call enamel.   370
Behind the gem, upon the lune's bright rim, the bangles,
Colliding with each other, made a pleasing noise.
The king commanded this lune added to the dish
With care; and then he placed eight earrings in the dish;
Of these, four, since they were adorned with precious
    gems   375
Of several kinds, like amethyst and beryl, glittered.
The other four were not inlaid with gems; and yet
These four had fancy lines entwining lovely knots,
Just as if with a brush one layered gold on glass.
The pearls and bangles jingled when the ear would move.   380
At last the king commanded thirty rings be made
Out of pure gold than which no better could be found,
In each of which he ordered them to mount and set
A ligure and a jacinth and a lovely beryl.
Of these, three were for giving to his bride-to-be,   385
Not large, but delicate, as women ought to wear.
And when the plates were filled with these imperial gifts
And were securely joined by nails with heads, the king
Then had them covered with a strong adhesive which
Had been combined with finely ground wheat flour, so   390
The flour could not be scraped off or washed away.

Quando dies venit, ad quam rex induci[avit,
quod deberet ei pie respondere clienti,
dixit principibus "Noster miles peregrinus
vult remeare domum carta revocatus h[erorum,   395
pro quorum causa patria caret, ut patet, ipsa.
En hic est carta; nunc vos audite, quid illa
dicat." Sic inquit et eam sciolus recitavit.
Carta perlecta fiunt ibi tristia corda,
compare tam fido tam miti tamque ben[igno,   400
tali tyrone regem seseque carere.
Et regi suadent, hunc vi prece seu reti[neret,
uxorem sibi det et honoribus hunc locupl[etet,
dicentes dignum comitatu quovis eund[em.
Rex ait "Absit, ut is de me tribuletur [sodalis,   405
a quo sum numquam minimam commotus in [iram,
quin irascentem me mitem redit ut ag[num,
totius fidei plenum se praebet in omni.
Nam sic e]xilii gravis est sibi sarcina longi,
qualiter i]n quoquam non hoc sentire valebam.   410
Nunc di]mittamus et eum patriare sinamus.
Has habeat gra]tes, si post sua sic veniat res,
quod non esse do]mi queat, huc bene posse reverti,
inveniat v]eteres ut apud nos commoditates."
Sic ait et p]uerum iubet, ad se quo vocet illum.   415
Is curren]s vocat hunc; ad regem venit is illuc.
Dum modicum] siluit, clementer rex sibi dixit
"Te nimis in]vite, mi kare, reliquero de me;
semper prom]ptus eras et in omni morigerebas;
hinc hab]eo grates tibi, dilectissime, grandes.   420
Invidus] es nulli sed plebi karus es omni.
Nunc mih]i dic verum, karissime cunctigenorum,
praemia dem t]ibi peccunia malisne sophia."
Is reputa]ns mente, sibi quid respondeat apte
"Non cupi]o, quod" ait "conponderat usus honori.   425
Census hab]et multos, ubi noscitur, insidiantes.
Pauperies mis]eros cogit plures fore fures;
in consanguineo]s parit invidiam vel amicos,
vel fratrem] stimulat, fidei quo foedera rumpat.
Est meliu]s, censu careat quis quam quoque sensu,   430
et quicum]que pia satagit florere sophia,
ille vel arge]nti semper sat habebit et auri,
quae vult] expugnat, quia telis intus abundat.
At memini] multos vidisse creberrime stultos,
qui opibus cunct]is per stulticiam nichilatis   435

vivebant in]opes, vitiose degenerantes,

When that day came on which the king had stipulated
That piously he would reply to his retainer,
He told his nobles: "Called home by a letter from
His lords, our foreign knight desires to return.   395
Because of them, it seems, he does without his homeland.
Behold, here is the letter. Listen now to what
It says!" He spoke, and then a scholar read it out.
When it was read to them, all hearts were saddened there,
Because the king and they were going to lose a friend   400
So loyal, gentle, kind, and such a warrior.
They urged the king to keep him there by prayer or force,
To give a wife to him, enriching him with honors,
And said that he was worthy to be made a count.
The king said: "Far be it from me to vex my friend,   405
By whom I never have been moved the least to wrath,
But who made me, when angered, gentle as a lamb,
And showed himself in everything completely loyal.
So grievous to him is his burden of long exile,
I never could observe its like in any man.   410
Now we must give him leave to go back to his homeland,
And thank him thus: if afterward it happens that
He cannot stay at home, he surely can return
To find his old advantages among us here."
He spoke, and then he told a page to summon him.   415
He ran and called him; that man came there to the king.
A moment's silence, then the king said graciously,
"Dear friend, I let you go, but most unwillingly;
For you were always ready at my every bidding.
For this I am extremely grateful, my beloved.   420
Nobody hates you; you are dear to all my people.
Now tell me truly, most beloved of all men,
Do you prefer rewards of money or of wisdom?"
He pondered then what he might properly reply.
"I do not wish," he said, "what custom ranks with honor;   425
For wealth, when it is known, has many ambushers,
While poverty turns many wretches into thieves.
It fosters hatred in both friends and relatives
And makes a brother break the bonds of loyalty;
But it is better to lack wealth than lack good sense.   430
Whoever is content to thrive in holy wisdom,
That man will always have enough of gold and silver;
He gains his wish since he is rich in inner weapons.
But I remember often seeing many fools
Who, after they had squandered all their wealth through
    folly,   435
Were living then in need and shameful degradation—

quos non iuvis]se sed opes patuit nocuisse.
Unde potes facile me verbum tale docere,

quod si servabo, quod id ipsum non temerabo,
tam karum quod erit, ceu pondo decem mihi quis det. 440
Nemo mihi rapit id inimicaturve nec odit
propter id et latro me non occidet in arto.
In camera regis census decet ut sit opimus,
pauper homo sat habet, si vi valet arteque pollet.
Non volo peccuniam, sitio gustare sophiam." 445
Hoc rex audito "Mecum" surgens ait "ito",
in penetralque pedant nullum secumque sinebant.
Rex residens, pro se tunc exule stante cliente,
dixerat in primis "Nunc audi cordis ab imis,
quae tibi praedico ceu verus amicus amico! 450
Non tibi sit rufus umquam specialis amicus!
Si fit is iratus, non est fidei memoratus;
nam vehemens dira sibi stat durabilis ira.
Tam bonus haut fuerit, aliqua fraus quin in eo sit,
quam vitare nequis, quin ex hac commaculeris; 455
nam tangendo picem vix expurgaris ad unguem.
Quamvis caenosa per villam sit via trita,
numquam devites callem, quo per sata pergas,
ne male tracteris careasque tuis ibi frenis
correptus per quem responsum dando superbum. 460
Quo videas, iuvenem quod habet senior mulierem,
hospicium tribui tibi non poscas iteranti;
in te nam magnam facis insons suspicionem.
Hic timet, haec sperat, fors inter eos ita versat.
Ast ubi vir viduam iuvenis teneat veteranam, 465
hospitium posce; non hic timet haec nec amat te,
tu[nc] ibi secure dormis sine suspicione.
Poscit ad occandum si te concivis agellum,
ut praestetur equa generandi tempore feta,
noli praestare, ni vis hanc degenerare; 470
nam perdet pullum, si planificabit agellum.
Non tibi tam karus sit contribulis tuus ullus,
quatinus hunc saepe soleas visendo gravare,
plusque solet rarum quam continuum fore karum,
nam cito vilescit homini quodcumque frequens fit. 475
Ancillam propriam quamvis nimium speciosam
non velut uxorem facias tibi consocialem,
ne contemnat te tibi respondendo superbe,
neve reatur, se domui debere praeesse,
si pernoctabit ad mensam sive sedebit. 480
Tecum manducans pernox tecumve repausans

And it was clear that wealth had hurt, not helped, those
   men.
And therefore you can easily give me advice,
Providing that I not reject but follow it,
As valuable as if someone gave me ten pounds.   440
No one will steal it from me, hate me or become
My foe for it; no thief will kill me in some alley.
Great wealth is fitting in the chamber of a king.
A poor man has enough if he has strength and skill.
I have no wish for money, but I thirst for wisdom."   445
When he heard this, the king rose, saying "Come with me."
They went all by themselves into his inner chamber.
The king sat down (the exile stood in front of him)
And first said, "Listen from the bottom of your heart
To what I will advise you as true friend to friend.   450
First, never let a redhead be your special friend.
If he is angered, he forgets his loyalty;
Indeed, his wrath is vicious, dreadful and long-lasting.
Nor will he be so good that he is lacking in
Deceit, by which you cannot keep from being soiled: 455
If you touch pitch, your fingernails will not get clean.
Although the traveled village road is full of mud,
Do not avoid the path and walk through planted fields,
Or you will be attacked and also lose your reins,
Rebuked by someone when you give a haughty answer.   460
When you see that an old man has a youthful wife,
Do not seek lodging there when you are traveling:
You bring suspicion on yourself, though innocent.
He fears, she hopes; for thus their fortune turns for them.
But where a young man has an older widow as   465
His wife, seek lodging: he fears not, she wants you not.
There you will sleep without suspicion, safe and sound.
And should a fellow-citizen request, to harrow
His little field, that he be lent a mare about
To foal, refuse unless you wish her to be ruined,   470
For she will lose the foal while leveling the field.
None of your kinsmen should become so dear to you
That you oppress him by your frequent visiting:
The rare is much more pleasing than the commonplace.
A man will quickly tire of that which happens often.   475
Though she is quite attractive, never treat your maid
As if she were your social equal or your wife,
So she will not despise you or give haughty answers,
Or even think she should be mistress of the house
Because she spends the night or sits there at your table;480
For if she eats with you and sleeps with you all night,

continuo domina cunctorum vult fore summa.
Talia famosum faciunt ignominiosum.
Si libet uxorem traducere nobiliorem
causa karorum generandorum liberorum, 485
tunc cognoscibilem conquire tibi mulierem
et nusquam, mater tibi ni quo consilietur!
Quam dum quaesieris, decet omnimodis ut honores,
tractes clementer; illi tamen esto magister,
litigium cum te ne quod praesumat habere; 490
nam vitium nullum maius valet esse virorum,
quam si subiecti sint, quis debent dominari.

Et licet in cunctis bene concordet tibi rebus,
numquam velle tuum debes sibi pandere totum,
a te correpta si post pro re vitiosa 495
improperare velit, ut nil tibi dicere possit,
unde pudor vel amor inter vos quid minuatur.
Nulla repentina tibi tam gravis ingruat ira,
quin pernoctare vindictam perpetiare,
maxime cum dubia res est, non ut tibi dicta, 500
forsan cras gaudes, animi quod frena tenebas.
Nunquam cum domino tibi lis sit sive magistro;
namque potestate, si non iuste superant te.
Nec quid eis praestes, veraciter id quia perdes.
Cum rogat, ut praestes, est tunc melius, sibi quo des, 505
inveniet culpam quia, tantundem tibi per quam
tollat; utrumque perit nec grates nec bona reddet.
'Grates' dicet 'habe,' cum despoliaberis a se,
tunc inclinabis dominum laudans, quod abibis
sanus cum vita, nihili pensans tua damna. 510
Et numquam sit iter quoquam tibi tam properanter,
ut praetermittas, quin, ecclesias ubi cernas,
sanctis committas illis te vel benedicas.
Sicubi pulsetur aut si quo missa canatur,
descendas ab equo currens velocius illo, 515
kattholicae paci quo possis participari.
Hoc iter haut longat, penitus tibi quin breviabit
tutius et vadis hostem minus atque timebis.
Abnuito numquam, si te cogens homo quisquam
oret amore pii ieiunia frangere Christi, 520
non ea nam frangis sua sed mandata replebis.
Si tibi sint segetes prope plateas generales,
non facias fossas, progressus ulteriores
in sata ne fiant; nam fossas circueundo
strata fit utrimque per siccum gente meante; 525

Then she will wish at once to be the highest mistress.
Such things will make a man notorious and disgraced;
And if it pleases you to wed a noble wife,
In order to engender darling children, then 485
Choose for yourself a woman of good reputation,
But not unless your mother so advises you.
When you have found her, you should honor her all ways
And treat her kindly; be her master, though, so that
She will not dare to have an argument with you, 490
Because there can exist no worse disgrace for men
Than when they are controlled by those whom they should rule.
And if she should agree with you in everything,
Still you should not disclose to her all your intentions,
So that if she, rebuked by you for some misdeed, 495
Might want to chide you, she cannot say anything
By which respect or love between you might be lessened.
No sudden wrath should be so strong that you cannot
Put off your vengeance overnight, especially
A doubtful case, not as it's told to you; perhaps 500
You will rejoice tomorrow that you reined your temper.
And never have a disagreement with your lord
Or master: they will win by force if not by law.
Don't lend them anything; you'll surely lose it; when
One asks, then better that you lend, since he will find 505
Some fault for which to take again as much; then double
Is gone: he will not give your goods back or his thanks.
He will say 'thank you' when you have been robbed by him.
Then you will bow and thank the Lord that you got off
Alive and safe, and place no value on your losses. 510
And never be in such a hurry when you travel
That you pass by where you see churches, and neglect
To pray to saints there and commit yourself to them.
Where bells are being rung or mass is being sung,
Dismount and then run very quickly to that place 515
So you are able to join in the Catholic peace.
Your trip will not take longer, but in fact be shortened;
For you will go more safely, fear your foes much less.
Do not refuse if someone urges you and begs
You for the love of holy Christ to break the fast: 520
You will not break it but be keeping his commandments.
If you have fields near public roads, do not dig ditches.
In this way you will keep more paths from being made
Upon your lands, since people going round the ditches
Will make roads on both sides by walking on dry land. 525

si non fodisses, damnum minus hinc habuisses."
Dum rex conticuit sapientia verbaque finit,
ambo prodibant rex inque throno residebat
et laudat cunctis virtutem militis eius
(econtra murmur laudantum multiplicatur), 530
qui grates regi populo referebat et omni.
Rex ait "Ito domum cunctorum plenus honorum
atque vide matrem totamque tuam pariter rem,
si potes in patria tamen esse tua velut ista,
solvere sique velint domini quae polliciti sunt. 535

Qui si fallant te, decet, ut fallantur et a te,
nec famuleris eis totiens delusus ab illis;
nulli servito parco nimis aut inhonesto.
Si tibi contingat, animus tuus unde vacillet,
taedeat ut patriae propriae te, si repetis me, 540
eiusdem velle contra te repperies me,
quo nunc te linquo; dubium non huius habeto."
Post nuerat digito prae se stanti paranimpho
et sibi secretim de more susurrat in aurem,
illuc ut peras camerarius afferat illas, 545
in quibus hi panes fuerant intus locupletes,
polline perfusi foris, intus pecuniosi.
Allatis peris rex inquit "Mi bone sodes,

hos geminos panes numquam, karissime, frangas,
primitus ad matrem venias quam tam tibi karam, 550
cuius in aspectu solius frange minorem;
cum sedeas nuptum cum sponsa, frange secundum.
Hinc et dilectis quantum vis detur amicis,
ut sapiant, qualis noster soleat fore panis."
Atque valedicens rex, oscula ter sibi figens 555

cum gemitu liquit. Miles lacrimando recessit.
Quem sequitur cunctus ad equum populus gemebundus,
cumque valedicunt, sibi flentes oscula figunt.
Inde recedente solo comitante sodali,
scutifer, enthecam qui vexit eo modicel[lam, 560
traxit sagmarium variis opibus oneratum.
Inter dilectos fit magna querela sodales,
tam breve tunc tempus quod ovarent alterut[rius;
nam non ni triduo simul ibant sermocin[ando.
Ad noctem mediam prolongant sumere cen[am. 565
Post mensam demptis ambobus calciamen[tis,
postquam dormitum decernunt visere lect[um,
aversi flebant taciti, lacrimando ge[mebant.

Had you not dug them, then you would have had less damage."
The king, when he completed his wise words, fell silent.
Both men came forth. The king sat down upon his throne
And praised the virtue of his knight to everyone.
In turn, the murmurs of those praising him increased.   530
And he expressed thanks to the king and all his people.
The king replied, "Go to your home, full of all honors,
And there see both your mother and all your possessions,
If you can live in your land just as you do here
And if your lords will wish to pay what they have
      promised.   535
If they deceive you, they should be deceived by you,
Nor should you serve them—you so often fooled by them.
Serve no one who is very stingy or dishonest.
If it should happen that you change your mind and grow
Disgusted with your land, if you return to me   540
Then you will find me just as well disposed toward you
As now when I dismiss you. Have no doubt of this."
He motioned with his finger to a page who stood
Nearby and whispered secretly into his ear,
As was his custom, that the chamberlain should bring   545
The sacks within which were the opulent bread loaves—
The outside flour-dusted, the inside full of money.
And when these sacks were brought, the king said, "My good
      friend,
Do not break open these two loaves, my dearest man,
Until you reach your mother, whom you love so dearly.   550
Then in her sight alone you break the smaller loaf;
When you sit at your wedding with your bride, then break
The next. Give all you wish to your beloved friends
From it, that they may taste how our bread tends to be."
The king then said farewell and kissed the man three
      times,   555
Dismissed him, sighing. Then the knight, in tears, departed;
And all the people sadly saw him to his horse.
They wept and gave him kisses when they said farewell.
He left, and was escorted only by his friend.
The squire, who had brought a tiny knapsack there,   560
Now led a pack horse loaded with assorted treasures.
A great complaint was made by the beloved friends
Because so brief a time remained for sharing pleasure.
At least three days they rode and talked together, and
Prolonged the eating of their dinner until midnight.   565
Once they had eaten, both of them removed their shoes,
And after they resolved to go to bed to sleep,
They silently turned back to back and, weeping, sighed.

Ut puer ille magis flet se quatiendo soda[lis,
a sibi tam fido quod disiungendus amic[o; 570
nescit, an hunc umquam fuerit visurus in [aevum;
pervigil insomnem vellet flens ducere noct[em,
ni cito quod somnus cor maerens opprimit eius.
Cumque diescebat, ambo simul evigilab[ant
surgunt, induerant se, prandent et fa[lerabant 575

insimul et pergunt, donec confinia cern[unt
alterius regni, qua sunt postremo dire[mpti;
exul et, ut potuit prae fletu, vix sibi dix[it
"Kare, meo domino de vero corde ve s[ancto
dic, precor, oramen vel devotum famula[men 580
omnibus atque suis mihi ceu cor semper am[andis."
Basia dum sibi dant, ambo nimis inti[me flebant
alterutrimque "vale" dicebatur sat abun[de,
discedunt a se sic in sua maestus u[terque.
Utque suae patriae iam coepit repropi[are, 585
rufus eum vidit ac currens se sibi i[ungit;
quando salutavit, hunc un[de m]eet r[ogitavit
ireve quo vellet, [c]omes [eius si] fore [posset.
Sat dedignanter respondit ei sapienter
"Est via] communis, quo vultis pergere quitis." 590
Rufus] parabolas incepit dicere multas,
quamquam res]ponsum de milite non capit ullum.
Increscen]te die cum ferre suam nequit in se,
ad sellam po]st se cappam solet ille ligare.
Rufus ut a]cquirat hanc, tota mente volutat. 595
Pergeban]t, veniunt ad aquam vel equos adaquabant;
mulcendo] tergum ceu detergendo caballum
ad se cor]rigiam furtim rapit indeque cappam,
hancque s]ub ascella tenet, usque recessit ab unda.

Tunc salien]s ab equo citat hanc intrudere sacco, 600
cum remor]aretur post hunc velut experiatur,
ungula quaeque] pedum clavos an haberet eorum.
Tunc ad se c]urrit et adulando sibi dixit
"Antea no]nne, bone, mihi cernebaris habere
in sella ca]ppam? Miror quod non video quam." 605
Cui miles] dixit "Est mirum me sed ubi sit."
Rufus ait "Sub aqua quid nescio diffluitabat;
sic ub]i potamus, ibi forsan perdideramus.
Ergo rev]ertamur, hanc si reperire queamus."
"Absit" m]iles ait simulans, sibi ceu nihili sit. 610
Vespere tunc] villae coeperunt appropiare,
per quam pl]atea vadit sat lata, lutosa.

Just like a child, his friend wept more, in agony
Because he must be wrenched from one so true a friend,   570
Not knowing if he ever would see him again.
He would have wished to spend a sleepless night in weeping,
Had sleep not quickly come upon his aching heart.
And when the morning came, both men awoke together.
They rose, then dressed, ate breakfast, saddled up their
    steeds   575
And then rode on until they saw the borders of
The other kingdom, where at last they separated.
The exile said to him (as best he could while sobbing),
"Friend, from my true and virtuous heart please tell my lord
And all his people, who are always dear to me   580
As my own heart, of my prayer and devoted service."
They gave each other kisses; both were sobbing deeply,
And said farewell repeatedly to one another.
And thus in sadness each departed for his home.
And just as he was drawing near his land again,   585
A redhead, seeing him, ran up and joined the man.
When he had greeted him, he asked from where he came,
Where he was going; if he could be his companion.
The man responded very scornfully and wisely,
"This is a public road; you can go where you wish."   590
The redhead tried beginning many conversations,
Although receiving no reply back from the knight.
Unable, as the day wore on, to wear his cloak,
He often tied it to the back part of his saddle.
The redhead thought intently how to steal the cloak.   595
At length they reached a stream and let their horses drink;
And while he stroked the horse's back, as if to wipe
It off, the redhead secretly removed the strap
And from it took the cloak, which he concealed beneath
His arm-pit, while he was returning from the stream.
Dismounting, he then rushed to stuff it in his sack,   600
While lingering behind the man as if to see
If each hoof of his horse's feet still had its nails.
Then he ran up to him and, fawning, said to him,
"Upon your saddle, sir, was there not earlier
A cloak? I marvel that I do not see it now."   605
The knight replied to him, "I wonder where it is."
The redhead answered, "Something did float off down stream.
Perhaps we lost it at the place where we were drinking.
Therefore, let us return and try to find that cloak."
"No," said the knight, pretending that he did not care. 610
Then in the evening they began to near a village,
Through which there ran a rather wide but muddy road;

Haut in e]quo quivis valet his exire lacunis
nec tran]sire via prope saepes tam lutulenta
quisque pe]dans posset ni pons artissimus esset,   615
quem sa]t temptando saepemque manu retinendo
vix devi]taret in caenum ne cecidisset
trames] at [est ar]tus e campo per sata tritus
qui dat iter]; callem rufus suadebat eundem,
dicens il]luvie caeni non posse meare,   620
nosse viam n]ullam tam caenosam vel aquosam.

Nobody on a horse could get out of these puddles;
Nor could a man on foot have crossed the muddy way
Next to the fence had there not been a narrow boardwalk; 615
But even if he held the fence and used the boardwalk,
A man would scarcely keep from falling in the mud.
There was a narrow path worn from the ground through fields.
The redhead urged them now to take this easy route
Because, he said, he could not ride through this morass, 620
And knew no other road so muddy or so wet.

VI.

"Posthac cum peccas, noceas cui, non ma[ledicas,
est quia valde grave duplex damnum tol[erare,
perdere quemque suum super hocque pati maledict[um."
E regione minas rufus satis egit inanes,
non pernoctari dicens quam sint mutilati   5
insculus n . .mos, quia vult incendere c[unctos.
Miles subrisit, sibi quid peius fore nam scit.

Ad villam propiant, ubi pernoctare volebant.
Sol petit oceanum monet hospitiumque pete[ndum;
rufus pastorem vocat unum conveniend[um,   10
illuc qui venit, quem rufus mox rogitavit
"Dic vicinorum mihi nomina praecipuorum;
est hic quis dives, nostri fore qui queat h[ospes?"
Pastor ait "Multi sunt hic, quos non stupefir[i
sat scio, si centum scutis comes appetat [unum,   15

quin his servire possint omni sub honor[e.
Esset homo pauper, nequeat qui sufficient[er
vobis servire vestros et equos stabulare.
Multi sint soliti licet hospitibus famu[lari,
inter eos omnes non suscipit advenientes   20
tam bene ceu iuvenis vel uti vetus u[xor illius."
Rufus ait "Viduam quid habet iuvenis veter[anam?
Vir vetus uxorem deberet habere vetern[am."
Pastor ait "Nusquam melius nupsisset ad ull[am.
Pauper erat nimium, prius is quam duxerat [illam.   25
Nunc dominatur ei, servivit cui vice ser[vi,
ac] veluti dignus, est nam pius atque benignus,
gratia sitque deo, qui sic miseretur ege[no."
Tunc dixit miles "Quae te rogo, dic mihi, sodes,
qualiter acciderit, inopi locuples quia nups[it."   30
Tunc ait i]s "Domine, dic, audieris, mihi, nonne
agna vetu]s cupide [va]s lingit salis amore
....ralta
quem] prius haec habuit, secum dirissime vixit.
Nam fuit in[gra]tus parcus rarissime laetus;   35
nunquam ri]dentem viderunt neve iocantem.
Quid], dix[it], pecorum vel apum fuerit vel equorum,

VI.

(After the redhead trespassed the fields to avoid the muddy
road, he was attacked by the owners of the land. Ruodlieb
is responding unsympathically to his complaints.)

"When you commit a crime, do not curse that man whom
You harm. A double hurt is grievous to endure:
To lose one's property and bear a curse besides."
In turn the redhead uttered many empty threats
And said they would be maimed before the night was over,   5
Because he wished to torch them all . . .
The knight smiled, knowing that this man would fare much
   worse.
They neared a village where they wished to spend the night.
The setting sun advises them to look for lodging.
The redhead called a shepherd to come toward him, and   10
When he came up, at once the redhead questioned him:
"Point out to me the names of your distinguished neighbors.
Say, is there here some rich man who could be our host?"
The shepherd said, "I know that many here would not
Be stunned if some count with a hundred shields should
   visit,   15
But could indeed receive them with full courtesy.
But he would be a poor man who could not give you
Sufficient lodging and a stable for your horses.
Though many people are accustomed to serve strangers,
Among them all none treats his guests as well as do   20
A young man and his aged wife." The redhead said,
"Why is a younger man wed to an aged widow?
Old men should have old wives." To this the shepherd said,
"He never could have wed a better wife at all.
He was extremely poor before he married her.   25
Now he is lord of her whom he served like a servant—
And worthily, because that man is kind and pious.
Thanks be to God who thus takes pity on the poor!"
The knight said, "Tell me, friend, what I now ask of you.
How did a wealthy woman wed a needy man?"   30
Then he said, "Tell me, lord, for surely you have heard
'The old ewe gladly licks the vat for love of salt.'
. . . .
She had a very wretched life with her first husband;
For he was dour and stingy, very rarely happy.   35
Nobody ever saw him laugh or tell a joke.
That man could scarcely count his cattle, bees and horses;

vix]; numerum nescit, quantum cuiusque sibi sit.
Rar]o tamen carnis propriae saturatur utervis,
cas]eolos comedunt duros seru[m]que biberunt, 40
qui]cquid habent, vendunt, precium cauteque recondunt.
Sua]vis is huc veniens iuvenis nudus vel egenus
vadi]t ad hunc, primo panem mendicat ab illo.
Qui] sibi buccellam sigalinam vix dedit unam;
han]c dum suscepit, reverenter stabat et edit. 45
Me]nsa sublata properat sustollere vasa,
ne m]ingat catta catulusve coinquinet illa,
sed]ulus ac lavit, post in toreuma reponit.

Cocl]ear in disco curat servare magistro,
ut] sibi praeponat, cum prandit quandove cenet, 50
app]osito cultro cum sale ve cum cocleari;
si be]ne conditum quid non sit, condiat hinc id,
seu] sit holus seu sorbicium seu quidque ciborum.
Haec] notat in corde senior, si non ait ore.
Nil] praetermisit iuvenis, quod opus fore vidit: 55
bov]es sicut oves adaquat, porcos ve capellas,
app]ortat faenum quibus annonat parafredis,
quae] fecit sponte sibi nemine praecipiente.
Si quid] alius erat opus, id studiosius egit.
Et c]um per triduum mansisset sic apud illum, 60
is n]isi buccellam sibi nil dedit ad comedendum,
cumque diutius esuriem sufferre nequiret,
inclinabat ei cupiens alio proficisci.
Ille sibi dixit, hunc cum secedere vidit
'Nunc hic esto dies binos tantummodo vel tres, 65
alterutrum nostros mores donec videamus.'
Consensit iuvenis, mox augetur sibi panis,
quadrans mane datur sibi sero dabatur et alter.
Interea rogat hunc, si quam cognoverit artem.
'Artem quam possem cognoscere, dic, meliorem, 70
quam quod nosco cibos lautos confingere pl[ures
vilibus ex causis, ex herbis sive farinis,
ad quae nil nisi lac posco modicumve sagi[men
et tantum salis, detur ut dulcedo sapori.
Est aliud, domine, nobis omnino necesse, 75
quod non irasci debes de me tibi dici.'
'Dic' ait 'id quid sit, non irascor.' Puer inquit
'En velut es, cunctis dives satis esse videris,
et tuus est panis solaminis omnis inanis,
furfuribus plenus fuscus lolio vel amarus. 80
Si praesentare mihi vis cuiusque farinae
vel modium vel dimidium panes faciendum,

He did not know how many he possessed of each;
And yet they rarely fed on meat from their own cattle.
Instead of this they ate hard cheeses and drank whey.　40
They sold whatever goods they had, then hid the proceeds.
This nice young man, arriving here both bare and needy,
Went to the husband, begging bread from him at first;
The man gave nothing but a crust of rye to him.
Receiving it, he stood respectfully and ate;　45
And when the table was removed, he rushed to put
Away the dishes, so that he could keep the cat
From pissing on them or the dog from fouling them.
He washed them carefully, then put them in the closet.
He saved a spoon to place upon the master's plate,
To set before him when he ate his lunch or dinner.　50
A knife was placed there also, with the spoon and salt,
With which he seasoned anything not seasoned well,
If it was cabbage, broth, or any other food.
The old man noticed this, though he did not speak out.
The youth omitted nothing that seemed necessary.　55
He watered cows as he did sheep and swine and goats;
And he brought fodder with which he would feed the horses,
And did this of his own accord, at no command.
If something else was needed, he did it with zeal;
And when he had remained three days at that man's house,　60
(That man who still gave him no food except some bread)
And when he could not bear his hunger any longer,
The young man, wishing to depart, bowed down to him.
The old man, when he saw him leaving, said to him,
'Now you remain here only two or three more days,　65
Until we have observed the habits of each other.'
The youth agreed; and his supply of bread was soon
Increased: a quarter pound at breakfast and at night.
Meanwhile the old man asked him whether he had learned
A skill. 'Tell me what better skill I could have learned　70
Than that I can cook up so many savory meals
From cheap ingredients—such as from herbs and flour,
To add to which I need just milk, a little grease,
Enough of salt to give some savor to the taste.
One other thing is absolutely needed, sir,　75
But you should not be angry when you hear of it.'
He said, 'Agreed. What is it? I will not be angry.'
The youth: 'You seem, just as you are, quite rich to all;
And yet your bread is lacking any taste whatever;
It is so dark and bitter, full of bran and darnel.　80
If you give me a peck, or even half a peck,
Of any kind of flour for making loaves of bread,

tot bene cribratos praesentabo tibi panes
semine conditos apii vel sale respersos,
et p[lacen]turas aliquas lardo superunctas 85
atque coronellas [pane]s ali[o]s, uti menclas.
Haec faciens numerum [non deminuo] tibi rerum.
Quicquid et excribr[o, cautissime vase recondo
atque tuis pullis dabo sive strepentibus au[cis.
In pueros panem si fregero distribuendum, 90
non ita [do] se[rv]is, ut eis lenis videaris;
haec faciendo domum totam tibi promptifi[cabo;
inspiciens] cuncta praesens sta, nitere furca."
Esset quod] iuvenis multum sapiens, homo cernens
procura]nda sua commisit ei bona cuncta, 95
res ut pro]videat puerosque suos, uti vellet.
Tali cau]tela facit hoc, tali quoque cura,
ut domi]no nil deficeret nullive suorum.
Ultra prae]bendam sibi nil tulit ille statutam,
saepe l]aborabat, quo se vestire valeret. 100
Sic fam]ulando fide domino summa, sine fraude
vixit] nescio quod. Posthaec moritur scelus illud;
sordidio]r nemo vixit vel amarior illo.
A paucis] fletur propriorum, dum tumulatur.
Nemo vet]at, vidua iuveni tunc fiat amica 105
corde te]nus, sed ad ecclesiam simul ire videmus,
ad me]nsam resident simul, ad lectum simul ibunt.
Matrem] iam dominam vocat hanc ast hunc ea natum.
Mox] famuli famulae patrem suescunt vocitare,
ille su]os liberos econtra nominat illos. 110
Nunqu]am maiorem nos cernebamus amorem
nec co]ntectales sibi tam bene convenientes.
Ianua], quae viduis prius est et clausa pupillis,
haec nu]nc divitibus semper patet atque misellis.
Illic] hospitium, si vultis, habebitis aptum; 115
stat vel] in ingressu villae grandis domus horum."
Tunc a]it rufus vanus nimiumque superbus
"Est vet]us hic aliquis, cui sit pulcherrima coniunx?"
Hic a]it "Est senior, multum bona cui fuit uxor;
pro d]olor, ah moritur. Is nupsit denuo nuper 120
et] duxit iuvenem stulta[m] nimiumque procacem.
Censet] pro nihilo, contemnit eum quia, crebro
huncce procis] stultis ludens inhonestius illis."

Then I in turn will give you bread so cleanly sifted,
Spiced and well seasoned with both parsley seed and salt;
And several spice cakes also, smeared on top with lard;   85
Some ring-buns, and some other breads shaped just like
    braids.
By doing this, I will not waste your meager wealth.
What I sift out, I then will place with care in dishes,
To feed this to your chickens and your squawking geese.
If I break bread for distribution to your servants,   90
I will not give so much to them that you seem lenient.
In this way I will win you all the household's favor.
Stand by, lean on your cane, inspecting everything.'
The man, realizing that this youth was very wise,
Entrusted all his property into his care,   95
To manage, as he wished, his servants and possessions.
He did this with such caution and such great concern,
No thing was lacking for the master and his household;
And taking for himself a set amount, no more,
He often struggled just so he could clothe himself.   100
He lived and served his master loyally, without
Deceit, for several years; but then that scoundrel died.
There never lived a viler or a meaner man.
But few of his own household mourned when he was buried.
No one objected to the widow's heartfelt love   105
For that young man; we saw them go to church together;
They ate together and would go to bed together.
He calls his lady mother; she calls him her son.
The servants, male and female, learn to call him father,
While he in turn addresses them as his own children;   110
For we have never seen a greater love or else
A married couple so well suited to each other.
Their door, which once was closed to widows and to orphans,
Is always open now to rich and poor alike.
In that place you will find fit lodging, if you wish,   115
A large house standing at the entrance of the village."
The redhead—vain and very haughty—said, "Is there
An old man who has wed a pretty wife?" He answered,
"There is an older man who once had a good wife;
But, sad to say, she died; he married recently   120
A younger woman—a stupid girl and impudent too.
She scorns him and thinks nothing of deceiving him
Disgracefully and often with her stupid lovers."

VII.

Panes ille secat et in illos distribuebat,
carnis de senis discis quod et accidit illis.
His consolatis, laetis ad doma reversis
hospes item dixit "Cum Christus quem mihi mittit,
tunc est Pascha meum mihi velque meis celebra[ndum, 5
sicut in hac nocte, dum laetificabimur a te.
Est mihi quod venit de te, Deus ut mihi mittat."
Cui mox de scapula partem mittit quoque sura,
in plures offas quam concidendo minutas
pro sacramentis pueros partitur in omnes. 10
Post haec sat cocti domino, sat ponitur assi,
potus at in patera summi tuberis nucerina
praecipui vini piperati sive medonis,
in qua bis bina sunt aurea flumina sculpta;
dextra dei fundo paterae confixa stat imo, 15
quam, dum pernoctat ibi, quidam summus ei dat.
Numquam gustavit tamen ex hac, ni sibi mittat,
cui servitur in hac, in opus servatur at istud.
Finita cena postquamque datur sibi lympha,
fertur ei vinum, de quo bibit et sibi misit, 20

qui dederat dominae prius et post ebibit ips[e.
De mensa surgit miles modicumque resedit,
sicque iacens tractat, hominem qui gratificar[et.
Tandem matronae, dederat sua pallia promp[te,
possit ut ecclesiam sic compta revisere sanctam. 25
Interea rufus quid agat non praetereamus.
Miles ut intravit, ubi tot bona repperiebat,

rufus, cur subeat, vetus est ubi simia, dixit.
Miles ait "Velles mecum, post forsan ovares;
quod volui reperi, sed quod tu quaeris habebi[s." 30
Asstantes multi rufo sunt consiliati,
deserat haut comitem, diver[tere tam bene nusquam.
At dedig]nanter discessit ab hoc properanter
currit et ad] neptem, nil nacturus nisi mortem.

VII.

(The redhead has decided to seek lodgings at the home of the old man with a young wife. Ruodlieb, meanwhile, has gone to the home of the young man married to the old widow. This couple has invited some poor people from the village to dine with them.)

He cut the bread, which he distributed to them
And gave them shares of meat from six large serving plates.
When they were satisfied and went home happily,
The host then said, "When Christ sends anyone to me,
My house and I must celebrate that day as Easter,   5
Just as this night on which we will be cheered by you.
It seems that God sends me whatever comes from you."
He cut for him some from the shoulder and the leg,
And this he cut up into many tiny pieces
That he gave out, like sacraments, to all the servants.   10
Then boiled and roasted meat were placed before the master;
A drink of excellent spiced wine or mead was brought;
There is a walnut cup made of the finest grain,
And on this cup four golden rivers had been carved;
The very bottom of the cup showed God's right hand.   15
A noble who had spent the night gave him this cup,
From which he never drank unless served by a guest
Whom he had served with it; the cup was saved for this.
When they had dined and water had been given them,
He was brought wine, from which he drank, then gave the
    other,   20
Who gave it to the mistress first, then drank himself.
The knight rose from the table and reclined a while,
And as he lay there thought how he could thank that man.
At last he gave the lady of the house his cloak,
So, clad in it, she could attend the holy church.   25
But meanwhile let us not leave out the redhead's actions.
The redhead asked the knight, as he was entering
The house where he discovered so much that was good,
Why he would go inside where some old she-ape lived.
The knight said, "Come with me, you might be happy later.
I found what I wished; you will get what you look for." 30
Then many bystanders advised the redhead not
To leave his friend, since nowhere else would he be housed
So well. Disdainfully he quickly left that man.
He hastened to his "cousin"—and to find his death.

Invenit] portam senioris saepe seratam. 35
Stat senio]r curte liberique sui duo prae se.
Tunc rufus] pulsat, quatiens portam nimis inquit

"quam cito qu]is aperi vel me praelinquere noli."
Cumque sene]x "Quis sit, per saepem prospice" dixit,
"vir quat]it et frangit portam" currens puer inquit. 40

Rufus] ait "Pande, rogitas quasi nescieris me."
Tunc sunt i]rati iuvenes nimis hinc stomachati.
Vim metu]endo mali iubet illi tunc aperiri.
Rufus pro]terve nimis incursando superbe
in curtem] mitram non deponebat et ensem 45
(desili]ens ab equo, freni loro sude iacto)
strinxit ut] insanus, prae se stetit utque profanus.
Sed rufu]s tandem ridens ait ad seniorem
"Si vos n]oscatis me, miror quod reticetis."
"Nescio qu]is sitis" ait is "stulte satis itis, 50
nescio qu]is sitis nunc nobis quidve velitis."
"Est uxor vest]ra mea neptis valde propinqua;
hanc ut] conveniam solus permittite solam."
Is dixit] "facite" iubet hanc ad eumque venire.
Quae venit; u]t vidit, ardens in corde cupivit, 55
gauden]s arrisit, ea congaudens sibi risit.
"Omne bon]um genitor tibi mandat vel tua mater.
Post dicam] solus ubivis et quicquid alius."
Ad portam] tunc stant ad saepem seque reclinant.
Rufus ait] "Primo quae dico corde notato, 60
nostrum col]loquium nam non debet fore longum;
non fle, non ride, te contineas seriose,
ne vetu]s ille canis sapiat nostram rationem;
si mihi] consentis, ab eo citius redimeris.
Est hic n]am iuvenis satur omnigenae probitatis, 65
haut b]revis haut longus sed staturae mediocris;
est similagineus totusve genis rubicundus,
in toto mundo non est speciosior illo.
Qui dum rescisset, tu quam speciosa fuisses
et quas aerumnas patereris cottidianas, 70
corde tenus doluit gemebundus vel mihi dixit
'Umquam si fueris mihi fidus, kare sodalis,
ito, dic illi mulieri martirizatae,
si velit, ut redimam se vel de carcere tollam,
audierit gracilem cras quando tubam reboantem, 75
ut dicens nulli sibi tam fidae mulieri
exeat e curte platea stans inopine,
donec accurram cum pluribus hanc rapiendam.

He found the old man's gate was barred and fenced around.   35
He stood, with his two sons before him, in the courtyard.
The redhead banged and shook the gate with violence,
     shouting,
"Hey! Open up right now! Don't leave me standing here!"
The old man said, "Look through the gate. See who it is."
"A man shakes and breaks down the gate," the boy said,
     running.   40
The redhead, "Open up! You act as if you do
Not know me." Then the young men grew annoyed and angry;
But fearing that fiend's strength, he ordered the gate opened.
The redhead, haughtily and boldly rushing in
The court, did not remove his cap. Dismounting from   45
His horse, he slung the reins around a post, then drew
His sword as if insane and stood there like a demon,
Then finally, while laughing, spoke to the old man:
"Your keeping silent, if you know me, is surprising."
"I know not who you are," he said. "You act quite foolish.50
I know not who you are or what you want with us."
"That wife of yours is my close relative, a cousin.
Allow me by myself to talk with her alone."
He said, "Agreed," then ordered her to go to him.
She came; he looked, and in his heart he burned with lust 55
For her. He smiled with joy, with joy she smiled at him.
"Your father and your mother send you their regards;
But later I will tell the rest in private, where
You wish." The two stood by the gate, leaned on the fence.
The redhead said, "First mark my words attentively,   60
Because our conversation should not last too long.
Don't cry or laugh. Conduct yourself quite seriously,
So that the old dog will not understand our plan.
If you consent to me, you will escape him quickly.
There is a certain youth, full of each kind of goodness, 65
Who is not short, not tall, but of just average height,
Of light complexion, but with very ruddy cheeks;
In all the world there is no one more handsome than
This man. He, when he learned how beautiful you are,
And heard about the hardships you endure each day,   70
Grieved deeply in his heart and groaning said to me,
'Beloved friend, if you were ever true to me,
Go, say this to that tortured woman: if she wants
Me to release her and to free her from her prison,
Tomorrow when she hears a horn resounding softly,   75
Without a word, not even to a trusted woman,
To leave the courtyard, standing hidden in the street
Until I come and with my troop snatch her away.

Posthac haec hera sit agat et sibi quodque placebit.'
Nunc sibi demanda quod vis, neptis mea cara." 80
Disciplinate stans hoc audivit ut omne,
interius gaudens tamen inquit ei quasi maerens
"Cuncta libens facio, sis certior, atque fidem do."
Accepta dextra rufus dubitans nihil ultra
"Ter mihi succumbas in mercedem volo laudes." 85
"Si decies possis, fac" inquit "vel quotiens vis."

"Sicut abire velim, facio, quod tu prohibeto"
adque senem rediit "mihi praecipitoteque" dixit.
Ille libens faceret, si prae muliere valeret.
Illa rogat multum, discedere ne sinat illum. 90
"Si velit, hic maneat, quod nobis sit, sibimet sit."
Duxerat in stabulum properantius illa caballum;
non ea nec rufus reminiscuntur magis eius,
manducet, si quid ibi graminis is reperisset.
Intrantemque domum neptis bene suscipit illum. 95
Insimul assidunt sat sermocinando ludunt,
insertos stringunt digitos, sibi basia figunt.
Ingreditur senior, quo non seriosior alter,
hispidus in facie, poterat quod nemo videre,
eius quid vultus fuerat, quia valde pilosus, 100
ni solus nasus curvus fuit et varicosus.
Stant oculi gemini velut effosi tenebrosi,
hosque retortorum superumbrat silva pilorum
neve foramen ubi sit in os, quit quisque videre,
sic se barbicia praetendunt longa ve spissa. 105
Ille parare tamen pueros iussit sat edendum.
Istorum nimius cum displicuit sibi ludus,
inter eos residet natibus disiunxit et ipsos.
Ad modicum reticent intersessosque dolebant;
prae se curvando fantur per plura iocando. 110
Cum pertaedebat, mensam velare iubebat
dixit et uxori "Satis est, iam parce pudori.
Non debet mulier sic esse procax, neque sed vir,
et praesente viro ludat decet haut alieno."
Sic dicens surgit, ad secretum velut iret, 115
respiciebat eo terebelli perque foramen.
Rufus et in solium salit infeliciter ipsum,
una manus mammas tractabat et altera gambas,
quod celabat ea super expandendo crusenna.
Hoc totum ceu fur rimans senior speculatur. 120
Quando redit, sibi non cedit, nam non ea sivit.
Tuncque sedens solio nimis indignando supremo,
saepe monet dominam, quo praecipiat dare cenam;

Then she may be my mistress and do as she pleases.'
And now, dear cousin, answer him as you desire." 80
She stood there calmly as she heard all this; although
Rejoicing inwardly, she said as if in sadness,
"Be certain I will gladly do all this; I give
My word." The redhead took her right hand, hesitated
No more: "For payment I want you to lie with me 85
Three times." She answered, "Do it ten times, if you can,
Or else as often as you like." "Then I will act
As if I want to leave, but you object," he said.
Returning to the old man, he said, "Grant me leave!"
He would have done so gladly, if he ruled his wife,
Who asked him often not to let the man depart. 90
"Let him remain, if he desires; what is ours
Is his." She quickly led his horse into the stable.
The redhead and the woman gave no further thought
To it: if it found any hay there, it would eat.
His "cousin," as he entered, warmly greeted him. 95
They sat together, talking very playfully,
And gave each other kisses and entwined their fingers.
The old man entered—no one was more dour than he.
He was so shaggy on his face that no one could
Discern what it might look like, since it was so hairy; 100
That is, all but his curved and varicolored nose.
The man's two eyes were black, as if two hollowed sockets,
And they were shaded by a forest of tangled hair.
No one could see where his mouth had its opening,
So long and bristly was the beard that covered it. 105
He had the servants fix some food to eat; however,
Because he did not like their flagrant play, he sat,
Squeezing between them with his buttocks. They were silent
A little while, upset since they were separated;
But then they leaned in front of him to joke some more. 110
Disgusted, he commanded them to set the table,
And told his wife, "That is enough! No more disgrace!
No woman, and no man, should be so bold; and when
Her husband's present, she should not play with a stranger!"
He rose, while speaking, as if going to the toilet, 115
But peering through a peep-hole he looked back on them.
The redhead, lucklessly, jumped right into his seat.
One hand caressed her breasts, the other touched her legs,
While she spread out her fur coat to conceal the fondling.
The old man saw all this while spying like a thief. 120
When he returned, the redhead did not move, nor did
She let him. Angry, he sat at the table's head
And often warned his wife to order dinner served.

quae subsannando cenam differt ioculando.
Is rogitat, cena, pueros, essetne parata   125
"Quam cito vos vultis" dicunt "cenare valetis."
"Nunc, hera, cenemus requiescendumque meemus
pauset et est tempus ut vester karus amicus
satque fatigastis hunc, nunc pausare sinatis."

But she delayed the meal with mocking and with joking.
He asked the servants if the dinner was prepared. 125
They answered, "You can eat as soon as you desire."
"Now, mistress, let us dine, then let us go to bed;
And it is time for your beloved friend to rest.
You have exhausted him enough. Now let him rest!"

VIII.

Venit is atque fidem sibi vult praedicere sanctam
Non valet is, "Credo" gemebundus ait nisi crebro
paeniteat, vel eum rogitat, mala quae faciebat.
Nutibus et verbis se paenituisse docebat.
Per domini corpus fit ab omni crimine mundus.   5
Exhalans animam domino commiserat illam
dicens "Christe pie mihi valde reo miserere,
his et dimitte, mihi vivere qui rapuere,
inspiresque meis, ut idem faciant, rogo, natis."
Sic dicens siluit, cito post haec vivere clausit.   10
Aurorante die populus convenit ubique
ante fit ecclesiam multus conventus et ipsam
et vicinorum maiorum sive minorum.
Rector eo venit, scelus ut miserabile rescit.
Utque resederunt ibi, quos residere decebat,   15
"Hic" ait "est" rector "miserabilis utique rumor,
quod sit percussus, quo non melior fuit ullus."
Flentes dicebant omnes, ibi qui residebant
"Ulciscatur ni, rescimus par iterari."
Misit post liberos, post mordritas simul ipsos.   20
Qui dum venerunt, coram rectore steterunt,
rufus ridendo, terram rea conspiciendo.
Rector, dum vidit, quod risit, "Pessime" dixit
"rides, cum cunctos hic flentes cum videas nos.
Quid succensebas, quod eum sic martirizabas?"   25
Rufus ait "Dentes mihi dempserat anteriores
ob nullam caus[am], n[i] quod sedi prope neptem."
Dixit et "Ancilla tua neptis si fuit illa,
cur hanc stuprabas, sceleri scelus adiciebas?"
Rufus ait "Cur me fur haec attraxerat ad se?   30
Cur [quaeram facere]? Facerem non, ni peteret me."
Quae tantum flevit, rivus lacrimis ibi quod fit.
Ex oculis sanguis posthaec fluxit sibi grandis.
Postquam convaluit, quod quid fari valet, inquit
"O nimis infide, cur sic mentire super me?   35
Exemplaris Adam, qui culpam vertit in Evam.
Non post te misi, non te prius, impie, vidi.

VIII.

(The redhead had intercourse with the old man's wife.
Caught in the act by her husband, he mortally wounded the
man. A priest has been summoned to perform the final rites
for the dying man.)

He came and wished to preach the holy faith to him.
The old man, groaning often, had no strength except
To utter "I believe." The priest then asked him whether
He was repenting of the evils he had done.
With nods and words he showed that he was penitent.
Then, through the body of the Lord cleansed of all sin,　　5
As he exhaled his soul, he gave it to the Lord
And said, "Have mercy on a sinner, holy Christ!
Forgive those two who snatched away my life from me;
And move my sons, I pray, to do the same." He spoke,
Then he fell silent, and soon afterward he died.　　10
At dawn the people came together from all sides;
And a large gathering of neighbors, great and small
Alike, assembled now before the church itself.
The judge went there when he learned of that heinous crime.
When those whose right it was to sit had taken seats,　　15
The judge said, "This is wretched news assuredly
That he than who there was no better has been murdered."
All who were sitting there in tears cried out, "Unless
He is avenged, we know the same will happen again."
The judge sent for the children and the murderers;　　20
And when they came there and they stood before the judge,
The redhead laughed, the woman looked down at the ground.
The judge, who saw that he was laughing, said, "You fiend,
You laugh when you see all of us are weeping here?
What made you so incensed to torture him that way?"　　25
The redhead said, "That man had knocked out my front teeth,
And for no reason but my sitting near my cousin."
The judge said, "If the woman really was your cousin,
Then why did you defile her, adding crime to crime?"
He said, "Why did the bitch seduce me? Why would I　　30
Attempt it? I would not, had she not asked me to."
She cried so much that she made there a stream of tears,
And then great drops of blood were flowing from her eyes.
When she recovered so that she could speak, she said,
"Why tell such lies about me, you most faithless man?　　35
You follow Adam's model: he cast blame on Eve.
I did not send for you, nor had I ever seen

Me cum promissis mendosis decipiebas.
Non ego defendo quod feci, sed mage damno
quod tu fecisti, me consiliante patrasti. 40
Non ego, confiteor, ulcisci me super opto.
Iudicium, rector, fieri differto parumper,
donec accusem memet, donec quoque damnem.
En, mea iudex sto, quia valde libens tolerabo.
Si me suspendi vultis super arbore grandi, 45
radite caesariem mihi, longam plectite funem,
stranguler ut per eam, per quam rea saepe fiebam.
Sed rogo, post triduum corpus tollatis ut ipsum
et comburatis, in aquam cinerem iaciatis,
ne iubar abscondat sol aut aer neget imbrem, 50
ne per me grando dicatur laedere mundo.
Inclusam vase vultis submergere si me,
deforis in vase quod feci notificate,
inveniant qui me, ne praesumant sepelire;
tantum vas rumpant in aquam vel reiciant me, 55
piscibus ut citius vorer aut diris cocodrillis.
Vultis in ignitum fumosum trudere furnum,
ingrediar sponte, quo non cremer igne Gehennae.
Ut caream vita, si vultis, mersa cloaca
(sum nimis inmunda, tali dignissima poena), 60
incidero prompte, quia tali gaudeo fine,
Tartareus foetor mihi post ne perpetuetur.
Quicquid supplicii reperitis adhuc gravioris,
omne libens patiar, multo peiora merebar."
Quae dum conticuit, rector miserans ita dixit 65

"Iudicat haec semet, vos dicite, si sat in hoc sit."
Omnes plorantes, nimium sibi compatientes
dicunt "Non opus est, rector rogitet super hoc plus."
Dicunt causidici "Vitam decernimus illi
donari tantum, si paeniteat male factum." 70
Eius privigni mansuefacti velut agni
volvuntur pedibus rectoris dando precatus,
ut vitam veniam sibi concedatque salutem,
esse domus dominam, velut ante fuit, sinat illam.
Quod dum promisit clementer, id illa recusat 75
"Amodo non dominam, sed me dicant homicidam;
vivere si vultis me, sed tamen, oro, salutis
ut mihi tollatis, quo me non debilitatis.
Nares truncate, quidquid sit et oris utrimque,
ut stent horribiles omni sine tegmine dentes, 80
ut nullum libeat posthac, mihi basia quo det,
in crucis atque modum me comburatis in altum

You, scoundrel. You tricked me with lying promises.
No, I will not defend my deeds, but I condemn
What you committed and you did with my connivance. 40
I do not, I confess, wish vengeance for myself.
Postpone, judge, handing down your verdict for a while
Until I can accuse and even damn myself.
Look! I stand here as my own judge and will endure
This gladly. If you want me hanged from a tall tree, 45
Cut off my hair and from it braid a length of rope,
To strangle me with that through which I often sinned.
Then after three days take away my corpse, I beg;
Cremate it, throw the ashes in the water so
The sun will not hide light or air refuse the rain 50
Or hail be said to harm the world because of me.
If you want to submerge me, shut up in a vessel,
Mark on the outside of the vessel what I did,
So those who find me will not dare to bury me.
But let them break it, throw me back into the deep, 55
For fish or awful crocodiles to eat. If you
Thrust me into a blazing smoky furnace, I'll
Go willingly, to keep from burning in the flames
Of Hell. If you wish me to die sunk in a sewer—
For I am filthy and deserve such punishment 60
I will jump in at once, rejoicing in that end,
So that the stench of Hell may not await me later.
Whatever graver punishments you still might find,
All will I suffer gladly, and deserve much worse."
When she was still, the judge, moved by compassion,
  spoke: 65
"She judges herself; you say if this is enough."
All, weeping, strongly sympathizing with her, said:
"The judge need not ask any more about this matter."
The jurors stated: "It is our decision that
Her life be spared if she repents her evil deed." 70
Her stepsons, who were gentle as if they were lambs,
Fell at the judge's feet while offering entreaties
To grant her life, forgiveness, safety, and to let
Her be the mistress of the house just as before.
But when he mercifully consented, she refused: 75
"Let them not call me mistress but a murderess.
If you want me to live, impair my body's soundness,
I beg you, although not enough to cripple me.
Cut off my nose and lips, in order that my teeth
Will be disgusting, with no covering at all. 80
From then on no one will desire to give me kisses.
On both my cheeks, which up to now have been as red

per geminas buccas rosa ceu tenus hac rutilantes,
noverit ut quisquam, propter scelus hoc mihi factum,
et dicat 'tibi vae, meruisti tale quid in te?' 85
ne grandis culpa penitus me sic stet inulta."
Tunc rector liberis hanc commisit senioris,
mater et ut domina sit eis nec, ut ante, noverca.

Quae vestes pulchras ornatus abicit omnes,
induitur tunica velut ex fuligine tincta. 90
Caesariem rasit, hinc resticulos ea plectit,
cum quibus et teneras constrinxerat illa mamillas,
restes vi mordent carnes, donec putrefiunt.
Tegmen pannosum caput omne tegebat et ipsum;
sic nil ni nares oculi cernuntur et eius. 95
Psalterium discit animae senis idque canebat.
Non manducabat, nisi stellam quando videbat
(tunc siccum panem comedens atrum cinerosum),
v[el bi]bit ex limpha tantum coclearia terna.
Ambulat haec pedibus nudis per frigus et aestus 100
dormit et in lecto nihilo palea nisi strato
et pro plumacio posito tantummodo ligno.
Ante diem surgit senis ad tumulum v[el adi]vit,
donec sudavit, donec plus stare nequivit;
tunc ruit in faciem, dum fontem flens ibi fecit. 105
Ningeret aut plueret seu sol torrendo cremaret,
venit ad ecclesiam, mox ut pulsatur, ad ipsam
et non inde redit, dum circumquaque diescit;
ad breve tunc rediit, donec faciem sibi lavit
presbiter ad missam vel pulsabat celebrandam; 110

tunc rediit, nonam post haec ibi mansit ad horam.
Nilque potestatis sibi vendicat, hanc sinit illis;
quod sibi dant, habuit, quod non dant, non ea quaerit.
Haec nunquam risit, cum nemine postea lusit,
cum rident alii, fletus dulcis fuit illi. 115

Hanc irascentem rixantem luxuriantem
nemo videbat eam, dum vitam deserit istam.
Illa commissa natis ab eisque recepta
rector ait populo "Quid agamus, dicite, rufo,
qui scelus hoc geminum patrat inter nos gemebundum?" 120
Rufus iudicii certus necis "Obsecro" dixit
"hic habeo comitem, prius hunc curate vocandum,
quam quid in his culpis ulciscendum rogitetis,

qui cuius generis sim, quit sat dicere vobis."

As roses, deeply burn the figure of the cross,
So all know this was done to me because of crime
And say, 'Alas, how did you earn such punishment?'   85
So my enormous guilt will not go unavenged."
The judge then bound her over to the old man's children
So that she might serve as their mother and their mistress,
But not their stepmother, as she had been before.
She cast off all her lovely clothes and ornaments,
And wore a coat which seemed to have been dyed in soot;   90
She shaved her hair and plaited it in little cords
With which she tightly tied her tender breasts together.
The cords bit fiercely in her flesh until it rotted.
She covered her entire head with ragged cloth,
So nothing could be seen except her nose and eyes.   95
She learned the Psalter, sang it for the old man's soul.
She did not eat until she saw the evening star,
And then ate only dry bread that was dark as ashes;
And then for drink she had just three spoonfuls of water.
This woman walked barefooted through the cold and heat;   100
She slept upon a bed with straw her only mattress,
And for a pillow merely used a block of wood.
Before dawn broke, she visited the old man's tomb
To pray until, perspiring, she could stand no longer,
Then fell upon her face and wept a flood of tears.   105
In snow or rain or in the scorching midday heat
She went to church soon as the bells were rung, and she
Did not return until it was day everywhere.
Then she went home a little while until she washed
Her face, and bells rung by the priest announced the
    mass.   110
Then she returned and stayed there until the ninth hour.
She claimed no power, leaving it to them. What they
Gave her, she took; what they did not, she did not seek.
She never laughed again or joked with anyone.
When other people laughed, from her there came sweet
    tears.   115
Until the time she left this life, nobody saw
This woman angry, quarrelsome or dissolute.
When she was given to and taken by the children,
The judge addressed the people, "Say what we do with
This redhead who has done this double grievous crime   120
To us?" The redhead, sure to be condemned to death,
Said, "Please, I have a comrade. Have him summoned here
Before you give thought to how these crimes should be
    punished;
He can say well enough what kind of man I am."

Mittere dum post hunc eius cupidi voluerunt, 125
militis hospes ait "Quem vos vultis citus asstat.
Hac mecum nocte mansit, quod non fuit iste."
Quem dum produxit, stantem rector rogitavit
"Dic, miles summe, socius tuus iste vir estne?"

When they, desirous of him, wished to send for him,   125
The knight's host said, "The man you want will soon arrive.
He stayed with me last night since he is not that sort."
When he brought him, the judge asked him as he stood there,
"Please tell us, noble knight, is he your friend or not?"

IX.

Qu..
obviat omnia quae............................
quae cum tempus erit, tibi dicere cuncta licebit.
Nunc falerare tibi iubeas unique clienti.
Nam cognoscunt te magis ac me compatriotae;   5
quando videbunt te, devitabunt penitus me.
Debes ire domum, si sit tua gratia mecum."
Cui cor mox hylarat, prae laeticia quoque flebat.
"Desine" miles ait...........................
....   10
scutiferum vocat.............................
....
ambo scutiferi...............................
....
qui mox ascen................................   15
....
scutiferos dico..............................
....
cursu veloci re..............................
....   20
quidve volun.................................
....
neve seram de................................
....

IX.

(Presumably the redhead was sentenced to death. Resuming his journey, Ruodlieb has met a young man, his cousin. The young man, who is involved with a courtesan, has begun talking to Ruodlieb about the affair, but Ruodlieb is urging him to delay the conversation.)

"When it is time, then you will be permitted to
Say everything. Now order one horse saddled for
Yourself and for one vassal . . .
For your compatriots know you much more than me.
When they see you, they will ignore me utterly.   5
You should go home, if you have any love for me."
At once this pleased his heart so that he wept for joy.
"Stop!" said the knight . . .

X.

Est ibi secrete prope secessus................
in quo sunt clavi plures in pariete fixi,
quis suspendere res potuissent quasque viantes,
ne noceant mures, cum non timeant ibi fures.
Cum dominis domina pedat ad solaria celsa,   5

qua dicebat eis "Multum bene nunc veniatis!"
Dum grates referunt, rogat illos, ut resinerent
atque iocarentur di..........................
....
et sibi quos vellent pis......................... 10
....
moles multigenae p...............................
....
tantum tres desunt..............................
.... 15
miles ait "Nunc piscari..........................
....
pulvere buglossae, [quo piscabamur et ante
....
est in aqua cimba............................... 20
....
assumunt virgam.................................
....
donec venerunt pisce[s, pilulas comederunt
.... 25
quas qui gustabant, [sub aquam resalire nequibant
....
quos miles virga perterrens cogit ad arva.
Miratur domina dominellarumque caterva,
contribulisque suus ovat in virtutibus eius.   30
Fit nimius risus manuum plaususve cachinnus
accurruntque coci, tollunt properantque parari.
Egressus lintre cuncto populo comitante
ad dominam repedat, ea quem bene suscipiebat.
"Piscator talis est nusquam, vos velut estis."   35
Tunc iubet exponi pisces in gramine molli,
ut, diversos quot, videat, lacus is generaret.
Tunc sunt expositi, quotquot fuerant ibi capti:
lucius et rufus, qui sunt in piscibus hirpus,
pisces namque vorant, illos ubi prendere possunt,   40
prahsina, lahs, charpho, tinco, barbatulus, orvo,
alnt, naso, qui bini nimis intus sunt acerosi,

X.

(Ruodlieb has convinced his cousin to return home with him. Accompanied by their squires, they have stopped at a castle where a widow lives with her young daughter. The widow is the godchild of Ruodlieb's mother.)

. . . An almost secret closet there
In which were many spikes which were nailed in the wall;
On these the travelers could hang their things, so mice
Would not harm them, since people here did not fear thieves.
The mistress then walked with the lords up to the
    sun-porch, 5
Where she addressed them: "Now you are most welcome here!"
When they expressed their thanks, she asked them to sit down
And jest with her . . .

(Ruodlieb is demonstrating the powers of bugloss.)

Then poking with the stick the knight drove them to shore.
The mistress and her retinue of ladies were
Amazed (his relative delighted by his skills). 30
Now laughter rose, applause and great hilarity.
The cooks ran up, took them, then rushed to cook the fish.
When he stepped from the boat, accompanied by all
He walked back to the mistress, who received him well:
"There is no other fisherman like you." And then 35
She ordered them to spread the fish on the soft grass
To see how many different kinds the lake produced.
Then all the kinds that had been caught there were displayed:
The pike and the red bass (which are the wolves of fish,
Since they devour fish when they can capture them); 40
The bream and salmon, carp, tench, barbel and the orf;

rubeta fundicola, truta digena, rufa vel alba,
in capite grandis capito post degener alis,
labilis anguilla vel per caput horrida vvalra, 45
asco, rinanch, ambo dulces nimis in comedendo,
ast agapuz ut acus in dorso pungit acutus,
praeterea multi pisces mihi non bene noti.
His visis tolli citius iubet illa parari.
Mensa parabatur, latis similis cumulatur. 50

Mittit et interea, cito quo veniat sua nata,
post quam mox agiles plures saluere tyrones,
texuit ex auro quae bina ligamina sponso,
post quemcumque sibi tribuat clementia Christi.
Quae dum procedit, ceu lucida luna reluxit. 55
Quam sollers esset, nemo discernere posset,
an volet an naret an se quocumque moveret

..............................rosa levabat
tunc hera poscit aqua]m, quam sumere iussit herilem.
Et post hospitibus datur, ultime sed sibi post hos 60
...........................unt insimul ambae.
Maior maiori, iunior consedit herili.
....................................iubet apte.
Eius contribulis conviva fiebat herilis.
Una sibi patera, sibi lanx etia]m datur una. 65
Prae quibus ille canis stat furti proditor omnis.
............................faciemque revertens
cauda blanditur, quid ei, monet, ut tribuatur;
contribulis quicquid sibi sponte d]at, ille recepit.
Excidit at sibi quid casu, non id repetivit. 70
Ille cani dixit malus quod] hoc homo coxit,
nunquam gustavit aut gustatum revomebat.
..................Dapifer calc]aria tollit
po[stmodo] scutellas dapifer cum posceret illas,
porrigat has sibi mox, cunctis lixis velut est mos 75
.................cani]s inspiciens male crebro,
insiluit tandem, lacerando trahit sibi vestem
atque momordisset, ni scutifer eripuisset.
Miles ridebat, plebs cetera cuncta stupebat.

Tunc dixit domina "Res cernitur haec mihi mira." 80
Miles ait "Furti canis est hic conscius isti.

The chub and broad-nose (both of which are full of bones);
The bottom-dwelling char; two trouts: one red, one white;
The large-head (big of head but lacking fins in back);
The slippery eel and catfish with its ugly head;   45
The grayling and the Rhine-trout (both are sweet to taste);
The perch, whose sharp back pierces like a pin, however;
And many fish besides which are not known to me.
These seen, she had them carried off and quickly cooked;
They set the table, piled it high with rolls brought
    there.   50
Meanwhile, she ordered that her daughter come at once.
She wove two bands of gold for the betrothed whom
The clemency of Christ might give to her someday.
When she came forth, she shone as brilliant as the moon.
How graceful was that woman! No one could discern   55
If she were flying, swimming, or just how she moved . . .

(The widow has invited Ruodlieb and his cousin to be her
guests at dinner.)

    . . . Water, which she told the girl to take;
And next the guests were served, but last of all the
    mistress . . .   60
. . . .
The older man was sitting with the older woman,
The younger with the daughter . . .
And she became the partner of his relative.
One cup and just one plate were given to them both;   65
Near them the dog that finds out any theft was standing.
. . . .
It wagged its tail to coax them to give food to it,
And took whatever that man's kinsman freely gave,
But did not take what fell to it by accident.   70
But if he told the dog, "An evil man cooked this,"
The dog did not taste that, but spat out what it chewed.
            . . . a waiter stole his spurs;
And later when the waiter asked them for their dishes,
He held them out at once, as was his way with servants . . 75
The dog was glaring at him, barking frequently;
At last it leaped upon him, pulled and ripped his clothes,
And would have bitten him had not the squire held
Him back. The knight laughed; all the others were
    astonished.
The mistress said, "This seems a strange event to me."   80
The knight then said, "The dog knows all about your theft;

159

Quod furabaris, nisi reddideris, morieris.
Vade, fer in medium quod fecisti cito furtum."
Currens absque mora retulit calcaria bina.
"Haec" ait "a sella denodavi modo vestra;   85
tunc ibi nemo fuit viventum nemoque vidit
neve canis sciret, a daemone ni didicisset."
Miles ait "Sibi da, cernas cui praebeat illa."
Quae sibi dum iecit, cuius fuerant ea reddit.

Hic dixitque cani "Nunc illa referto sodali."   90
Quae dat scutifero caudam persaepe movendo.
"Ante pedes cadite furis veniamque rogate."
Qui se prostravit caput inque pedes sibi ponit
et veluti fleret veniam poscens ululavit.
"Nunc tu dic: surge vel amici simus ut ante."   95
Quod cum dixisset, surgens canis exhilarescit,
nunc hunc nunc dominos nunc gratificat residentes.

Miles ait "Vestrum sibi quis captando capillum,
accipiat baculum, velut ulciscendo reatum."
Quod duo dum faciunt "Cur furabaris?" et aiunt,   100

insiliebat eos canis hunc ab eisque redemit,
mordens in suras illos nimium dolituros,
sic se lusisse, cum quo prae pacificat se.
Quidam ridebant, quidam nimis inde stupebant.
Prandia cum cena sic sat fiunt opulenta.   105
Fercula post multa, post pocula tam numerosa
limpha datur; modicum residetur, dum biberetur.
Tempus pomorum non tunc fuit ulligenorum,
ni pueri veniunt, de silva fraga ferebant,
quaedam pars vasis, pars corticibus corilinis,   110
quae singillatim legerunt undique passim.
His esis mensa removetur, sumitur aqua.

..............................it se discaligandum.
Ille ligaminibus de Lukka crura coemptis
.......................cca sibi fluitaret.   115
Atque super pedules se calceolos sericatos
..............................nxit sericosis.
Contribulis rubeos soccos sub curduanellis
..................................gestans operosis.
Ambo ligaturis coniunxit crura gemellis   120
........................re sunt margine cunctae,
a quibus et multae dependent undique bullae.

160

And you will die unless you give back what you stole.
Go, quickly bring into our midst what you have stolen."
He ran and brought the two spurs back without delay.
He said, "Not long ago I took these from your saddle;   85
No other man alive was there, and no one saw.
The dog would not know, had it not learned from a demon."
The knight said, "Give it them, and see to whom it takes
The spurs." Thrown them, the dog returned them to their
    owner.
He told the dog, "Now take them back to my companion."   90
And with a wagging tail it gave them to the squire.
"Fall down before his feet and ask the thief for pardon!"
It bowed down, and it placed its head between its paws,
And as if crying howled as it sought his forgiveness.
"Now you say, 'Rise, let us be friends just as before!'" 95
And after he said this, the dog rose up rejoicing,
Thanked first the thief and then the lords, those sitting
    there.
The knight said, "Someone grab the culprit by the hair,
And hold a stick as if to punish his misdeed."
When two of them complied and said, "Why did you
    steal?"   100
The dog jumped up on them and from them rescued him,
And bit their calves so that they would be very sorry
That they mocked him with whom it had been reconciled.
Some laughed, while others were quite stupefied by this.
The courses of the meal were very sumptuous;   105
And after many dishes, after many drinks,
They brought the water; while they drank, they sat a while.
Fresh fruits of any kind were not in season then,
Though boys were bringing, from the forest, strawberries
(Some carried them in vessels, some in hazel bark)   110
Which they had picked one at a time from all around.
When they had eaten these, the tables were removed,
And water was provided . . . .

. . . . to remove their shoes.
He bound his shins with bands that he had bought in
    Lucca,   114
. . . .
And over socks of silk he wore his shoes . . .
. . . .
The kinsman wore red socks beneath cordovan shoes . . .
He bound both shins with bands . . .   120
. . . .
From which hung down, all over, many ornaments.

Post haec pellicium mox in]duerat varicosum,
prae vel post fissum vel circumquaque gulatum,
....................crus]inam ponendo profundam 125
fibro limbatam lato nimis atque nigello.
Sumpsit, herilis quem sibi donavit digitalem
ad minimum digitum bene vix tum convenientem
.......................interulam male lotam
mantel mardrinum senio sudoreque fuscum 130
.......................m]ox ad dominas repedabant,
quas ad cancellos invenerunt speculantes.

He put on after this a many-colored coat,
Slashed in both front and back and trimmed with marten fur.
. . .a very long fur cloak   125
That had a wide black border made of beaver skin.
He took the ring that the young woman gave to him;
It barely fitted on his little finger . . .

       . . . an undergarment badly washed,
And marten cloak all dark with age and sweat.   130

       . . . they went back to the ladies, whom
They found were looking through the lattice.

XI.

Tunc sibimet comedunt [satis] et pullis tribuerunt.
Cum per aperturas in domate quis sibi micas
praebet, mox illo concurrebant adhiando
captantes avide, quod quit contingere cuique.
Sic consuefactae sunt post modicum cito cunctae; 5
quin post, ostiolum sibi cum fieret patefactum,
in manibus resident, quod eis datur accipiebant,
dumque fiunt saturae leniendo manuque politae,
doma sua sponte certatim mox subiere
et componendo rostris pennas residendo, 10

sic gaudendo, diem quod non siluere per omnem.
Oblectamentum fit herili deliciosum,
cum nimis insuave senibus sit tale quid omne.
Pabula nulligena, vel limpha stat in domicella
sturnorum, sed eos duxere fame domitandos, 15
ut per aperturas poscant escas sibi dandas,
quod primo veteres nimium renuere parentes.
Cum pullis non dant, has illi deseruerunt,
qui digitum praebent, his illi mox adhiabant.
Eligitur sciola super hos doctura magistra 20
nostratim fari "Pater" et "noster" recitare
usque "qui es in caelis" lis lis lis triplicatis,

Staza soror, "canite canite" doceat geminare,
quod pulli discunt, veteres quam discere possent.

Interea miles, consanguineus simul eius 25
cum domina vadunt, harpatores ubi ludunt.
Miles ut audivit, male quam rithmum modulavit
inter eos summus illius artis alumnus,
ad dominam dixit, ibi si plus harpa fuisset.
"Est" ait "hic harpa, melior qua non erit ulla, 30
in qua, dum vixit, meus heros simphoniavit,
cuius clangore mea mens languescit amore,
quam nemo tetigit, is postquam vivere finit,
in qua, si vultis, rithmos modulare valetis."
Quam iubet afferri sibi, quam citat is moderari 35

. . . .

XI.

(The guests have been amusing themselves with some trained
birds.)

They took food for themselves and then gave to their young.
When someone offered crumbs between the cage's bars,
At once they hurried to that spot with gaping mouths
To seize with eagerness whatever came to each.
Eventually they all grew used to doing this.   5
But later, when the door of their cage was left open,
They perched on hands, accepting what was given them.
When they were full, and smooth from being stroked by hand,
Then on their own they quickly raced inside their cage,
And as they perched they groomed their feathers with their
   beaks,   10
So happy that they were not quiet all that day.
This did provide a pleasant pastime for the maiden,
Although the older folk disliked this sort of thing.
The starlings' cage contained no type of food or drink.
The people caused them to be galled by hunger, so   15
They'd ask that food be given them between the bars.
The older birds, the parents, first resisted strongly.
The chicks deserted them, since they gave them no food,
And soon were pecking at the ones who offered fingers.
A trainer was assigned to them to teach them how   20
To speak and say the Lord's Prayer in our tongue up to
"Who are in heaven" (with "-ven -ven -ven" said three
   times).
Let Sister Staza teach them to repeat "sing sing."
The young birds learned this trick before the old birds
   could.
Meanwhile the knight, together with his relative,   25
Went with the mistress where the men were playing harps.
The knight, when he heard their best student of that art
Playing the melody so clumsily, then asked
The mistress if there was another harp nearby.
She said, " There is no better harp than this one here,   30
On which my husband used to play when he was living.
The music from it makes my mind grow faint with love.
Nobody else has touched it since he passed away.
On this you can play melodies if you desire."
She ordered that harp brought to him, which he makes
   haste   35
To play . . .

pulsans mox laeva] digitis geminis, modo dextra
tangendo chordas dulces reddit nimis odas,
multum distincte faciens variamina quaeque, 40
quod pede saltandi manibus neumas vel agendi
nescius omnino citus haec perdisceret ambo.
Qui prius audacter chordas pulsant ioculanter,

auscultant illi taciti modulare nec ausi.
Sic tribus insolitis actis dulcissime rithmis 45
quartum poscit hera faceret petit et sua nata.
Eius contribulis quem saltaret vel herilis.
Quem per sistema sive diastema dando responsa
dum mirabiliter operareturve decenter,
surrexit iuvenis, quo contra surgit herilis. 50
Ille velut falcho se girat et haec ut hirundo;
ast ubi conveniunt, citius se praeteriebant;
i]s se movisse, sed cernitur illa natasse,
neutrum saltasse neumas manibus variasse
nemo corrigere quo posset, si voluisset. 55

Tunc signum dederant, ibi multi quod doluerunt,
deponendo manus, finitus sit quia rithmus.
Insimul et resident et in alterutrum nimis ardent
lege maritali cupientes consociari,
illius id matre fieri nimium cupiente 60
atque facultante, quod vellent, sermocinare.
Hunc dominella rogat, quo secum tessere ludat,
annulus ut victi donetur ter superanti.
Tunc is "Qui ludum, quem ludamus modo primum,
acquirat," dixit "digitalis uterque suus sit." 65
Haec] ea laudavit ludens et eum superavit,
gratis perdente iuvene gratis sibi dante.
Quae nimium laeta, se sic habuisse trophaea,
ludendo proprium cito perdebat digitalem,
quem trahit a digito iaciebat eique rotando. 70
In cuius medio nodus fuerat cavus intro;
hunc ni laxaret, digito non inposuisset.

Now striking chords two-fingered with his right hand, now
His left, he coaxed forth very lovely melodies,
While sounding many variations so distinctly   40
A man who was completely ignorant of dancing
Or keeping time by clapping could learn both skills quickly.
Those who had plucked the strings in bold and jesting
    fashion
Now listened silently and did not dare to play.
When he had played three unfamiliar songs most sweetly, 45
The mistress and her daughter asked him for a fourth,
To which his relative and the young girl could dance.
And while restating themes in scales and intervals,
He played the music with both elegance and skill.
The youth stood up; the girl rose and stood opposite.   50
He whirled just like a falcon, she just like a swallow,
But when they came together, quickly passed each other;
He seemed to glide along and she appeared to float;
And no one, even if he wished, could have improved
The way they danced or clapped their hands to keep the
    time;   55
And then by lowering their heads they gave a sign,
Which many there regretted, that the dance was over.
They sat together, and they burned for one another;
And they were eager to be joined by marriage bonds.
Her mother wanted very much for this to happen,   60
And gave them chances to talk over what they wished.
The maiden asked the youth to play at dice with her:
The one who wins three times receives the loser's ring.
Then he said, "No, whoever wins the first game which
We play right now, let both the rings belong to him."   65
Then she approved of this, and beat him when they played.
The youth lost gladly, gladly gave the ring to her.
So very happy that this trophy now was hers,
She quickly lost her own ring when they played a game.
She pulled it from her finger, tossing it to him.   70
Inside it in the middle was a hollow knot.
Unless the youth untied this knot, he could not put
It on his finger.

XII.

Nunc, hera, commatrem quam proxime videris [ipsam,
dic mihi, si valeat, si tranquille sua res stet,
quandoque commater fieret tua, si mihi frater
ex illa sit, quem de fonte levaveris, inque,
anne tuam natam de fonte levaverit ill[a. " 5
Obstupefacta nimis dictis hera militis ist[is
"Ah, quid dixisti, quod eam nupsisse putasti,
cui fuerat sine te non ipsum vivere dulce;
nam flendo visum post te iam perdidit ipsum.
Illa meam natam de fonte levaverat istam 10
et pro natabus propriis nos post habet amb[as,
saepeque nos visit vel nobis tunc aliquid fert."
Audit ut hoc miles, matri compassus ait flens
"An queo septimana revenire domum vel in ist[a?"
"Cras" ait "ad seram matrem quis cernere karam, 15
sed panem missi penes hanc volo prima mereri."
Est divulgatum, commatris eum fore natum,
inter mancipia fit laeticia cito magna,
congaudent matri reditu pro sospite nati.
Tunc hera direxit missum, quem dicere iussit 20
commatri, natum praesente die rediturum.
Interea iuvenis pariter ludunt et herilis.
hunc ea ter vicit, hanc is totiens superavit,
alterutrim victi gaudentes omine pacti,
virginis is quod erat, iuvenis quod virgo manebat, 25
non se vicisse, sed victor succubuisse.
Haec suus, ille sua vocitabantur vice versa,
mutato sexu soloecismi scemate facto.
Nec iam celarunt, se quin ardenter amarent,
mater si sineret, vel in ipsa nocte coirent. 30
Illa tamen sineret, sibi si non dedecus esset;
ut praestoletur, tunc virgo vix superatur.
..................lus non dominetur
..................velit ire sinatur
..................domino dominaeque placebat 35
..................um, domini faciendum
..................s resident quibus illi
..................m]ulta viando loquentes
..................os videt a matre missos
..................omnibus oscula praebet 40
..................matris amorem
..................um prius intueatur
..................deus utque remittat
..................debemus famulari

XII.

(Ruodlieb has struck up a conversation with the widow about his mother.)

"Now, mistress, how long since you saw your godmother?
Please tell me, is she well? And does she live in peace?
Please tell me, when did she become your godmother?
Has she borne me a brother whom you raised from that
Baptismal fount, or did she raise your daughter from   5
The fount?" The knight's words utterly amazed the lady.
"Ah me, what have you said? Do you think she has wed,
For whom her life has lost its sweetness without you?
For she has lost her vision from her tears for you.
That woman raised my daughter from the fount and from   10
That time considers both of us to be her daughters.
She often visits us and bring us gifts." When he
Heard this, the knight was moved by pity for his mother;
He wept and said, "Can I still go back home this week?"
"Tomorrow night," she said, "you can see your dear
          mother.   15
But I want to be first to earn the envoy's bread
At her house." Word spread that he was the son of her
Godmother. Quickly joy arose among the servants,
Who shared the mother's joy at her son's safe return.
The mistress sent an envoy to tell her godmother   20
That on that very day her son would come back home.
The young man and her daughter meanwhile played again.
She won three times, and three times he defeated her.
Defeated mutually, they liked this omen of
Their marriage: he was hers, and she belonged to him.   25
They liked not winning, but surrendering defeated.
She was called his boy, he vice versa called her girl.
They changed their sexes in a form of solecism.
No longer did they hide their passion for each other;
And if the mother had allowed, they would have slept   30
Together on that very night; and even so,
She would have, were it not dishonorable for them.
The girl could hardly be prevailed upon to wait.

(The marriage has been agreed on. Ruodlieb and his cousin have resumed their journey. His imminent arrival has been reported, and a servant is sitting in a cherry tree in order to be the first to see his master.)

```
.................rediisse videmus              45
.................noribus amplificatum."
.................tes vobis et habebo
.................atri bonitatis
.................spondent et ovantur
.................s accuset apud te             50
.................lli debueramus
................. et ante non utu servos
.................ius ad haec famulari?
.................r non venere nisi tres
.................ectant here nostri             55
.................endum facientes
.................dans oscula dixit:
.................s grandis fit in illis
.................ibi fuit atque bibebant
.................herum comitantur ovantes       60
.................m cum reliqua re
.................q]ualiter omnia starent
.................diceret omnia stare
.................d nocuisse suorum
.................nitus iacuisset agrorum        65
.................erat omnipotentem
.................cerasiorum
sederat hinc speculans prae se pendentia spernens
.................rantia mora.
Nunciet ut primus, dominus com venerit eius     70
.................monedula supra
explorans quid agat, cur cerasiis ita parcat
.................hoc ea prodat.
Ille magis dominum cupit ut videat equitantem,
.................e curre venique                75
idque monedula discit et ad dominam revolavit
.................,precor, audi."
Quae dixit "Loquere." "Ruodlieb here, curre venique."
.................e gementem,
omnes risere, volucrem quid tale notare.        80
.................sedeas ubi supra
quod dicatque nota, si clamet, tu quoque clama."
.................monedula verba
ipsius pueri Ruodlieb venientis avari
.................quando veniret                 85
prospicit, e silva socios emergere densa;
primo contribulis, iu]xta quem scutifer eius,
postremo dominus meat officialis et eius
.................quaeque suarum.
Tunc puer exclamat "Dominus, gaudete, propinquat." 90
```

He sat there looking out, ignoring all the cherries
That hung in front of him. . .
He wished to be the first one to announce his lord's   70
Arrival . . .
Above him perched a jackdaw which examined what
He did and why he was abstaining from the cherries,
To report this later . . .
The servant wanted more to see his master riding . . .   75

The jackdaw learned this, then it flew to her and said,
What he said, "Master Ruodlieb, now hurry, come!"

All laughed because the bird had noticed such a thing.   80
. . .above the boy and take note what he says; and if
He calls out, you call out as well. . .
The jackdaw listened to the words said by the servant
Who wanted Ruodlieb to come. . .
At last he saw his friends emerge from the dense forest. 85
First came the kinsman, next to whom his squire walked,
And last the master with his squire . . .
And then the boy exclaimed, "Rejoice, the master nears!" 90

171

XIII.

Barbiciam] scabit, quod non pilus unus ibi sit.
Quod tam nemo vafer sit, qui discernere possit,
clericus an mulier inberbes an esset alumnus,
est tam iocundae tam virgineae faciei.
Dum se tondebant sordes limphaque lavabant, 5
exierant butinam. Lavacralem mox sibi laenam
scutifer imposuit, qua lectum tectus adivit,
donec siccetur aestusque sibi minuatur.
Post modicum surgit, sua calciamenta requirit.
Sic pedat ad mensam comes insed. . . 10
non tamen in solio voluit residere supremo,
sed subiective matris dextrim velut hospes
atque libens totum sibi permisit dominatum;
haec quod ei dederat, reverenter suscipiebat.
Incidens panem turbam partitur in omnem, 15
transmisit cuivis discum specialibus escis,
cum vino pateram, mittens aliquando medonem.
Ruotlieb contribulis conviva fuit socialis,
ex uno pane comedunt, una quoque lance,
ex uno cyato biberant communiter ambo. 20
Matri conviva solet esse monedula sola,
cui pilulam micae cum dat, capit illa, superbe
perspacians, mensam transversim transilit omnem.
Fercula post multa post pocula totque secuta
tunc hera poscit aquam, camerarius attulit ill]am. 25
Ad mensas quasque summo iubet hanc dare cuique.
Posthinc pincernae passim potum tribuere.
Mensis amotis mensalibus atque plicatis
laeti consurgunt dominae gratesque dederunt
dicunt gaudere, Ruotlieb sanum rediisse, 30
quo consoletur matrem, ne plus tribuletur,
primitus ut saepe, dolet illo cum caruisse.
Est divulgatum cito per totam regionem,
Ruotlieb venisse locupletatum sat abunde.
Dum sibi post placuit dum secretumque sibi fit, 35
intrat conclave cum dilecta sibi matre
scutiferumque iubet, enthecam quo sibi ferret.
De qua multiplices extraxit opes preciosas

XIII.

(Ruodlieb and his cousin have arrived at Ruodlieb's home,
where they are preparing themselves for a banquet arranged
by Ruodlieb's mother in honor of his return.)

He shaved his beard so closely not one hair remained.
Nobody there was shrewd enough to notice if
He was a cleric, woman, or a beardless schoolboy,
Because he had a face so cheerful and so girlish.
When they had shaved and washed away the dirt with water,   5
They left the tub; the squire covered them at once
With robes; and clothed in these they then went to the
     couch,
Where they remained until they were dried off and cooled.
Arising somewhat later, they put on their shoes. . .
The knight went to the table and sat down . . .   10
He did not wish to sit up at the head, however;
But like a guest sat humbly on his mother's right,
And gladly he gave her complete authority.
Respectfully he took that which she gave to him.
She cut the bread and passed it out to all the group,   15
And passed to everyone a dish of special foods;
She sent around a bowl of wine, and sometimes mead.
His relative was there as Ruodlieb's companion.
They ate from one loaf, also from a single plate;
Both even drank together from a single cup.   20
The jackdaw liked to be the mother's sole companion.
When she gave it some crumbs, it took them and then hopped
Along the whole length of the table, strutting proudly.
Then after many dishes and as many drinks,
The mistress called for water which the chamberlain   25
Brought there; she had it served the nobles at each table.
And then the waiters served a drink to everyone.
And when the tables were removed and tablecloths
All folded, happily they rose and thanked the mistress,
Expressing joy that Ruodlieb had come back safe   30
To bring his mother comfort and to end her worry,
As she had often grieved that he had gone from her.
The news spread rapidly through the entire region,
That Ruodlieb returned abundantly enriched.
When later he received the privacy he wished,   35
With his beloved mother he went to his room,
Commanding that his squire bring his pack to him.
From this he took a multitude of precious riches,

in chrusinis, in pelliciis census et alius,
exul quae denis nanciscebatur in annis.   40
Post poscit peras, quas scutifer attulit amb[as.
Extrahat ut panes, iubet hunc, factos aput Afr[os.
Quos dum produxit, matri ioculanter is inquit
"Hos deservivi, tenus hac, mater, ubi mansi.
[Hos mihi rex dederat m . . .   45
[mater ait "Famulos nobis, reor, ante vocandos;]
quam bene sint] sapidi, videant, panes africani."
Is dixit "Melius] puto, quo soli videamus."
Educens cultrum], quo panem dissec[at] unum,
percipit arge]ntum lancis, sub quo fuit aurum.   50
Pollen ut abra]sit iubar argentique reluxit,
clavis coniun]ctos cernens tria per loca lances,

comminuens] lima cito clavorum capitella,
dissolvens] lances videt aureolos ibi nummos
tam strictim] iunctos, quod suppingi nequit unus.   55
Ruodlieb exult]at domino grates et agebat.
Nec cunctan]s parilem manibus sustollere lancem,
tergendo p]ollen, clavos limando minutim,
nummis confert]am vario censuque repletam
cernit et ob]stupuit; nimium sua mater ovavit,   60
tunc gemitus e]dens, in mente sat ast hylarescens
perfusis] oculis grates Christo dat in altis,
quod locupletat]um dederat sibi tamque beatum.
Miles humi dat] se terram premit oreque saepe,
ceu se pro] regis pedibus domini daret eius.   65
Tunc nimium plo]rans faciem lacrimandoque tingens
orabat "Dom]ine, num par tibi quis valet esse,
qui clemens] illum miserum dignaris homullum
sic locuplet]are vel honoribus amplificare,
eius nec vitiis] reminiscere quod patereris?   70
Nunc mihi des, d]omine, quo non moriar, precor, ante
quam rursus v]ideam, quem pauper egensque petebam,
qui manda]nte te clementer suscipiens me
fecit tantar]um consortem deliciarum
et miserum d]enos secum retinendo per annos   75
amplificavi]t me, queo quod posthac sat honeste
vivere fi]denter, haec si tracto sapienter."
Ruodlieb cum m]atre, dum sat gaudent super hac re,
lances conclu]dunt, cautissime quam valuerunt,
et prendunt, cen]sus secum fert quicquid alius.   80
Accurrunt] plures proprii servi iuniores.

Consisting of both pelts and furs and other wealth
Which he had gained in his ten years of exile; then   40
He sought the knapsacks, both of which the squire brought.
He had him take the loaves out baked in Africa.
As he showed them, he told his mother jokingly,
"I earned these, mother, where I stayed until this time.
The king gave them to me . . ."   45
His mother said, "I think we first should call the servants
To see how tasty are these loaves from Africa."
He said, "I think it better if we see alone;"
And pulling out a knife, with which he cut one loaf,
He saw the silver of the dish—beneath it, gold.   50
When he rubbed off the flour, the radiant silver glittered.
When he observed that three nails joined the plates
    together,
He quickly used a file to scrape away their heads,
And loosening the plates he saw there golden coins
So tightly packed that not one more could be wedged in.   55
Then Ruodlieb rejoiced and gave thanks to the Lord.
Without delay he seized the other in his hands,
And wiping off the flour he filed down the nails.
He saw it filled with coins and crammed with varied wealth.
He was astonished, and his mother was elated.   60
Then heaving sighs, though very joyful in her heart,
With tear-filled eyes she offered thanks to Christ in heaven
That He had given her a son so rich and blessed.
The knight fell to the ground and often kissed the earth,
As if he lay there at his feet before his lord   65
The king. Then weeping much and moistening his face
With tears, he prayed, "Lord, who indeed can be your equal,
Who in your mercy thus have deigned both to enrich
And magnify a wretched little man with honors,
And to forget what You have suffered for his sins?   70
Now grant me, Lord, I pray, before I die, to see
Again the man whom I approached when poor and needy;
For he received me mercifully, as You commanded,
And he made me his partner in such great delights;
And while he kept this poor man with him for ten years,   75
He so enriched me that I can live honorably
And faithfully, if I will manage this wealth wisely."
He and his mother, very happy with the outcome,
Then closed the plates as carefully as possible,
And took the other treasure he had brought with him.   80
Then many of their younger servants ran toward them.

XIV.

"..................pueris ceu credo venire
quidam karorum nostri consanguineorum,
qui quando veniant, haec dum firmentur, ibi sint.
Ad vos nunc illam vos invitate puellam,
vestri communes veniant utrimque fideles." 5
Quae cum venisset hanc hi circumque stetissent,
curtis amicorum cito plena fit advenientum.
Quos Ruodlieb bene suscepit, quibus oscula praebet,
et prandere rogat satis illis et tribuebat.
Amotis mensis dominabus et inde reversis 10
ad sua secreta, praecedit eas ea nata;
post illasque pedant, sibi qui plumatia portant,
et plures alii comitantes his famulari.
His vinum ferri iubet illo pro famulari;
dumque bibit quisque, sibi vicino dedit, usque 15
pincernae pateram reddebant evacuatam.
Inclinant, abeunt Ruodlieb dominosque revisunt.
Tunc Ruodlieb dixit "Quia vos deus huc glomeravit,
nunc audite mihi curate vel auxiliari,
connubium quoddam quo fiat nunc stabilitum, 20
est quod laudatum, sic ad nos induciatum,
ad quod praesentes mihi vos cupio fore testes.
Contigit, ut iuvenis meus iste nepos et herilis
mutuo diligerent sese, dum tessere ludunt,
lege maritali cupientes consociari." 25
Dicunt "Hoc cuncti debemus consiliari,
indolis ut tantae vir tam virtutis opimae
non dehonestetur, citius sed ut eripiatur
a scorto turpi digne satis igne cremari"
et laudant dominum, quod in hoc cosmo fuit usquam 30

femina, quae magicam de se divelleret ipsam.
Tunc surgit iuvenis, grates dabat omnibus illis,
quod tam clementes sibi sunt communiter omnes,
inquit et, horrere penitus se seque pudere
sic dehonestatum per id execrabile scortum. 35
"Nunc opus uxore nimium mihi cernitis esse,
quam quoniam facile nunc possumus hic reperire,
hanc desponsari desidero vel mihi iungi,
ut sitis testes et ad hoc mihi, quaeso, libentes,
alterutros cum nos dotabimus, est veluti mos." 40

XIV.

(Ruodlieb has taken care of the arrangements for his
cousin's marriage to the daughter of his godmother.)

. . ."Invite too some of our dear relatives
To come and be there when the marriage is contracted.
Now send that girl an invitation to your house,
And ask those who are friends of both of you to come." 5
When she arrived, and they all had surrounded her,
The court was quickly filled with friends who were arriving,
Whom Ruodlieb then welcomed cordially and kissed.
He asked them to have lunch and gave them much to eat;
And when the tables were removed, the ladies went 10
Back to their chambers, with the daughter going first.
Behind them walked the servants who were holding pillows,
And many others who were there to offer service.
He ordered wine brought them as payment for their service.
When each had drunk, he passed it over to the next, 15
Until the waiters carried back an empty bowl.
They bowed, left, went back to the lords and Ruodlieb.
Then Ruodlieb said, "Since God has assembled you,
Now hear me and take care to offer your assistance,
So that a certain marriage now may be confirmed 20
Which has been sanctioned and entrusted then to us.
I want you to be there with me as witnesses.
It happens that my youthful cousin and this girl
Fell mutually in love while they were playing dice
And now desire to be joined in lawful marriage." 25
They answered: "All of us should counsel that a man
Of such great natural talent and the highest virtue
Ought not to be disgraced but quickly snatched away
From that vile whore who well deserves a death by burning."
And then they praised the Lord that somewhere in this
    world 30
There lived a woman who would rip that witch from him.
And then the youth arose and thanked them all because
They all alike had been so merciful to him.
He said that he shuddered and that he felt deep shame
At being so disgraced by that accursed whore. 35
"Now, as you see, I have a great need for a wife.
Because now we can find her here so easily,
I wish her to be affianced and joined with me;
I ask that you be willing witnesses to me
In this when we exchange our gifts, as is the custom." 40

Qui dicunt "Prompte tibi subveniemus in hac re."
Ruodlieb post dominas pariter direxit eas tres,
quae cito venere nata praeeunte mo[deste.
Contra quas agmen surrexit eis ad honorem.
Cuncti dum resident, spatium breve conticuerunt, 45
tunc Ruotlieb surgit et ut auscultent sibi poscit.
His post contribulis pactum dixit vel amicis,
hic] quod et haec ferveret in alterutrius amorem.
Hanc hunc uxorem suimet si vellet haber[e
....
illam.................................... 50
illum si vellet, rogitant; parum quoque ridet,
post ait "An servum nolim ludo superatum,
tessere quem vici sub talis fenore pacti,
seu vincat, seu succumbat, soli mihi nubat.
S]erviat obnixe, volo, quo mihi nocte dieque, 55
quod quanto melius facit, est tanto mihi karus."
T]unc risus magnus fit ab omnibus atque cachinnus,
tam praesumptive loquitur quod tam vel amice.
E]ius at ut matrem cernunt haec non renuentem
e]t genus amborum par posseque divitiarum, 60
discutiunt caute, bene conveniant quod utrimque,
hanc desponsari sibi censent lege iugali.

S]ponsus at extraxit ensem ve piramide tersit;
anulus in capulo fixus fuit aureus ipso,
affert quem sponsae sponsus dicebat et ad se 65
"Anulus ut digitum circumcapit undique totum,
sic tibi stringo fidem firmam vel perpetualem,
hanc servare mihi debes aut decapitari."
Quae satis astute iuveni respondit et apte
"Iudicium parile decet ut patiatur uterque. 70
Cur servare fidem tibi debeo, dic, meliorem,
quam mihi tu debes? Dic, si defendere possis,
si licuisset Adae, maecham superaddat ut Evae,
unam cum costam faceret deus in mulierem;
quam de se sumptam cum proclamaverat Adam, 75
dic, ubi concessas binas sibi legeris Evas.
Cum meretricares, essem scortum tibi velles?
Absit, ut hoc pacto tibi iungar; vade, valeto
et quantumcunque scortare velis, sine sed me.
Tot sunt in mundo, tibi ceu quo tam bene nubo." 80
Sic dicens gladium sibi liquerat et digitalem.
Cui dixit iuvenis "Fiat, dilecta, velut vis.
Umquam si faciam, tibi quae dedero bona perdam,
istius capitis abscidendique potens sis."

They said, "We will support you readily in this."
Then Ruodlieb sent for the three young mistresses
Together, who came quickly, the daughter properly
In front. The line of guests rose up to pay them honor.
When all sat down and had been silent for a while,   45
Then Ruodlieb stood up and asked the two to listen.
He told their relatives and friends about their pact,
That he and she were burning with a mutual love.
Then they asked if he wished to have her as his wife. . .
....   50
If she desired him. She smiled a little, then
Replied, "Should I refuse a servant beaten in
A game, whom I defeated playing dice with this
Agreement: win or lose he would wed me alone?
I want him night and day to serve me zealously.   55
The better he does this, the dearer he will be
To me." Then everyone began to smile and laugh,
Because she spoke so boldly and so genially.
Perceiving that her mother did not disapprove,
And that both families had equal wealth and power,   60
They carefully decided that the couple were
Well matched and thought she should be pledged to him in
    marriage.
The bridegroom drew his sword and wiped it at its point.
Set in the very hilt there was a golden ring,
Which he as groom gave to his bride and said to her,   65
"Just as the ring embraces your entire finger,
I pledge to you my constant and enduring faith.
You must preserve the same for me or lose your head."
Both cleverly and suitably she answered her
Young man: "The same rule should apply to both of us.   70
Why should I, tell me, be more true to you than you
To me? Speak, if you can maintain that Adam was
Allowed to have a mistress in addition to
His Eve, when God formed just one woman from his rib.
When Adam cried out that his rib was gone from him,   75
Tell where you read that two Eves were conceded him.
When you go fornicating, would you like that I
Become a whore for you? No, far be it from me
To marry you on such conditions. Go! Good-bye!
Go whore however much you like, but not with me.
The world has many men like you for me to wed."   80
She spoke, but left his sword and ring behind for him.
The youth told her, "It will be as you wish, my darling,
If ever I do, I'll lose the goods I gave to you.
And you will be empowered to cut off my head."

Quae modicum ridens ad eum seseque revertens   85
inquit "Ea lege modo iungamur sine fraude."
Huius amen dixit procus et sibi basia fixit.
His ita coniunctis aenesis fit maxima plebis,
laudantes dominum cantizabant hymenaeum.
Ruotlieb pellicium dederat bene valde gulatum   90
sponso vel crusinam limbo terrae crepitantem,
dat et equum celerem sibi compte sat faleratum.
Munerat et sponsae consanguineo sociatae;
huic tria dat spinthra, quae velent pectora pulchra,
atque dat armillas sibi bis binas operosas   95
et pariter sibi tres dat gemmatos digitales
datque superductam cocco crusinam migalinam.
Cetera turba sua sibi dant sponsalia magna.
Qualiter inter se concordent, quid mihi curae?

She smiled a little bit, turned back to him and said,   85
"By this law, without fraud, let us now be united."
Her suitor said "amen" to this, then gave her kisses.
When they had thus been wed, the people shouted their
Acclaim; they praised the Lord and sang the wedding song.
Then Ruodlieb gave to the groom a coat well trimmed   90
With neck-fur and a cloak whose border brushed the ground,
And a swift stallion, handsomely caparisoned.
He gave gifts to the bride now married to his kinsman:
To wear upon her lovely breast he gave three brooches;
He also gave to her four decorated bracelets;   95
He gave her also three rings set with precious gems,
A cloak of ermine that was trimmed with scarlet cloth.
The others too gave lavish wedding gifts to them.
What worry do I have how they will get along?

XV.

Quamvis..................................[senectus
parcere quae nescit pariter cunctos domi[tavit.
Femina, quae lunae par est in flore iuv[entae,
par vetulae simiae fit post aetate senectae.
Rugis sulcata frons, quae fuit antea pl[ana,   5

ante columbini sibi stant oculi te[nebrosi;
deguttat nasus sordes nimium mucul[entus.
Dependent buccae quondam pinguedine t[ensae.

Dentes oblongi moti stant ut ruitur[i,

per quos lingua foras pellit locutura fa[bellas,   10
et verbum profert, plenum ceu pollinis o[s sit.
Utque recurvatum resupinum stat sibi m[entum,
os et risibile, quod plures allicit in se,
Stat semper patulum, populum terrere vel [aptum.
stat collum gracile deplumatae quasi p[icae,   15
extantes mammae, iam ceu trochi tub[erosae,
molles ut fungi suci pendent vacu[ati.
Et prius usque nates [qui] crines auricolore[s
pendent discretim dorsum velando pil[atim,
extant horribiles terrentes inspici[entes,   20
per saepem caput ut anuatim sit sibi t[ractum;
inclinata caput humeris extantibus [umbrat
ut tardus vultur, ubi scit iacuisse cad[aver.
Et quae discincta consueverat ire iuve[nta,

alte succingit tunicam, ne sordifica[ret,   25
calcatura fabas veluti pultem coquitu[ra.
Calciamenta sua, quae iam fuerant nim[is arta,
cum soccis laxa, ligo ceu, stant, ante sup[ina,
sustollunt luti nimium calcando limo[si.
Et graciles digiti, quondam pinguedine pl[eni,   30
nunc super ossa cutem, sucosi, carne care[ntem
sordent rugosis nimis ex fuligine nod[is,
unguibus incisis longis squalore nige[llis.
Sic agilem iuvenem senium domat ut mu[lierem.

XV.

(Ruodlieb's mother is urging him to get married. She is
describing the horrors of old age.)

                                        . . . Old age
Which knows not how to spare, has conquered all alike.
A woman who in bloom of youth is like the moon,
In dotage afterward is like an old she-ape.
Her brow, which once was smooth, is deeply etched with
    wrinkles;   5
Her eyes, which once were just like doves, are murky now;
Her nose is full of mucus and is dripping filth;
Her cheeks, which once were plump and firm, are hanging
    down;
Her crooked teeth, through which her tongue thrusts words
    when she
Would speak, are loose, as if about to tumble out;   10
She utters words as if her mouth were full of flour.
Her chin is curved and tilting upward in an arc;
Her smiling mouth, alluring once to many men,
Is always gaping, and is apt to frighten people.
Her scrawny neck is like a magpie's after plucking.   15
Her jutting breasts, which used to be like firm round balls,
Are flabby and are hanging down like shrivelled mushrooms.
The golden-colored hair that once hung to her buttocks,
Bound up in separate braids and covering her back,
Sticks up grotesquely, terrible to see, as if   20
Her head had just been drawn, arse first, through shrubbery.
Her hunching shoulders shade her drooping head, just like
A sluggish vulture when it knows a corpse has fallen.
Though in her youth she always walked with skirts
    free-flowing,
She hoists her cloak up high to keep from soiling it   25
As though she were about to trample beans for porridge.
Her shoes, which once fit very snugly, now are loose
Despite her socks, and, curled up like a hoe in front,
Scrape up much slimy mud with every step she takes.
Her graceful fingers, formerly both plump and full   30
Of juice, are now mere skin and bones devoid of flesh,
And are extremely fouled with soot, their knuckles gnarled,
Their fingernails uncut and long and black with dirt.
Age overcomes an agile man as it does woman . . .

....	35
....................s sibi celsior est ubi tellus	
....................at quis crus sellam super ipsam	
....................m suspendat se socialem	
....................et girans si sella vacillet	
....................etum fuerit si forte iumentum	40
....................dum latum saliens super amnem	
....................aculo sese sustollere crebro	
....................n post multa levamina tandem	
....................n post se transit tussi quatiente	
....................eas cernit girare choreas	45
....................us iuvenis fugitabit amarus	
....................bunt cuncti vel ei maledicunt	
....................vel in his iuvenilis ovabat	
....................idit quid cantent aure notabit	
....................uit digitis neumas agitabit	50
....................meros huc huc vertens hilarescens	
....................os ad sese respicientes	
....................es optant rediisse priores	
....................fieri si posset eundem	
....................let dum sponte libens obiisset	
....................do suspirans intime flendo	
....................um dicens saepissime secum:	57

"Mors humanorum] finis tu sola malorum
cur mihi ser]a venis? Cur non me carcere solvis?
....................li languore dolore	60
....................quos tolerare debet	
....................licet id sibi vivere mors sit	

donec quando] iubet deus, eius spiritus exit;
haec nam lex do]mat omne quod est, volet, ambulet aut net:
principium quod] habet non quodam fine carebit."
Non cessat ma]ter Ruotlieb minitare frequenter   65
quae sic languis]set et id effugitare nequisset
....................et alius nil habuerunt	
....................quicquam tractare suarum	
....................fili, tua magna sophia.	
....................e plus quam claresc............	70

(The horrors of a man's old age are described. In his
youth, no mountain was too steep, no horse too wild, no
river too wide. Now he must use a cane, is racked by
coughing, and is jeered when he tries to dance.)

. . . . .saying often to himself, 57
"Death, you who are alone the end of human woes,
Why do you come for me so late? Why do you not
Release me from my prison? . . ."
Which he must suffer, though his life is death for him, 61
Until that time his soul departs at God's command.
This law rules everything that is: which flies or walks
Or swims . . .
That which has a beginning will not lack an end.
His mother, who had grown so weak that she could not 65
Escape her death, did not cease giving Ruodlieb
Her frequent warnings. . .

XVI.

"Haeres tunc valeat, si filius haut tibi fiat!
Si sine, dic, liberis, quid erit, fili, morieris?
De nostris rebus erit altercatio grandis.
Deficiunt vires omnino mihi iuveni[les;
nam denos annos, quos tu fueras apud [Afros,   5
cottidie curis angebar in omnibus hor[is
post te maerendo pro nostra reque tuenda,
nique revertisses, citius iam caeca fuisse[m.
Sed iuvenescebam, cum te remeare scieb[am,
contineo melius et me modo quam mea sit v[is.   10
Vellem, si velles, quo nostros congenerales
et nobis fidos nunc conveniamus amicos,
quorum consilio quorumque iuvamine fido
possis in uxorem reperire tibi muliere[m,
esse parentelae quam noris talis utrimque,   15
claudicet ut neutrim vestri genitura [vicissim,
per cuius mores tibi nec minuantur hono[res,
quam tibi demonstret clemens deus ac tibi i[ungat."

Ruodlieb respondit, matri placidissime [dixit
"Cras demandemus consanguineis et ami[cis,   20
ut nos conveniant quam velocissime possi[nt.
Quod mihi consilium dant, si censes id agendum,
non praetermittam, quod vultis quin ego solv[am."
Missis legatis et amicis conglomera[tis,
ad se dum veniunt bene suscepti[que sibi sunt,   25
Ruotlieb disposuit sedilia, ceu bene [novit,
in quo quisque loco sedeat sibi certificato,
dans geminis unam mensam dominis ad h[abendum,
et matri solium fieri iubet altius un[um,
ut super aspiceret cunctos, ibi qui resi[derent,   30
solaque manducet, hera cerni sic fore [posset.
Sic et honorando matrem dominam vel h[abendo
a populis laudem sed ab omnipotente coronam
atque diuturnam vitam meruitve bea[tam.
Dum manducavit, mensas removere] rogavit   35
claudunturque] fores, quos observant duo fortes,

qui non ire sinun]t intro quem neve foras quem,
donec consili]um diffiniretur id ipsum.
Tunc Ruodlieb] surgens modicum sileant, rogat omnes,

XVI.

(Her arguments concerning marriage continue.)

"Unless you have a son, bid farewell to an heir!
Son, tell me what will happen if you should die childless?
A bitter fight about our property will happen.
The vigor of my youth now fails me utterly.
The ten years that you spent among the Africans,   5
I was beset by cares each day and every hour.
I mourned for you and looked out for our property.
If you had not returned, I would have soon gone blind;
But I felt youthful when I learned you were returning,
And I am holding up more than my strength allows.   10
I should desire, if you do, that we now call
Our relatives and loyal friends together, that
With their advice and with their loyal help you can
Find for yourself a wife, a woman who you know
Is of such noble lineage on both sides that   15
On either side your offspring will not be deficient,
And by whose character your honors will not be
Diminished. May God in His mercy point her out
To you, and may He join her to you." Ruodlieb
Replied, and he spoke very gently to his mother:
"Tomorrow we will tell our friends and relatives   20
To gather here with us as quickly as they can.
If you think we should follow the advice that they
Give me, I will not fail to carry out your wish."
The messengers were sent and the friends were assembled.
When they arrived and had been greeted cordially,   25
Then Ruodlieb arranged the seats, as he was skilled
At doing, showing in what designated seat
Each was to sit, and placing two lords at each table.
He ordered one seat elevated for his mother,
So that she could look over all those seated there,   30
And eat alone, thus signifying her as mistress.
By honoring his mother and by making her
His mistress he has earned praise from the people, but
From God a crown and a long-lasting blessed life.
When he had dined, he ordered them to clear the tables.   35
The doors were closed and they were watched by two strong
    men,
Who gave no one permission to go in or out
Until all the deliberations were concluded.
Then Ruodlieb stood up and asked them all for silence

quo sibi notific]et, propter quod eos glomeraret. 40
Cum sileant, dix]it, genitrix sua ceu sibi suasit
"Nunc audite, m]ei consanguinei vel amici!
Quanto maerore] mea mater quove labore
pertulerit m]ulta, patris atque mei viduata,
curando cun]cta, vobis in re patet ipsa. 45
Nunc se defi]ciunt vires et membra fatiscunt
nec quidquam facere] valet amodo, quivit ut ante,
quod mihi vel cre]bro narrat vel id ipse videbo.
Hinc mihi sponsa]ri non cessat consiliari.
Quare nunc ad v]os misi me conveniendos, 50
ut reputare qu]eat sibi quisque vel hoc mihi dicat;
nam nimium paucae] mulieres sunt mihi notae
nec valeo] scire, quo me vertam mihi fauste;
vos mihi dicatis], super hac re quid faciatis,
uxorem nobis] si quam reperire queatis, 55
quae non indecor]et nostrum genus, id sed inauret
moribus ingen]ita vel vitae nobilitate."
Respondent p]ariter "Id quam faciemus ovanter,
ut natum carum d]e te videamus obortum
heredem morum], virtutum sive bonorum, 60
quis locupleta]vit te Christ et honorificavit."
Adnuerat quis]que, se spondens haec agitare.
Unus at exsurg]ens, cui notae sunt regiones
et noti domini bene], qui fuerant ibi summi,
is "Dominam" dixit] "unam scio, quae tibi par fit 65
moris honestate] virtute ve nobilitate.
Hanc vellem vi]deas, cum videris ut fatearis,
in mundo] nullam quod vidisses dominellam
omnem virtut]em tam strennuiter facientem,
talis quae fuer]it, ut quemque virum decuisset." 70

That he might tell them why he had assembled them.   40
When they were hushed, he spoke just as his mother had
Advised: "Now listen here, my friends and relatives.
You know with what great toil and grief my mother has
Endured so much, bereft of both me and my father,
While she took care of everything—all this you know.   45
Her strength is failing now, her limbs are growing weak,
Nor, from now on, can she do things as she once could.
She often tells me this, and I see it myself.
Hence she does not cease from advising me to marry.
And so I sent for you just now to gather here,   50
For each of you to counsel me about this matter;
For I do not know very many women, nor
Do I know where I might begin auspiciously.
Now say what you can do about this situation,
And whether you can find a wife for me, one who   55
Will not disgrace our family but gild it with
Her character and her inborn nobility
Of life." They said together: "We will do this gladly,
So that we may behold a dear son born to you,
The heir of the good character, the virtues, and   60
The goods with which Christ has enriched and honored you."
Each person nodded, promising to do these things.
One man, who was familiar with the regions and
The lords who were the noblest there, arose and said:
"I know a woman comparable to you in her   65
Integrity, her virtue and nobility.
Please see her, so that when you do you will confess
That you have not seen any other woman in
This world who practices each virtue so intently.
A woman such as she is fit for any man."   70

XVII.

Apportans patera nunc ipsamet optima vina
auratis vasis dulcorem saepe medonis,
stans de virginibus rogitabat compatrioti[s,
cuius sint famae, formosae sint an honestae.
Subridens ille "Scio, quod, minime, rogitas me. 5
Nil minus intromisi me, quam tale notare,
quid facerent dominae; morem talem sino scurr[ae.

Sicubi praetereo, dominas ubi stare videbo,
illis inclino, quo mens est ire vel ibo.
Qui respondere Ruotlieb nunc vis, hera, per m[e?" 10
Dixit "Dic illi nunc de me corde fideli
tantundem liebes, veniat quantum modo loub[es,
et volucrum vvunna quot sint, tot dic sibi m[inna,
graminis et florum quantum sit, dic et honor[um."
Qui dubitans minime, huic illam nubere p[osse, 15
dum se dimitti petit, ut mutus subito fit,
et veluti stupidus loquitur vix ut gemeb[undus
"Qualiter acciderit mihi quam male quam vici[ose,
me pudet id fari; peius non contigit ulli.
Nam sigillata misit tibi xenia parva." 20
Pixiden e caliga trahit, in qua sunt ea dona.
Quam dum suscepit, ab eo properando recedit
adque fenestellam stans solvit pixiden [illam,
in qua subtilem dum cernebat fore pan[num
sigillis cum bis binis suimet digitalis 25
tam bene munitum, quid sit, mirans ea [multum,
sigillis fractis panni nodisque solutis,
dum tam praeclarum convinctum viderat ostr[um,
id pandens cydarim reperitve ligam[ina crurum,
quae cecidere sibi, dum clericus iungitur i[lli. 30
Haec cum vidisset, ubi perderet et memi[nisset,
contremit] et pallet per totum corpus et alget

nec ver]us dubitat, quin is sit, qui simulabat,

190

XVII.

(Ruodlieb subsequently agreed to court the woman; however, he learned of her involvement in a clandestine affair with a priest. Having first obtained evidence of her indiscretion, he has sent a messenger to her with a box containing the evidence. The messenger, who does not know what the box contains, has just related a marriage proposal from Ruodlieb to the woman.)

As she now brought the very best wine in a bowl,
Or sometimes bringing honeyed mead in golden vessels,
She stood and asked about the women of his homeland—
What was their reputation, beauty, character.
"I have no knowledge of what you ask me about,"   5
He answered with a smile, "for nothing matters less
To me than following things like the doings of
Our ladies. I leave such behavior to the dandy.
If I walk by a place where I see ladies standing,
I bow to them and keep on my intended way.
What do you wish to answer Ruodlieb through me,   10
My lady?" She then said, "Now from my faithful heart
Bring him from me as much of love as there are leaves;
Bring him from me as much amour as birds have joy,
And bring him honors equal to the grass and flowers."
He did not doubt at all that she would marry him.   15
He was requesting leave when he was suddenly
Struck dumb and, groaning, as if dazed, could barely speak:
"How bad, how evil what has happened to me is,
I am ashamed to say! Worse has befallen no one;
For he sent little gifts, sealed in a box, to you."   20
He drew a box, in which those gifts were, from his boot.
When she received the box she left him hurriedly,
Then, standing by a window, opened up the box,
In which she saw there was a delicate kerchief
Which was so well secured by four seals from his ring   25
That she was very curious what they might be.
She broke the seals and loosed the knots made in the cloth.
She found a stunning scarlet cloth tied up as well.
Untying this, she found her headdress and her garters,
Which fell from her while she was coupling with a priest.   30
When she saw these, recalling where they had been lost,
She trembled, blanched and felt cold chills all through her
   body.
She did not doubt that he who was pretending told

conspexit modo que]m nimis insipienter agentem.
"Usque pudicam] me plebes omnes habuere"   35
tractat; vis an]imi coepit firmata reverti,
ad missum rem]eat, si sciret eumque requirit,
munera, quid fu]erint, quae sic signata fuerunt,
num praesens fuerit], in pixide cum posuisset.
Iuravit nosse] per eum, quem nil latet, haut se   40
munera, quidquid s]it, mirans cur id rogitarit,
id sigillatum quia] sit, quod erat sibi missum.
Tunc ait illa "Tu]o dic contribuli vel amico
usquam si nullus] vir plus foret, is nisi solus,
ille vel in dotem] mihi mundum si daret omnem,   45
nubere nolo sibi], dic tu veraciter illi."
Missus ait dominae], qui factus tristis ab hac re
"Miror, cur in e]am deveni suspicionem
certo posse qui]dem videor tibi solvere fraudem."
Illa "Tace cito] nunc" ait "absque vale modo vade."   50
Nuntius absced]it ad Ruodlieb reproperatque.
Is simulac vid]it, subridens dixit ad illum
"Quod bene sis potu]s, scio, tractatus saturatus;
qualiter accept]a sint demandamina, narra;
num bene suscepta], non haesita, sunt mea dona?"   55
Sic dicens gaudet] sese quatiendo cachinnat.
Missus ait sibi] quod amicum perderet ipsi
sive petens iterum] tunc se faceret sibi missum
....................t Ruodlieb sibi serio dixit
"Dic nunc, contribul]is, ea dixisset quid herilis,   60
illi quando] meum magnum narraris amorem."
"Quod demandasti sibi, cum plenissime dixi,
omnino siluit, mihi prandia summa paravit,
apportans vinum satis et super atque medonem.
Respondere tibi quid velit cumque rogavi,   65
dixit 'Dic illi de me de corde fideli
tantundem liebes, quantum veniat modo loubes,
et volucrum vvunna quot sunt, sibi dic mea minna,
graminis et florum quantum sit, dic et honorum.'
Quando licentia quo detur mihi vel rogitavi,   70
obmutui subito vel ei, quid sit mihi, dico,
oblitum simulans, tua non sibi dona dedisse.
Quae dum suscepit, de me iubilando recessit.
Post modicum rediit nimis indignanter et inquit
'Dic mihi, si nosti, quid sint quae dona tulisti!'   75

Iuravi per eum, qui cuncta scit, omnipotentem,
numquam vidisse penitus, quid sint ea, scire;
nam sigillatum patuit mihi scire negatum.

The truth, and saw him acting very innocent.
"All people up to now have thought that I am chaste,"   35
She pondered, as her self-control revived, now strengthened.
Returning to the envoy, she inquired if
He knew what gifts those were which had been sealed inside,
And had he been there when they were placed in the box.
He swore by Him, whom nothing can escape, that he   40
Knew nothing of the gifts and was surprised why she
Asked this, since that which had been sent was under seal.
Then she said, "Tell your relative and friend that if
There were no other man alive save him alone,
And if he gave to me the whole world as a present,   45
I do not wish to marry him. You tell him truly!"
The envoy, saddened by this turn, said to the lady:
"I wonder why I have come under such suspicion.
I think that I can settle this misunderstanding."
She said, "Be quiet now! Just go. Don't say good-bye!"   50
The envoy left and hastened back to Ruodlieb,
Who as soon as he saw him, smiled and said to him,
"I know that you were treated well and filled with drink.
Report to me how my petition was received;
And were those gifts of mine—don't hesitate—well liked?"55
He was rejoicing as he spoke and shook with laughter.
The envoy told him he would lose his friendship, if
He asked him to serve as his envoy ever again. . .
. . .but Ruodlieb addressed him seriously:
"Tell now, my kinsman, what did that young lady have   60
To say, when you told her about my potent love?"
"When I reported fully what your message was,
She fell completely silent, then prepared for me
A sumptuous meal, and served more than sufficient wine
And mead. When I asked what reply she wished to make   65
To you, she said 'Now from my faithful heart bring to
That man from me as much of love as there are leaves;
Bring him from me as much amour as birds have joy,
And bring him honors equal to the grass and flowers.'
When I asked leave be given me, I suddenly   70
Went speechless, then explained what had occurred to me,
Pretending I forgot to give your gifts to her.
Receiving them, she joyfully went out and
Returned a little later, very angry, saying
'Now tell me if you know what were those gifts you
    brought.'   75
I swore by God Almighty, who knows everything,
I never looked inside or knew what those gifts were,
For obviously the seal prevented me from knowing.

Tunc ait illa 'Tuo dic contribuli vel amico,
usquam si nullus vir plus foret, is nisi solus, 80
ille vel in dotem mihi mundum si daret omnem,
nubere nolo sibi, dic tu veraciter illi.'"
"Nunc opus est aliam, reor ut, mihi poscere sponsam,
quae non furtive quem suescat amare super me."
Sed Ruodlieb mater, quodcumque potest, operatur 85
in Christi miseros viduas orbos peregrinos.
Inde merebatur, quod Ruodlieb valde beatur.
Namque revelat ei, velit hunc quam glorificare.
In somnis geminos vice quadam viderat apros,
hos grandisque suum comitatur dente minacum 90
turba velut bellum cum Ruodlieb inire minantum.
Ille sed utrique caput apro diripit ense,
quodque suum fuerat ferientum, strage cadebat.
Post mater tiliam latam videt et nimis altam,
in cuius summo residere cacumine fulchro 95
Ruodlieb cernebat, circa quem plurima stabat
in ramis turba veluti bellare parata.
Post modicum nivea venit speciosa columba
rostro gemmatam preciosam fertque coronam,
inponens capiti Ruodlieb mox assidet illi 100
savia figendo, recipit quae non renuendo.
In visu mater haec cernens praemeditatur,
quid queat hoc omne, quod vidit, significare.
Et quamvis sciret, quod honorem praetitularet,
inde superbior haut ea fit, sed humillima mansit, 105
nil sibi sed domini dans gratuitae pietati,
quicquid tantorum Ruodlieb concedat honorum.
Post triduum narrat, deus illi quaeque revelat,

de suibus, capita quibus abscidit truculenta,
et de strage suum geminos apros comitantum, 110
qualiter in tiliae summo videt hunc residere
in ramisque suos sub se vidisset alumnos,
quodque columba sibi ferat advolitando coronam
in manibusque sedens sibi dulcia savia praebens.
"Haec dum cernebam, subito mox evigilabam 115
atque pigebat me nimium sic evigilasse.
Id vigilare scio, quia signat me morituram
esse prius, rerum veniat quam finis earum.
Nate, recordare quam saepe sua bonitate
te deus adiuvit et ab ipsa morte redemit, 120
et quod in exilio multum tibi subveniendo
sospes vel locuples patriam dat quod repetebas.
Nunc scio, maiores nacturus eris quod honores,

Then she said, 'Tell that relative and friend of yours
That if there were no other man, save him alone, 80
And if he gave to me the whole world as a present,
I do not wish to marry him. You tell him truly!'"
"I think that I must seek another bride, who is
Not wont to love in secret other men than me."
The mother of that Ruodlieb, as best she could, 85
Helped Christ's unfortunates: the widows, orphans, pilgrims,
And thus she earned that Ruodlieb be greatly blessed.
For Christ revealed to her how he would glorify
Her son. Thus in her dreams one night she saw two boars,
These followed by a multitude of sows which bared 90
Their teeth as if to threaten war on Ruodlieb;
But with his sword he hacked the head off of each boar,
And all that herd of charging sows fell in the slaughter.
His mother later saw a linden tree, both broad
And very tall, and on its top saw Ruodlieb 95
Was sitting on a couch; around him, on the branches,
A huge troop stood as if prepared to go to war.
A little later came a lovely snow-white dove,
Which carried in its beak a precious jeweled crown
Which it placed on the head of Ruodlieb, then perched 100
Beside him, giving kisses he accepted and
Did not refuse. When she saw these things in her dream,
His mother pondered what all that she saw could mean.
Although she knew that it prefigured honor, she
Did not grow prouder, but remained extremely humble, 105
Not giving credit to herself but to the Lord's
Unselfish mercy for whatever honors He
Gave Ruodlieb. She told him three days later what
God had revealed to her: she told him of the boars
Whose savage heads he had cut off, and told him of
The slaughter of the sows which followed those two boars,110
How she had seen him sitting on the linden's top,
And saw his servants on the branches underneath;
Then how a dove flew down to him, brought him a crown,
And perching on his hands had given him sweet kisses.
"While I was watching this, I suddenly awoke, 115
And was exceedingly annoyed at waking up.
I know that this awaking signifies that I
Will die before the end of these things comes to pass.
Remember, son, how often in his goodness God
Has helped you and has rescued you from death itself, 120
And that He often helped you when you were in exile,
And let you come back to your homeland safe and wealthy.
I know that now you will obtain still greater honors;

et timeo valde dominum sic retribuisse
nobis ambobus, umquam siquid faceremus 125
quod placuisset ei, caveas quod dicere, fili;
nam quid possemus, qui nil, nisi quod dat, habemus?
Sed bene seu male contingat tibi, da sibi grates."

But I fear very much to say the Lord has thus
Rewarded us for ever doing anything   125
Which has pleased Him—my son, beware of saying this!
What could we do, who have nothing but what He gives?
But whether you fare well or badly, give Him thanks!"

XVIII.

Exiliens et abire volens salit undique clamans,
dum lassus cecidit vix spiramenque recepit.

Cui vigor ut rediit, ad Ruodlieb humillime dixit
"Parce mihi misero, scio quod gratum tibi dico.
Si me non occideris atque manus mihi solves, 5
monstro tibi censum binorum denique regum,
et patris et nati, qui tecum proeliaturi
(nomen habet genitor Immunch, sed filius Hartunch)
a te vincuntur ambo per te perimentur.
Filia sed regis haeres tunc sola superstes 10
regni totius Heriburg, pulcherrima virgo,
est tibi lucranda, sed non sine sanguine magno,
ni quod consiliar, facias, ego quando resolvar."
Ruodlieb ait nano "Non occidendus es a me.
Te cito solvissem, tibi si confidere possem; 15
si me non fallis, a me sanus remeabis.

Quando potens fueris tuimet, nil post mihi dices."
"Absit, ut inter nos umquam regnaverit haec fraus;
non tam longaevi tunc essemus neque sani.
Inter vos nemo loquitur, nisi corde doloso. 20
Hinc nec ad aetatem maturam pervenietis;
pro cuiusque fide sunt eius tempora vitae.
Non aliter loquimur, nisi sicut corde tenemus,
neve cibos varios edimus morbos generantes,
longius incolomes hinc nos durabimus ac vos. 25
Non mihi diffidas, faciam, mihi quod bene credas.
Si mihi diffidas, mea coniunx sit tamen obses."
Hanc vocat ex antro, quae mox processerat illo,

parva, nimis pulchra sed et auro vesteque compta.
Quae ruit ante pedes Ruodlieb fundendo querelas 30
"Optime cunctorum, vinclis mihi solve maritum
meque tene pro se, donec persolverit omne."

III.

(Ruodlieb has captured a dwarf.)

Then jumping up and wishing to escape, [the dwarf]
Was shouting and was leaping to and fro, until,
Exhausted, he collapsed and gasped for air. But when
His strength returned, he spoke to Ruodlieb most humbly,
"Spare wretched me; I'll tell you what I know will please.
If you do not kill me, and if you free my hands, 5
I will in turn show you the treasure of two kings,
A father and son, who will then fight with you
(The father's name is Immunch; Hartunch is the son);
But both of them will be subdued and killed by you.
The king's own daughter, Heriburg, a lovely girl, 10
Will be the sole surviving heir of all the kingdom.
She will be won by you, but not without much bloodshed
Unless you do what I advise when I am freed."
Then Ruodlieb said to the dwarf, "No, you will not
Be killed by me. I would have freed you quickly if 15
I could trust you; if you do not deceive me, you
Will go away from me unharmed. When you are your
Own master, you might tell me nothing afterward."
"Far be it that such fraud prevail among us dwarves!
For then we would not be so long-lived or so healthy.
Among you, no one speaks unless deceitfully; 20
And therefore you will not attain a ripe old age.
Each man's life span accords with his fidelity.
We speak not otherwise than we hold in our hearts,
Nor eat the various foods that bring on illnesses;
And therefore we stay sound much longer than you do. 25
Do not distrust me! I will make you trust me fully.
If you distrust me still, my wife will be your hostage."
He called her from the cave, and she came from there promptly.
Small, very beautiful, decked out in gold and clothes,
She fell at Ruodlieb's feet, uttering complaints: 30
"Best of all men, release my husband from his chains!
Hold me for him until he settles his whole debt."

Textual Notes

WALTHARIUS

Dedicatory Preface: Schaller (1965) argues that these prefatory verses constitute a "Widmungsgedicht"; that is, Gerald is sending Erkambald a work by another poet. It should be noted, however, that the preface seems clearly modeled on the preface by Prudentius to his own *Psychomachia*. Prudentius' preface has twenty lines; Gerald's has twenty-two, the last two of which ask for the bishop's prayers on his behalf. Prudentius begins by invoking Christ; Gerald, by invoking the Trinity.

6. The identity of Erkambald has not been positively established.

13. Strecker: *omnitenentem. omnitonantem* BPT. I prefer *omnitonantem* on the basis of the manuscript evidence.

20. Strecker: *perlectus longae + vi stringit in ampla diei longevi* P; *longe vi* T.

Narrative:

1. Supporters of Ekkehard's claim to authorship point out the strong interest in geography at St. Gall in the tenth century.

3. *Relligione* is an unusual but not unprecedented form for *religione,* used because the poet needed a long syllable.

4. Literally "are known to live."

23. The poet makes frequent use of the particle *forte* to complete his hexameter lines.

28. The poet's invention, perhaps to tie the poem even more clearly to the classical epic tradition.

52. Von den Steinen (1952, pp. 40-44) cites this passage, which places Chalon-sur-Sâone in Burgundy, as historical

evidence for dating the composition of the *Waltharius* in the ninth century. He cites also the idenfication of Aquitaine as a *regnum* (line 77) and the reference to Metz as a *metropolis* (line 644) to support his belief that the *Waltharius* was written during the Carolingian period.

123. The poet seems to have invented this name for Attila's wife.

177. *Virtus* is used by characters in the *Waltharius* to mean "courage" or "bravery." Contrast the use of *virtus* in Gerald's preface.

210. Strecker: *timpora. timpora* P *tempora* BT. I prefer *tempora* here and *tempus* in line 1394. Compare *Aeneid* 5.539: *cingit...tempora lauro.*

216. *Equitem* here means "horse." It is also used by the poet in its more usual sense "horseman" (as in line 748).

224. *Tallum* is an unusual word. Niermeyer suggests "goblet."

254. Strecker: *prae multis.*

266. Strecker: *Pannonicarum. Pannoniarum* PT.

288. For a detailed discussion of the banquet scene and its aftermath see Dronke 1971 and Kratz 1980, pp. 26-31.

291. Strecker: *septam.*

322. Perhaps an allusion to the legend of the burning of Attila's palace which occurs in the *Nibelungenlied*.

331. An unusual form for *itineri*, probably as earlier (see note to line 3) for the sake of the meter.

337. This second sword figures prominently in the climactic episode.

411-412. Notice the connection drawn between the desires for fame and wealth.

496. The phrase *apta latronibus* is rich with irony. The place is dangerous, for thieves may be lurking there. On the other hand, Walter is a thief who has stolen from Attila; and Gunther will seek to become a thief by stealing the treasure that Walter is transporting.

513. Lines 513-515 contain a striking allusion to Prudentius' description of the sin of Pride in *Psychomachia* 253-256.

552. *Qui* may refer grammatically to either *Deus* (God) or *gladius* (Walter's sword). Walter's words contain a reference to the Bible (2 Cor. 1.10: *qui de tantis periculis nos eripuit*) in which *qui* clearly refers to God. I believe that the ambiguity of this passage is intentional, and meant to point out the confusion of Walter's own values.

578. *Homonem*. Another extremely rare form (cited by Priscian as being used by Ennius) needed for the meter. The form occurs also in line 933.

617. Hagen's dream foreshadows the ending of the narrative.

633. Strecker: *ullum*. *ullum* P *ulli* BT.

652. Strecker omits this line. For consistency and to avoid confusion with all critical studies (which of course use his edition) I have adopted his numbering of the rest of the *Waltharius*.

761. For a discussion of this and other trans-language puns in the *Waltharius* see Morgan 1972.

774. Walter replies in the proper form. *Transponit* is the word most often used in Latin for "transplanting" a tree.

857. This speech is central to the design of the *Waltharius*. Hagen equates the desire for praise, which motivates Batavrid, with the sin of avarice. The death of Batavrid will provide Hagen's motivation for fighting Walter; and Hagen will reject Walter's offer of treasure in order to perform a "memorable deed."

965. Wayland or Wieland in Norse mythology is the god of smiths.

993. See Lucan *Bellum Civile* 10.720.

1148. For the significance of this line, see note to line 1351.

1189. Taprobane is an island in the Indian Ocean, probably the modern Sri Lanka.

1190. *Eous* refers to the morning star.

1235. See also line 1348. The concern with Fortune suggests that the values of Gunther (and later Walter) are misguided. Pickering 1967-1976 has made an exhaustive study of the topos of Fortune in medieval literature. Those who call on this goddess tend to be concerned with transitory values rather than permanent moral goods.

1351. An example of the poet's fondness for punning. In German *Hagedorn* means a "hawthorn" or "thorn-bush." Therefore, the narrative contains several references to him as "thorny." Hence Walter's fear of "thorns" in line 1351 turns out to be symbolically prophetic. See, for example, line 1421.

1371. This passage, in which Walter's sword shatters and is thrown away by the angry hero, alludes to scenes in both the *Aeneid* and *Psychomachia*. In the *Aeneid* (12.729-741) it is Turnus who throws away his useless hilt in his climactic battle against Aeneas. In the *Psychomachia* (132-144) the sword of Anger shatters. Neither reference is flattering to Walter.

1391. The poet calls attention to this dagger in line 337.

1394. Strecker: *timpus*. See note to line 210.

1401. See Kratz 1980, pp. 48-51. The relevant passages from the Bible are Mark 9:42-48 and Matthew 5:29-30.

1404. Perhaps another pun: Avars and avarice.

1426. *Wantis* is OHG for "gloves."

1435. The Sicambrians were a Germanic tribe. I have tried to recreate the play of sounds in *lusce Sicamber*.

1445. One last example of word-play. The adjective *disiecti*, which I have translated with the phrase "their separate ways," also contains the meaning "mutilated."

RUODLIEB

I.

1. The narrative begins without a prologue. The hero is simply "a man."

4. The poet links a participle (*famulans*) and a finite verb (*potuit*) by the conjunction *et*. In my translation I have not reproduced such uses.

7. The man (that is, Ruodlieb) has been willing to perform acts of vengeance. This line introduces a theme, the rejection of vengeance as taught by the Greater King, central to the *Ruodlieb*.

11. He blames Fortune for his situation (see also I.66). For some implications of this passage, see note to *Waltharius* 1235.

12. This is the first of many instances of the poet's changing verb tenses, for no apparent reason other than metrical, within a sentence.

17. Compare *Aeneid* 4.350: *extera quaerere regna*.

49. An allusion to *Aeneid* 12.65: *perfusa genas*.

58. An allusion to *Aeneid* I.209: *spem vultu simulat, premit altum corde dolorem*.

123. The hero is always careful to provide for his horse. The redheaded man whom he meets later in the narrative, by contrast, lets his animal fend as best it can (see VII.94-95).

II.

1. The herb bugloss, or oxtongue, is in fact mentioned by Pliny; however, not all the powers described by the author of the *Ruodlieb* are cited by Pliny. A fifteenth-century book on fishing from Tegernsee does mention the use of bugloss as bait, and it was not uncommon in the medieval period to hunt wolves with poison. See Zeydel 1959, pp. 144-145.

57. *Compatres* (also *commatres*) is the technical term for godparents.

63. *Vverra*: "war." This is an OHG borrowing.

III.

7. The idea of eschewing vengeance is introduced.

37. Scholars have long wondered whether the author of the *Ruodlieb* had read the *Waltharius*, for several scenes in the later work bear a strong similarity to the earlier. Compare this scene with *Waltharius* 215-220.

IV.

6. *Crisis* = French *gris*. The *pellicium* is a short-cropped fur, usually worn only by the wealthy. The *crusina* was made of a longer fur. Other passages in the *Ruodlieb* describe it as reaching to the ground (XIV.91), edged with beaver (X.126), or even trimmed with ermine (XIV.97).

103. *Abbatibusque*: Zeydel.

162. Zeydel (1959, p. 145) calls this the earliest literary reference to "Gertrudenminne." She is the saint of peace.

187. See Gamer 1954. This is one of the earliest mentions of chess in Western literature. Although the *Ruodlieb* begins with reminiscences of the *Aeneid* and Ruodlieb is in many respects like the wandering Aeneas, the poet has chosen not to include the scenes of warfare that one would expect in an epic. Instead we find an emphasis on peace negotiations here and in the following fragments; and in this fragment we find a "bloodless" battle over a chess board.

V.

1. I have adopted Strecker's conjectured beginning for this line. Ford's suggestion is *cancellis lata*; however, since the letters *eg* are visible in the manuscript, that reading is impossible.

11. *Sinaxis* is a Greek word. A gloss in the margin states that it means *cursus vel hora*.

16. *Prandium* refers to the early afternoon meal; the evening meal is the *cena*.

101. The notion that a gem could be formed from lynx urine was common. Grimm (1838, p. 15) thought that the idea came from a typically medieval "folk etymology" in which *ligurina* was associated with *lynx urina*.

223. The first mention of the hero by name. The name was added over an erasure, apparently by the author. The hero is not called Ruodlieb again until much later in the narrative.

234. Compare I.17.

324. The lines are difficult. I understand the coin to have on one side Christ; on the other, an emblem of royal power with its hand on the king, symbolizing the legitimacy of his kingship. Zeydel (1959, pp. 147-148) believes that the treasure described in this passage is based on a treasure owned by the Empress Gisela, wife of Henry III.

363. I prefer Seiler's conjecture *inventi* to Ford's *orti de*.

364. I have adopted Zeydel's conjecture *rerum* rather than Ford's *rorum*.

402. Compare Ospirin's plan to keep Walter in Pannonia by having him marry the daughter of one of the Huns' noble families.

448. The most thorough discussion of the king's maxims is to be found in Braun (1962, pp. 58-68).

474. Seiler (1882, p. 162) quotes a similar aphorism from the work of Froumond of Tegernsee (965-1008).

559. The friend is the hunter who befriended Ruodlieb when he first entered the land ruled by the Greater King.

VI.

6. No convincing suggestion has been made to complete this lacuna.

57. *quibus...parafredis* = *parafredis...quos*. An idiosyncratic use of "attraction" by the poet.

87. Ford's conjecture is *panum*. I suggest *rerum*.

VII.

12. An example of *ekphrasis*, the extended depiction of a work of art. Compare the mention of the elaborately designed cups in *Waltharius* 308-309. This passage contains one of the earliest known references to wooden cups adorned with carvings.

VIII.

11. For an analysis of the legal procedures described in this episode see Vollmann 1979.

20. *Mordrita* as "murderer" here only. In legal language the term usually refers to the victim.

X.

39. Wehrli (1969, p. 132) points out that this catalogue could be derived either from literary sources or from the poet's own knowledge. Many of the fish are mentioned in the fifteenth-century book on fishing mentioned in the note to II.1.

71. I print Zeydel's conjecture here.

73. *Dapifer* is Zeydel's suggestion.

114. The northern Italian town of Lucca was famous for its production of luxurious cloth thigh-bands.

XI.

21. Probably "in human speech" rather than referring specifically to German.

51. The first literary depiction of a courtly dance.

XII.

1. All other editors have printed *nunc matrem*; however, I accept as probable the emendation *commatrem* offered by Vollman (1981, pp. 227-228). The manuscript has a lacuna.

4. Other editors read *illam*. I prefer Vollmann's suggestion *illa*.

28. The solecism refers to a grammatical mixing of genders and not to any moral flaw or incorrect mingling of two people from different social classes.

75. The name Ruodlieb here occurs for the first time since V.223.

XIII.

The Munich manuscript contains only the first nine lines of this fragment completely. It also contains portions of lines 31-55. The St. Florian manuscript contains lines 10-81 with the exception of lines 45 and 46.

21. Above *monedula* is written the German gloss *taha*.

42. The first mention of the Greater King's people as "Africans." Presumably southern Italy is meant. See Dronke 1970, pp. 38-39.

57. This opening of the second loaf is contrary to the instructions of the Greater King. See V. 552-554.

XIV.

1. It is my interpretation that in this passage Ruodlieb is addressing his mother. Zeydel (1959, p. 123) suggests that Ruodlieb is addressing the mother of the bride.

18. Gellinek (1967) argues that the scene offers a realistic depiction of a marriage ceremony called a *Friedelehe*.

43. I print *modeste* rather than Ford's conjecture *morose*.

63. I translate *pyramis* as referring to the point of the sword. Zeydel (1959, p. 152) argues that it refers to a column in the substructure of a stairway.

88. *Aenesis*. Another example of the poet's fondness for foreign words, in this instance Greek.

XV.

The *descriptio puellae*, or portrait of the beautiful young woman, is a staple of medieval rhetoric. Here we have a brilliant example of the opposite topos.

1. Certainly the word *senectus* appears in this line.

17. Ford prints *succi*. I read the manuscript as *suci*.

61. I print Zeydel's conjectured ending to this line.

XVII.

11. A famous and much discussed love greeting. Walther (1928) traces the *tot-quot* form through medieval literature back to Ovid.

49. I print Zeydel's conjectured beginning to this line.

56. I print Zeydel's conjectured beginnings to lines 56-58.

83. Note the dramatic change in the narrative; however, the handwriting in the manuscript is the same as for all the rest of the *Ruodlieb*. The author has not changed, but his design of the poem seems to have been altered.

89. Animal dreams are common in German literature. See Schach 1954.

94. Braun (1962, p. 72) argues that this aspect of the dream connects Ruodlieb with Christ.

For Product Safety Concerns and Information please contact our EU representative GPSR@taylorandfrancis.com
Taylor & Francis Verlag GmbH, Kaufingerstraße 24, 80331 München, Germany

www.ingramcontent.com/pod-product-compliance
Lightning Source LLC
Chambersburg PA
CBHW071821300426
44116CB00009B/1387